CLASSIC STUDIES
IN
PSYCHOLOGY

CLASSIC STUDIES IN PSYCHOLOGY

STEVEN SCHWARTZ

University of Queensland, Australia

Mayfield Publishing Company

To Gregory

Published in the United States by Mayfield Publishing Company by arrangement with Angus & Robertson Publishers, Unit 4, Eden Park, 31 Waterloo Road, North Ryde, NSW, Australia 2113, and 16 Golden Square, London W1R 4BN, United Kingdom.

First published in Australia by Angus & Robertson Publishers in 1987. First published in the United Kingdom by Angus & Robertson (UK) Ltd in 1987.

Library of Congress Catalog Card Number: 86-062208
International Standard Book Number: 0-87484-796-6

Manufactured in the United States of America

10 9 8 7 6 5 4 3

Mayfield Publishing Company
1240 Villa Street
Mountain View, California 94041

Science is nothing but trained and organised common sense, differing from the latter only as a veteran may differ from a raw recruit; and its methods differ from those of common sense only as far as the guardsman's cut and thrust differ from the manner in which a savage wields his club.

T. H. Huxley, *Collected Essays*

CONTENTS

PREFACE

"Psychology", according to pioneer psychologist Hermann Ebbinghaus, "has a long past but only short history". This rather cryptic remark is easier to understand if a distinction is made between psychology's subject matter — behavior — and its investigative methods. Although attempts to understand behavior go back thousands of years (every ancient philosopher had a psychological theory), experimental psychology is barely 100 years old. Even today, many people find it strange to think of psychology as an experimental science. Partly this is because psychology laboratories bear little resemblance to the laboratories depicted in science-fiction movies. There are no glass beakers heating above Bunsen burners, no ominous white gases flowing through tubes and, often, no technicians in white coats. Nevertheless, psychological studies have been conducted in laboratories around the world for many decades. Some of these studies, the ones described in this book, have even changed the way we view ourselves and our place in the world. The main goal of this book is to show how these classic studies help us to understand human and, to a lesser extent, animal behaviour.

All psychology textbooks review research results, but the traditional format precludes an in-depth analysis of any single study. The result is that students learn *what* scientists do but not *why*. Because the social and cultural backgrounds of researchers can influence their work almost as much as their theoretical views, students gain a deeper appreciation of the research process when experiments are placed in their appropriate historical and theoretical context. For this reason, I have attempted to make psychological research more "real" by describing not only the details of each study but also the backgrounds of the experimenters involved. In addition, the aftermath of each study — its impact on subsequent research — is reviewed and evaluated. Sufficient detail about each experiment has been included to make the book a suitable adjunct to an introductory psychology course as well as to a course in experimental psychology or history and systems. As my aim was to produce an intelligible and, I hope, entertaining book while at the same time maintaining scientific accuracy and rigor, the book may appeal not only to students but to anyone who is interested in science in general and psychology in particular.

The main difficulty with an exercise such as this is deciding which studies are really "classic". Some experiments (Pavlov's dog, for example) are so famous they practically choose themselves. Selecting from the thousands of less famous studies in the psychology literature those that are enlightening, entertaining and at the same time classics is not quite so easy. Inevitably, someone's favorite is omitted. The criteria used to choose the studies described in this book are three: the study must deal with a topic of substantial interest to the general reader; it must have exerted a strong effect on subsequent research; and it must possess an elegance and clarity that can be appreciated by readers not intimately familiar with the history of psychology. Studies that meet these three criteria were chosen from the broad categories of physiological, perceptual, cognitive, social and developmental psychology.

I should note that not all the results described in this book have gone unchallenged. In fact, several have produced findings that were ultimately refuted by subsequent research. This does not mean that these studies were not important in their own right. Even mistaken research based on ideas can be informative.

In preparing this book, I was helped by many people, but particularly by Carolyn Schwartz. I am also indebted to Mandy Little and Richard Walsh, without whose encouragement this book would never have been written.

Steven Schwartz

INTRODUCTION:

PSYCHOLOGY AND SCIENCE

Imagine the following scene. A professional water dowser, who makes his living by discovering underground streams, is walking across a rural landscape carrying a special Y-shaped tree branch he calls a divining rod. He holds a fork of the branch in each hand with the long end pointed downward and slowly sweeps the ground as he walks. Suddenly he stops and the branch begins to vibrate mysteriously. The dowser has all he can do to keep the branch from flying out of his hands.

"Here is the spot!" he shouts. "Dig here and you're sure to find water."

The landowner, who has been standing by with digging equipment, gets to work. Within the day, water is discovered just where the dowser said it would be. The landowner, who was something of a sceptic before this demonstration, is now convinced. Professional dowsers (at least this one) can find water by tuning in to the vibrations produced in a Y-shaped stick. After all, seeing is believing.

Much of our everyday knowledge comes from observations just like the landowner's. We are presented with a theory (dowsers can discover water) and then with a demonstration that appears to substantiate it. The result is increased belief in the theory. Unfortunately, knowledge gathered this way is often unreliable, and almost never scientific.

The problem is that the observations made by the landowner were not systematic. While it is true that the dowser was successful this time, it would be useful to know whether he is routinely successful. He could just have been lucky. One important feature of the scientific method is *replicability*. Observations must be repeatable to be scientific. But replicability alone is not enough. Scientific observations must also be *controlled*. That is, alternative explanations for a phenomenon have to be ruled out. For example, a possible alternative explanation for the dowser's success is his familiarity with geological and topographical cues to water's presence. In other words, he knows there is water present not because of his sensitivity to vibrations transmitted through his stick but because he recognises the geological formations indicating underground water. Since the landowner did not include a control for this possibility, his observations were not very scientific. His observations would have been more scientific if he had the dowser perform his water-finding feat blindfolded, but even then a previous tour of the land could have allowed the dowser to memorise a promising location. If the landowner really wants to examine the dowser's ability scientifically, he will have to create a more carefully controlled situation; he will have to do an experiment.

Although everyone knows that scientists do experiments, it is not always clear just how experiments differ from other types of observations. In this introductory chapter the nature of psychological experimentation is described and the mechanisms by which experiments give rise to scientific knowledge are examined. The chapter begins with a description of the experimental method and a definition of its most important terms.

WHY PSYCHOLOGISTS DO EXPERIMENTS

An artificial, but carefully controlled, experiment designed to examine dowsing ability could be conducted as follows. The landowner (now turned experimenter) arranges 10 covered buckets in an otherwise empty room. Only one of the buckets has water in it, the other nine are empty. The dowser, accompanied by his stick of course, is invited into the room and asked to identify the bucket containing the water. As there are no geological cues to help him (these cues are said to have been *controlled*), any success he has cannot be attributed to his geological knowledge.

Let us assume that the buckets are arranged as described and the dowser is invited in. What do you think happens next? He wanders up and down the row of buckets until he feels his stick begin to vibrate. He points to the nearest bucket and identifies it as the one containing water. The landowner checks and, much to his surprise, the dowser is correct. But the landowner, who has become rather a hard case, is still not satisfied. While it is true that geological clues can no longer account for the dowser's success, there is still another explanation. He may have made a lucky guess. To be certain that the dowser was not just lucky, the landowner requires that the dowser perform the experimental task 100 times. Before each attempt, the dowser is asked to leave the room while the water-containing bucket is moved to a new position. The landowner's reasoning goes something like this: since there are 10 buckets, the probability that the dowser will choose the correct one by chance alone is 10 to one or .10. In 100 attempts, therefore, the dowser would be expected to find the water 10 times purely by chance ($100 \times .10 = 10$). If the dowser does better than this, lucky guessing can be ruled out as an explanation for his success. This approach to testing dowsing ability is not purely hypothetical. It has actually been carried out several times. Each time the results are the same. In the controlled conditions prevailing in the laboratory, dowsers do no better than chance in predicting which bucket contains water. Similar tests have been conducted on other phenomena attributed to ESP, usually with the same results.

Controlled tests constitute the essence of the experimental method. Instead of just noting the dowser's success in the field, the experimenter relies on tightly controlled laboratory procedures to rule out alternative explanations for the dowser's ability. Not surprisingly, the landowner's original conclusion (that the dowser's abilities were real) changed to quite the opposite after testing his ability in the laboratory. This is one of the main reasons for doing experiments — to rule out alternative explanations for an observed phenomenon. But it is not the only reason. The next section describes how experiments also provide knowledge unobtainable by any other means.

WHAT EXPERIMENTS TELL US

Although scientists do experiments, not all scientific knowledge is experimental. In fact, some scientists never do experiments at all. Astronomers, for example, merely observe the heavens, making careful recordings of what they see. Geologists, palaeontologists, ethologists and many comparative biologists do not perform experiments either, relying instead on systematic observations of natural phenomena.

Naturalistic observation can be a powerful way to gather scientific information. Charles Darwin, for example, relied on it exclusively in formulating his theory of evolution. He toured the world noting the variations produced by nature as well as by animal breeders and botanists, all the while trying to devise a theory that could account for the phenomena he observed. Superficially, naturalistic observations appear little different from those made by the landowner watching the dowser discover water. But there is, in fact, a difference. Scientific observation requires a theory, a set of constructs and concepts which guides observations. A theory allows the scientist to classify facts and to make observations that confirm or disprove hypotheses. Much valuable psychological knowledge on child development, social behaviour and even thinking has been gained by carefully observing behaviour in naturalistic settings.

An experiment is also a way of testing a theory. But instead of passively observing nature, experimenters actively interfere in natural phenomena. To use Francis Bacon's famous phrase, the goal of an experiment is to "put nature to the question". Experimental psychologists accomplish this by manipulating factors hypothesised to produce behavioural effects and then observing what happens. Experimenters call the factors they manipulate *independent variables*. In psychological experiments, sensory stimuli (lights, tones), new teaching methods or even new types of psychotherapy may all be independent variables. The *dependent variable*, on the other hand, is whatever is affected by the independent variable — usually the behaviour of a person or animal. Thus, noticing a light, hearing a tone, improved learning with a new teaching method, or psychological improvement after psychotherapy are all dependent variables. In their experiments, psychologists manipulate independent variables in order to produce changes in dependent variables. In a sense, then, the value of the dependent variable *depends* on the value of the independent variable.

Since experiments involve manipulating one or more independent variables and observing the effect on one or more dependent variables, the 10-bucket dowsing task just qualifies as a simple experiment. The independent variable is the number of empty buckets and the dependent variable is the dowser's accuracy. However, as no experimental manipulations were involved (the number of buckets never changed), the 10-bucket situation is an example of an intermediate type of scientific exploration called a *controlled demonstration*. Some of the classic experiments described in this book fall into this category. Although I have called them experiments, they are not really experiments at all but examples of controlled scientific observation.

The ideal experiment demonstrates a direct relationship between a single independent variable and a single dependent variable. For example, an unexpected loud noise (independent variable) almost always produces a fearful startle (dependent variable). Unfortunately, in the real world there are very few psychological problems so straightforward that one independent variable will invariably produce the same effect on an experiment's outcome. Typically, many other factors besides the independent variable may affect the dependent variable. In order to keep these *extraneous* influences from clouding the experiment's results, they must be held constant. Holding extraneous factors constant while permitting the independent variable to vary requires careful experimental design and an understanding of the concept called *control*.

Clearly, it is a waste of time to conduct an experiment in which factors other than the independent variable are permitted to vary. The experimenter would never know whether changes in the dependent variable were the result of his manipulations of the independent variable or the result of the action of one of these uncontrolled extraneous influences. Consider, for example, an experiment designed to test a new form of psychotherapy for a phobic fear of heights. We could find a sample of sufferers, perhaps referred by a psychiatrist, have them undergo the psychotherapy and see if their fear disappears. The problem with this approach is that even if patients improve, we cannot be sure the therapy was responsible. It may be that height phobias improve by themselves (spontaneous recovery), or it may be that something in the therapeutic situation other than psychotherapy itself (having someone to talk to, for instance) was responsible for their improvement. As things stand, it is impossible to tell whether it is the therapy or some other factor that is responsible for the improvement. The only way to find out for sure is to *control* for these extraneous factors by conducting a true experiment. At the very least, this means having a second group of phobic patients (called the *control group* to differentiate them from the treated *experimental group*) who do not undergo the therapy. If they improve as much as the group receiving therapy then spontaneous recovery becomes a likely explanation for their improvement.

Although a control group helps to rule out spontaneous recovery as an explanation for improvement, it is still not possible to conclude that the psychotherapy itself was effective. This is because there were important differences in the way the two groups were treated. The members of the experimental group not only received therapy, they also had a kind therapist to talk to and just having someone who cared about their problem may have led to improvement. So, an adequate control group to evaluate the effects of psychotherapy is not a group of phobic patients who receive no attention at all but a group of patients who meet each week with a considerate therapist to whom they can talk about their problems but who do not receive any specific psychotherapy. Researchers call such a group a *placebo control group* because their visits to the therapist are considered equivalent to the placebos (inactive drugs) used in medical research. If they improve as much as the group receiving therapy then the experimenter can conclude that it is not the therapy itself which is effective but just having an interested therapist to talk to.

Although comparing a therapy group with a placebo control group is the only way to determine whether the therapy itself is responsible for any improvement, the researcher cannot be certain that the experiment's results are reliable unless the experimental and control groups are equivalent before the experiment begins. If one group has more severe phobias than the other, it will be more difficult for them to improve. Ideally, then, the experimental and control groups should be chosen to ensure that their phobias are equally severe. They also should come from the same social class, be about the same age and contain equal numbers of males and females because these factors can also affect treatment outcome. Since, in practice, it is difficult to match the experimental and control groups on all possible relevant variables, a compromise technique is employed. Phobic patients are assigned at random to experimental and control groups. Experimenters hope that random assignment will equalise the groups.

An experiment's value is directly proportional to the standard of its control groups. Indeed, some of the experiments described in this book are classics mainly because of the skill the experimenters exercised in controlling extraneous variables. Because there are so many possible extraneous variables that can affect behaviour, psychologists must be even more concerned with adequate controls than other scientists. Failure to control an important factor can lead to unrepeatable experimental results and, as already noted, phenomena that cannot be replicated under similar experimental conditions are, by definition, unscientific. Indeed, the main reason why many scientists have refused to accept ESP phenomena is their difficulty replicating them under controlled scientific conditions.

Although the experimental method is accepted by scientists as the best way to gain scientific knowledge, the need to identify separate variables and to keep all others controlled restricts its use to only certain problems. There are some cases where attempting to isolate a particular variable can destroy the phenomena the scientist wishes to study. This is particularly a problem for social-psychological research where the context in which a behaviour occurs may define what the behaviour actually means. Take non-verbal gestures, for example. Raising the arm above the head can mean anything from a friendly greeting (or goodbye) to a threat or a display of exuberance depending on the context. An experiment designed to measure the effect of a gesture (independent variable) on an observer (the dependent variable), with the context held constant, would yield trivial results at best and meaningless ones at worst. Experiments are best suited to questions in which isolating one property does not seriously change its nature.

It should be obvious that the ideal experiment, one that meets all of the requirements described here, is not easy to achieve. Indeed, few of the classic experiments discussed in later chapters meet all of these requirements. Never-theless, they remain classics because they tackle psychological questions in an original way. What they lack in rigour they more than make up for in originality. In every case, later researchers carried out more sophisticated experiments in attempts to substantiate the findings of the classics.

Psychological experiments, then, involve controlled observations of the effects of a manipulated independent variable on some dependent variable. But how do psychologists decide what variables to manipulate and what phenomena to study in the first place? This is the subject of the next section.

WHERE DO EXPERIMENTAL IDEAS COME FROM?

Ideally, experiments are suggested by scientific theories. Consider, for example, early theories of learning. Based on the work of the Russian physiologist Ivan Pavlov, as well as his own research, Clark Hull of Yale University developed an elaborate theory designed to account for various phenomena observed when animals and humans learn to make conditioned responses. One aspect of this theory dealt with the role of practice in learning.

Let us take a simple example. We start with a white laboratory rat in a cage facing two levers. Our aim is to teach the rat to press the left-hand lever each time a red light goes on but not to press the right-hand lever. Each time the animal presses the appropriate lever in response to the signal, it receives a food reward and one conditioning (learning) trial is said to have occurred. Although in the beginning the rat sometimes hits the wrong lever or fails to press either lever, after a number of conditioning trials correct responses begin to outnumber incorrect ones. Eventually, the animal makes no mistakes at all. According to Hull's theory each successful (rewarded) conditioning trial contributes a small amount of learning. These small amounts accumulate so that eventually the rat learns the required response perfectly. However, there is another aspect of Hull's theory that is also relevant. This is the problem of fatigue. In addition to an increment in learning, each conditioning trial produces fatigue (or what Hull called *reactive inhibition*). Fatigue temporarily inhibits learning but its effects tend to dissipate with rest.

The contrasting effects of reactive inhibition and learning led researchers to the following hypothesis. If conditioning trials are spaced over fairly long intervals, rats will learn to make the correct response more efficiently (they will require fewer conditioning trials) than if the conditioning trials are bunched together. This hypothesis is derived directly from Hull's theory. Massed practice trials should lead to a rapid build-up of fatigue which will inhibit learning. Spacing the trials allows fatigue to dissipate between each trial and should, therefore, lead to more efficient learning. Experiments were designed to test this hypothesis. In these experiments the time between conditioning trials (short or long) was the independent variable and the number of trials required by the rats before they learned the correct response was the dependent variable. The findings of these experiments were largely in line with Hull's hypothesis and served as experimental support for at least part of his learning theory.

Hypotheses specifying the relationship between independent and dependent variables are always part of psychological experiments. Psychologists may hypothesise that giving children enriched learning environments will improve their school performance or that teaching people to relax will lower their anxiety level. (Enriched environments and relaxation training are independent variables, school performance and anxiety levels are dependent variables.) Although experiments make their greatest contribution when they are designed to test hypotheses derived from theories, this is not necessarily a requirement. Many hypotheses, in fact, are derived from naturalistic observations. For example, most of the antipsychotic medications that have been so effective in helping mental patients live outside institutions were discovered quite by accident when someone observed what appeared to be a potentially beneficial effect of drugs developed for quite another purpose. Although the value of antipsychotic drugs has been confirmed by many experiments, their discovery was not the result of any theory and, in many cases, we still do not know why these drugs work.

Although experimental hypotheses can come from anywhere, they are most useful when drawn from psychological theories. Not only can the results of such experiments be used to confirm or disprove theoretical predictions, they may also be used to develop new theories. The past 100 years have seen several changes in psychological theory. Some formerly popular views are today of merely historical interest; other theories have remained important for decades and are still influencing research today. The following section briefly reviews the history of experimental psychology since its founding 100 years ago. It is instructive to note how the questions psychologists ask, and the way they try to answer them, is influenced by the popular psychological theories of the day.

THE DEVELOPMENT OF EXPERIMENTAL PSYCHOLOGY
In western countries psychology first developed out of theology, philosophy and ethics. When some academics began to refer to themselves as scientific psychologists, they were trying to separate their view of mankind from the theological views favoured by philosophers and clerics. The new psychologists set out to study behaviour scientifically. Instead of merely arguing about ethics and semantics (the "armchair" approach to understanding people), scientific psychologists set out to observe and measure behaviour in the real world. Problems that could not be solved by observation and experimentation (for example, do people have free will or are their actions entirely determined by outside forces?) were simply ignored or left to philosophers.

The experimental method's success in the physical sciences soon led the new psychologists to try studying psychological phenomena experimentally. And so, about 100 years ago, experimental psychology was born. It is usually agreed that the first experimental psychology laboratory was established by the German philosopher-psychologist Wilhelm Wundt at Leipzig University in the 1880s. Experimental psychology became popular almost immediately and by the close of the century, experimental psychology laboratories had been established in major universities around the world.

The first experimental psychologists were mainly concerned with studying what they called "the mind" and what today is known as consciousness. Typical experiments involved presenting physical stimuli (lights, tones and so on) and noting their effect on a subject. The major goal of these experiments was to develop measures of subjective sensations. In other words, psychologists wished to discover the relationship between changes in a physical stimulus (making a light brighter, for example) and the subjective experience of that stimulus. Related research was concerned with how the various senses (sight, hearing, touch, taste, smell) work. Much that we now know about the operations of the various sense organs was first discovered by the nineteenth-century experimental psychologists. By the close of the last century, experimental psychologists had broadened their subject matter considerably; they were conducting experiments dealing with such phenomena as visual imagery, memory, reading and problem solving.

FIG. 1. *Wilhelm Wundt (1832–1920), founder of the first psychology laboratory in Germany 100 years ago*

Another stream of experimental psychology which developed around the same time, but quite independently of human research, was the study of animal behaviour. Influenced by Darwin and the nineteenth-century physiologists, animal behaviourists were interested in the relationship between physiology and behaviour. Their work is epitomised by Ivan Pavlov, whose research on the digestive system of dogs led to the first demonstration of what was later to be called the "conditioned reflex". Pavlov's work began independently of human psychology, but the two research streams were soon joined together by psychologists who appreciated the relevance of his research for human learning.

By the early twentieth century, divisions began to develop among experimental psychologists concerning just what psychologists should be studying and how they should be doing it. One school of thought became known as *structuralism*. Structuralism's main concepts were derived from Wundt's original research but were greatly elaborated by his most famous student, Edward Titchener. Titchener was an Englishman who studied with Wundt before emigrating to America just prior to the turn of the century. He established a laboratory at Cornell University where he became structuralism's most famous spokesman. For Titchener and the structuralists, the goal of psychology was to elucidate the elements that constitute consciousness. Using an analogy with chemistry, they claimed that what psychologists should be doing was discovering and defining the basic components underlying sensations, images, thoughts and feelings. These components, like chemical elements, were thought to constitute the basic building blocks of mental life. Also, like chemical elements, they believed that mental components could be combined to produce higher mental processes.

The favourite experimental method of structuralists was introspection. Subjects were required to taste foods, for example, and report their subjective sensations. If they reported sweet "sensations", they were given other foods that produced sour sensations and still more foods that gave rise to salty sensations. The procedure continued until no further new sensations were reported, at which time all of the component elements underlying taste were thought to have been isolated. A similar procedure was used to isolate the mental components of other modalities. For instance, a subject would be required to introspect about

FIG. 2. *Edward Titchener (1867–1927), leader of the structuralist school*

the mental sensations produced by various colours in order to determine their basic mental components.

The structuralists were not happy simply to identify the basic elements of conscious experience, they also wanted to know how these elements combined to produce more complex sensations. To take but one example, experimenters were not satisfied to have subjects report that purple sensations are composed of blue and red ones; they also wanted to know whether purple is more *reddish* or *bluish*. Unfortunately, this is where the structuralists began to get into trouble. Different subjects would frequently disagree. Some people saw purple as more blue and others more red. Arguments about whether purple is more bluish than reddish raged in the psychological literature but eventually died out without being resolved. Introspection was simply too subjective an experimental approach to yield reliable data.

While Titchener tried vainly to keep the structuralist enterprise going, back in Germany other psychologists were questioning the whole notion that consciousness is divisible into elements. These psychologists, particularly Max Wertheimer, Kurt Koffka and Wolfgang Kohler called their alternative viewpoint *Gestalt* psychology, from the German word meaning "form" or "figure". For them, consciousness was not a matter of elements acting singly or in combination, but the total result of all the sensory input an organism experiences at a particular moment. The Gestalt psychologists argued that when a listener hears a familiar tune he does not hear a set of isolated notes but rather a coherent pattern or melody. This melody, or Gestalt, is not merely the sum of its constituent elements but something quite separate. Their point is easily demonstrated. Simply play the tune in a different key. The notes (the basic elements) are all different and yet the tune is easily recognisable. Gestaltists summarised their views with the simple statement: the whole is more than the sum of its parts. Not surprisingly, a great deal of their research was devoted to proving the truth of this dictum. They also tried to identify the principles by which elements are organised into coherent wholes. Although the Gestaltists made a deep impression on the psychology of their day (the 1920s to 1940s), particularly on the study of perception, their position appeared to have little to offer to psychologists interested in learning and thinking.

These latter psychologists turned to a school called *functionalism* which developed under the leadership of John Dewey and James Angell in America. Like the Gestalt psychologists, the functionalists also objected to the structuralists' approach, but for rather different reasons. The functionalists believed that psychology should be concerned not so much with what the mind is comprised of as what it does. Their focus was on adaptation, how the "mind" changes with experience. Their research focused on learning and the behavioural changes that accompany child development. Although their emphasis on the function of behaviour heralded the modern era in experimental psychology (by and large, most of today's experimental psychologists are still concerned with function), they were quickly overshadowed by another school of psychology known as behaviourism.

Behaviourism's founder, John Watson, was a psychologist at Johns Hopkins University in Baltimore in the early years of this century. Rejecting all previous psychologies as subjective and largely speculative, Watson insisted that what psychology should be studying was not thoughts or sensations or even consciousness but behaviour — the observable activities of humans and animals. For Watson, searching for mental elements was like searching for ghosts in the head. Instead, he emphasised the importance of the conditioned reflex (which he adopted from Pavlov) in determining behaviour. In fact, he saw all complex behaviour as constructed from complicated arrangements of simple conditioning. In this regard, he was a sort of structuralist, but unlike their mental sensations, his "basic element" could be easily observed and measured and it had some physiological reality. Watson avoided any study of mental elements. In fact, the term "mentalistic" was the most pejorative adjective Watson could think to bestow on a theoretical concept. Watson also denied that inborn instincts were in any way important determinants of human behaviour. All behaviour, he believed, was learned by conditioning. Since Watson's time, behavioural research has been dedicated to explicating the relationship between environmental stimuli and rewards on the one hand and conditioned responses on the other.

Unlike the structuralist and Gestalt psychology schools, behaviourism is still an important school of psychology today. Its most famous adherent, B. F. Skinner, has devoted a lifetime to showing how environmental events affect behaviour in various conditioning experiments. However, by the late 1950s it became clear to many psychologists that a strict behavioural approach eliminated many important phenomena from scientific study. For example, behaviourists had relatively little to say about the way in which people solve mathematical problems, the underlying basis for language, the uses and nature of imagery and many other issues which both Watson and Skinner would characterise as mentalistic. Prior to the 1950s, psychologists could find no adequate way to conceptualise these problems without lapsing into the mentalism decried by Watson. However, with the advent of computers things began to change. Experimental psychologists began to view mental activities as a type of information processing. Their main idea was that when individuals engage in mental activity, they are actually modifying, comparing and storing information in much the same way as a computer. This change in viewpoint was a major breakthrough. Mental activities were no longer the ghosts that Watson worried about but could be characterised in objective and specific terms. The development of information-processing models of thinking led to an explosion of research into cognitive phenomena that continues to the present. Indeed, experiments concerned with cognition and information processing make up the vast majority of psychological research today, with strict behavioural studies falling very much in second place.

This brief look at the history of experimental psychology is meant to do no more than provide a feel for how theory and research interact and some of the changes that have occurred over the decades since experimental psychology was born in Wundt's laboratory. It should be obvious that not all psychological theories have been mentioned. For instance, Freud's psychoanalytic theory has been omitted. The reason is that psychoanalysis has not traditionally been a fruitful source of experiments. In fact, many psychoanalysts argue that the theory cannot be evaluated by experiments and the only relevant data are those collected within the psychoanalytic session. Although psychoanalytic theory has not itself generated any classic experiments, it has had a strong influence on other theories. Many psychological theories have been developed solely to account for psychoanalytic phenomena (the unconscious, for instance) and some theories have been developed solely to criticise the psychoanalytic point of view. For this reason Freud's ideas are frequently mentioned in this book.

Although the present focus is on the work of individual experimenters, no scientist works in a vacuum; all great discoveries are built on the work of earlier scientists. In a way, dividing the continual flow of scientific discovery into discrete "classic" units distorts history by presenting an artificial view of how discoveries actually are made. Thus, it is worthwhile keeping in mind that although the classic experiments described in the following chapters all represent important landmarks in the history of psychology, not one could have been carried out without the contribution of earlier scientists.

Most of the issues discussed in this introductory chapter are dealt with in greater detail where they relate to the classic experiments described in the remaining chapters of this book. In reading these chapters, it will become clear that while psychological theories have changed over the years, one thing has remained steady — a commitment to rigorous scientific methods.

This book is divided into four parts. The first part, *Bodies and Minds*, contains experiments concerned with the relationship between biology and behaviour. The second part, *Perceiving, Remembering and Feeling*, deals with experiments on each of these important aspects of behaviour. Part 3, *The Social Animal*, examines social behaviour, and the fourth part, *Critical Periods in Development*, is concerned with how behaviour changes over time.

Further Reading

Boring, E. G., *A History of Experimental Psychology*, Appleton-Century-Crofts, New York, 1950.

McCain, G. and Segal, E. M., *The Game of Science* (second edition), Brooks/Cole, Monterey, California, 1973.

PART 1

Bodies and Minds

Except for radical behaviourists, psychologists frequently try to explain behaviour by invoking activities and processes that occur in the "mind". Unfortunately, it is not always clear what they mean. Sometimes psychologists appear to believe that the mind is something that exists separately from the physical body; at other times they act as if all mental functioning is synonymous with changes in biological states. The relationship between the body and the mind is one of the oldest and thorniest in philosophy. René Descartes, and many other philosophers, spent most of their professional lives unsuccessfully trying to mend the "mind–body" split. Even comedians have had their say. Woody Allen, for example, poses the question: "If there is a mind–body split, which would you prefer?" There are many amusing answers to this question, but one theme predominates. That is that, for most people, the answer depends on the situation. Scientific psychologists appear to operate similarly, altering their definition of mind according to currently popular theories and the requirements of a particular research paradigm.

Although there is a long way to go, it is fair to say that we know more today about the relationship between the body and the mind than ever before. To a great extent this knowledge derives from the experiments described in the next three chapters. All of the experiments are concerned with the relationship between the brain and behaviour; otherwise, there is little similarity among them.

CHAPTER ONE

THE CONDITIONED REFLEX

What properties would a potato have to have in order to be conscious?

This rather odd question appears at the beginning of "Mind and Mechanism", an article published by American psychologist and historian Edwin G. Boring in 1946. In case you have not already guessed, Boring's question was strictly hypothetical. He was not interested in creating a Frankenstein-type monster from a vegetable, but in constructing an inventory of basic psychological functions. Included in his inventory were *memory*, *learning*, *insight*, *attitudes*, the ability to *react* to the environment, and the ability to *symbolise*. Boring argued that any potato possessing these skills would, by definition, be conscious. He put it this way: "If we could find a potato that is Socrates' peer in performance, then we should have, for all practical purposes, Socrates." As you can see, Boring was a *behaviourist*.

CONSCIOUSNESS AND BEHAVIOURISM

Of course if a sceptical enquirer were to look inside both the potato and Socrates, differences between the two would immediately become apparent. Boring admitted as much but claimed that psychologists should not look inside the organisms they study. "In science," he wrote, "things are what they do." Since it is impossible to observe mental functions directly, Boring believed psychologists had no choice but to infer their presence from external behaviour. This is the basic behaviourist dictum: we know what an organism thinks, believes or feels by the way it behaves. If a baby begins to cry during a thunderstorm, we say it is afraid; if the same child reaches for a new toy, we say that the toy has aroused the child's interest.

Boring advocated giving all psychological variables objective definitions. The best way to do this, he believed, was to define theoretical concepts in terms of the observable operations performed to measure them. *Intelligence*, for example, can be defined as a score on an intelligence test; *memory* by the number of items one can recall after some time period and *thirst* by the amount an organism drinks. If all psychological traits are defined objectively, then Boring's comment about the potato being Socrates is not as strange as it first sounds. So long as its behaviour meets our objective definition of how a conscious organism should act, the potato is conscious, no matter what its insides look like.

The idea that inanimate objects may be considered conscious so long as they behave like humans is not peculiar to Boring. The English mathematician, Alan Turing, had the same idea in mind when, in 1950, he proposed the following game. One person, the examiner, is put in a room furnished with only a desk and teletype terminal. The examiner must use this terminal to communicate with two respondents; one respondent is another person, the other a computer. The examiner's task is to decide which respondent is human solely on the basis of their dialogue. The rules permit the examiner to ask any question except "Are you a computer?". A sample dialogue might go like this:

Question: How much is 23,440 and 34?
Answer: 23,474.

Question: Have you studied history?
Answer: Yes.

Question: When was Scotland united with England?
Answer: 1603.

Question: Are you depressed?
Answer: I never get depressed.

Turing believed that any computer clever enough to pass this test deserved to be considered conscious. At the time he proposed it, Turing's test, like Boring's "potato" question, was completely hypothetical; modern computers had not yet been invented. Even today, no computer can pass Turing's test, but there is a good chance such a machine may be created in the future. Suppose that in the next few years engineers were able to create a computerised robot smart enough to pass Turing's test. Would this robot be conscious? Both Boring and Turing would say that, provided we stick to operational definitions (and do not care about what is going on inside), the answer is yes. If a computer behaves like a person, then it is one, behaviourally speaking.

It is no accident that Boring and Turing's papers appeared within a few years of one another. The 1940s and 1950s were years when behaviourism reigned supreme over experimental psychology. Both writers were simply expounding one of behaviourism's main tenets — psychologists can only study overt activity. From the behaviourist's viewpoint, what goes on inside an organism is unknowable and, for scientific purposes, irrelevant. This chapter is concerned with two classic experiments in the history of behaviourism: Ivan Pavlov's discovery of the conditioned reflex and John Watson's famous "Little Albert". Both experiments were performed in the early decades of this century by scientists who were influenced by similar philosophical ideas and who were both reacting against the sterile research of their contemporaries. Before reading of their experiments, it is useful to know the context in which they were performed.

PHYSIOLOGY OF THE MIND

The mind–body (or mind–brain) problem has a long history in philosophy and psychology, one which is discussed in more detail in Chapters Two and Three. For the present, it is sufficient to note that in the modern era, philosophical discussions about the relationship between the brain and the mind are usually considered to begin with the writings of the French philosopher René Descartes. Descartes believed that the body is merely a machine and something quite separate from the mind or soul. (The distinction between mind and soul is difficult to make in French where the same word applies to both.) Descartes believed that the mind is a sort of spirit that lives in the brain's pineal gland where it directs behaviour by giving orders to the body through the brain. Although the pineal gland no longer features importantly in philosophical thought, even today there are philosophers who view the mind and the brain as two separate entities.

Descartes' *dualist* view of the mind–body split was opposed by philosophers holding the opposite (*monist*) theory. Monists equate the mind with the brain, seeing them as pretty much the same thing. Since the eighteenth century, monist philosophers have been known as *materialists* because they reject Descartes' spiritual notion of mind. Instead of a spirit, materialists believe the brain is only a machine; it secretes thoughts the way the stomach secretes digestive juices.

Although it is doubtful that the mind–body debate will ever end, the monist position has become increasingly popular as more is learned about how the brain works. Many particularly important breakthroughs took place in the second half of the nineteenth century. For example, improved microscopic methods made it possible to visualise the neuron (the nerve cell) for the first time. It was also during this period that the speed of the nerve impulse was measured. But perhaps the most important discovery of nineteenth-century neurophysiology, at least as far as psychology was concerned, was the delineation of the mechanism underlying the *reflex arc*.

Of course, reflexive behaviour was observed long before the nineteenth century. Descriptions of the familiar "knee-jerk" reflex and the pupillary reflex (the contraction of the pupil in response to light) go back thousands of years. Even the word *reflex* was not coined in the 1800s. Descartes used it hundreds of years before. What had not been known previously was how reflexes work. We owe our present understanding of reflexes to many physiologists, but one was particularly aware of the profound importance reflexes hold for psychology. This scientist was the Russian Ivan M. Sechenov.

In his book *Reflexes of the Brain*, Sechenov tried to show that all complex forms of behaviour can be viewed as "brain reflexes". For Sechenov, so-called voluntary movements — those involved in playing tennis, for instance — are simply chains of reflexes built up over a lifetime. In a similar manner, he viewed emotional reactions (sadness, joy) as reflexive responses to certain environmental events. Sechenov believed that even thoughts are brain reflexes, albeit with their motor components inhibited. To back up this latter claim, he performed an experiment in which salt was placed on the top end of a frog's severed spinal cord. The salt inhibited spinal reflexes, thus demonstrating that brain inhibition is possible.

With the possible exception of his demonstration of inhibition, Sechenov's contribution to science was not so much empirical as theoretical. He not only insisted that all psychological phenomena can be understood as reflexive responses to environmental stimulation, he also believed that new reflexes could be learned. For Sechenov, the elucidation of the various reflexes (what stimuli set them off, how they are inhibited) and the mechanisms by which new reflexes are learned is what psychology should be all about. As far as he was concerned, studying the contents of the mind through introspection — the common preoccupation of nineteenth-century psychologists — was not only unscientific but also a waste of time.

Sechenov's ideas were not well received by the Tsar's committee of censors which charged him with advocating a "materialist theory" that "reduces even the best men to the level of a machine devoid of . . . free will, and acting automatically". And, as if that were not bad enough, the committee also found his views "opposed to both Christianity and the Penal Code" and conducive to the "corruption of morals". Despite this and other attacks, Sechenov's book was well received by Russian scientists who welcomed it as a blueprint for the creation of an objective science of psychology. His strong belief that psychology should confine itself to studying only overt behaviour makes him a direct forerunner of twentieth-century behaviourists.

Sechenov's book exerted an especially profound effect on the Russian physiologist Ivan Pavlov, who was 20 years his junior. It was Pavlov who eventually performed the experiments necessary to provide Sechenov's theories with an empirical base. But Pavlov did not set out to become a psychologist, or even a neurophysiologist. His first research, for which he was to become very famous, was concerned with blood circulation and digestion. Yet, as will be shown, his psychological research grew out of these earlier investigations.

IVAN P. PAVLOV: FATHER OF BEHAVIOURAL PSYCHOLOGY

Ivan Petrovich Pavlov was born on 14 September 1849 in the ancient Russian peasant village of Ryazan, about 300 kilometres from Moscow. He was the eldest of 11 children. Pavlov's early years were harsh and filled with manual work; but the work seemed to suit him and throughout his long life he enjoyed gardening and other forms of manual labour. When he was seven, Pavlov fell off a stairway, sustaining a severe blow to his head from the hard tile floor. The concussion must have been quite serious: for four years it left him unable to attend school or to pursue any task that required mental effort.

Pavlov recovered, however, and at the age of 11 he was sent to a nearby theological seminary to prepare for the priesthood. Although those were hardly enlightened days in Russia, this theological seminary was not nearly so sheltered as others of the time. Pavlov had access to and read many "progressive" books and journals. His reading got him interested in the larger world, particularly in science. Eventually his scientific interests outweighed his religious commitment and he gave up his plans for a religious career in favour of a scientific one. In 1870

FIG. 3. *Ivan Pavlov (1849–1936), discoverer of the conditioned reflex*

Pavlov entered St Petersburg University intending to study physics, but he soon switched to physiology, a science that was enjoying explosive growth in those years. He proved an apt student and won the university's gold medal at his graduation in 1875.

For the next eight years Pavlov pursued medical studies, working in the research laboratory of the local veterinary institute. The Tsar and the feudal lords who ruled Russia in those days had little interest in scientific research and funded such activities accordingly. As a consequence, those interested in research careers had to learn to make do. Pavlov, for example, had to pay for his experimental animals out of his wretchedly inadequate wages, leaving little extra for rent. He learned to cope by sleeping in the laboratory and eating only when necessary. Even after he married in 1880 Pavlov lived and slept in the lab while his young wife lodged with her brother-in-law. In 1883 Pavlov received his doctorate as well as the title "Professor". It was also a year of tragedy for him as his first child, a boy, died after a prolonged illness.

Pavlov spent the next two years studying at the ancient University of Leipzig in Germany before returning to Russia to pursue physiological research into blood circulation and digestion. In 1887 he published a well-received book on this research. But, though his reputation grew, he and his family continued to live in very poor circumstances. In fact, although he was close to 40, Pavlov had no proper job and his wife was often forced to live with relatives. He applied for several positions, but received few offers. Eventually he wound up at the Military Medical Academy in St Petersburg, the same institution in which Sechenov had worked.

Pavlov began at the Academy as Professor of Pharmacology but after a short time was given the Chair of Physiology which he held for over 30 years. In addition to his work at the Academy, Pavlov founded the physiology laboratory at the Institute of Experimental Medicine which he headed for 40 years and where he performed most of his important research. For a time he also ran a third laboratory at the Academy of Sciences.

Pavlov's research into circulation and digestion revealed basic facts about both systems. In recognition of his accomplishments, he was awarded the Nobel Prize in physiology and medicine in 1904. However, Pavlov did not rest on his laurels. In fact, the research he conducted after receiving the Nobel Prize is more famous today than his earlier work. His experimental work was slowed down a little by the First World War and the revolution of 1917, but even during those terrible times he kept doing experiments. When there was no electricity or gas for light, he worked by the light of wooden torches. When there was no heat in the laboratory, he worked in coat, cap and boots. Sometimes it got so cold in the lab that the animals froze, but Pavlov kept on working. It seems almost as if Pavlov was making up for the weakness that left him unable to perform mental tasks as a young child by doing the work of three men as an adult. Between the ages of 47 and 72 Pavlov published 40 books and lectures on psychology, psychiatry and brain physiology. Many of these lectures continue to be cited as authoritative even today. He did not begin to slow down until he was almost 80 and, even then, he tried to keep up with developments in physiology and psychology.

Pavlov died in 1936 at the age of 87. At the time of his death he was the world's most famous physiologist and second only to Sigmund Freud in his influence on modern psychology. Since the 1920s Pavlov's name has appeared in every psychology textbook ever written, and probably always will. Although he accomplished much in his long lifetime, the work that he is best known for is surely one of the most famous experiments in psychology — his demonstration of the conditioned reflex.

CLASSIC EXPERIMENT 1:

THE CONDITIONED REFLEX

If a hungry young puppy, newly weaned from milk but never given meat to eat, is shown a piece of steak, it shows no reaction other than idle curiosity. If the puppy is allowed to put the meat in its mouth, however, it immediately begins to salivate and before you know it, the steak is gone. After the puppy has tasted steak on several occasions, a change will be noticed in its behaviour. The puppy now begins to salivate as soon as it sees the meat, before the food reaches its mouth. Some puppies have even been known to begin salivating as soon as they hear the footsteps of the person who usually feeds them. There is nothing particularly startling about these observations; dog owners have been making them since the beginning of time. Pavlov also noted changes in salivation habits while pursuing his research on digestion (he used dogs as subjects). The difference between Pavlov's observations and those of millions of other dog owners is that Pavlov began to wonder about them. It is often this way in science. Simple everyday phenomena that most of us take for granted strike a brilliant scientist as worth studying, and sometimes important insights result.

Pavlov's earlier experiments showed that puppies (and other animals) are born with an innate salivation reflex which is triggered by placing food in the mouth. Actually, there is more than one such reflex. The amount and even the type of saliva a puppy produces depends on the nature of the food in its mouth. Pavlov called the salivation stimulated by food a *psychic secretion* because he believed it was the result of a brain reflex.

Pavlov knew that nerve fibres from the mouth convey information about the food to the brain where it stimulates another brain site that controls the amount (and type) of saliva produced in the digestive glands. But what sets off the reflex when the food is just seen rather than placed in the mouth? And why should a few tastes of meat cause a puppy who previously did not salivate at the sight of meat to begin salivating whenever meat comes into view? Can reflexes work "at a distance"? Can they be learned? These were the questions Pavlov sought to answer.

Before he began doing his own research, Pavlov consulted with psychologist colleagues to see how they would approach such an obviously psychological problem. But he did not like the advice he received. Psychology at the turn of the century was still largely dualist in orientation. Its main goal was describing subjective experiences and its major method was introspection. To be sure, psychologists did experiments — rats ran through mazes, people pushed buttons — but the results of these experiments were interpreted in terms of how the subjects (animal or human) subjectively felt about what was happening to them. A typical psychological explanation for a rat's behaviour in a maze might be: the rat turned left because the right corridor produced fearful feelings arising from previous electric shocks received there. In this same spirit,

Pavlov was told that to find out why a dog salivates at the sight of meat, he should try putting himself in his subject's place and think like a dog.

Pavlov, however, was a monist. Like Sechenov, he believed that the mind is not separate from the brain and that introspection is not an adequate scientific method. He rejected the introspective approach and resolved to design a method for observing the human mind from the outside. Following Sechenov's recommendation, he decided to study reflexes without reference to inner mental states. Preparing to begin this research, he wrote:

The first and most important task before us, then, is to abandon entirely the natural inclination to transpose our own subjective condition upon the reaction of the experimental animal, and instead, to concentrate our whole attention upon the investigation of the correlation between the external phenomena and the reaction of the organism.

In other words, Pavlov set out to study "the mind" as a physiologist studies any other organ of the body — by performing overt experiments and seeing what happens. For the rest of his life Pavlov insisted that what he was doing was properly called physiology rather than psychology. Even to this day Russian scientists interested in learning and conditioning are known as physiologists rather than psychologists as in the West.

Pavlov's classic experiment was conducted in 1905. (Actually, there were several experiments, but all illustrate the same point.) Pavlov had always used dogs as subjects and he already knew a great deal about salivary reflexes, so he decided to use both in his experiment. However, this experiment was different from any he had done in the past. Now he was after the general principles of learning rather than the physiology of digestion. There is nothing special about salivation in this regard, he could have used any reflex and obtained the same findings (a fact confirmed by many subsequent researchers).

Pavlov's experiment required that a dog be placed in a special apparatus. The idea was to keep the dog from moving about too much and to keep its head looking forward. A cup fastened to the dog's cheek collected saliva flowing from its parotid salivary gland which had been surgically redirected to the outside of the cheek through a fistula (duct). The saliva passed from the collection cup into a tube which was connected to an instrument designed to measure with great accuracy every drop of saliva the dog secreted.

The experiment took place in a sound-proof room while Pavlov observed what was going on through a viewing port. Using mechanical "arms", he could move a food pan within the dog's reach or place some food into its mouth without entering

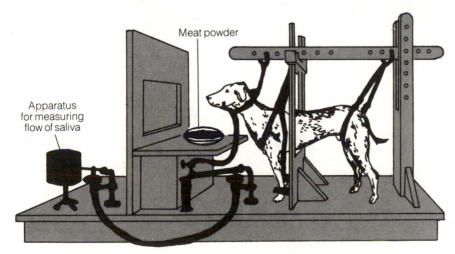

Meat powder

Apparatus for measuring flow of saliva

FIG. 4. *Pavlov's conditioning apparatus*

the room. Pavlov also had the ability to present the dog with a variety of different stimuli: lights, buzzers, bells, even a metronome. In later research Pavlov found that any stimulus will work in a conditioning experiment, so long as the animal notices it.

In the classic experiment, Pavlov began by sounding the bell and noting that the dog did not salivate. And there was no reason why it should. At the outset, there was no connection between the bell and salivation. Then followed a series of trials during which the sound of the bell was immediately followed by the presentation of food. On these trials, saliva did appear in response to the food. After the bell and food were paired a few times, Pavlov presented the bell alone, not followed by any food. This time, the animal salivated to the bell even though no food was presented. The paired (bell followed by food) trials were resumed and after a few more pairings, the bell was again presented alone. Now the dog produced more saliva to the bell than it did before. By alternating paired trials with presentations of the bell alone, Pavlov showed that the salivary response was becoming stronger. Thus, a formerly neutral stimulus, the bell, became associated with the food and came to produce salivation. This is all there was to Pavlov's classic experiment — no control groups, no elaborate statistical procedures — merely the repeated pairing of two stimuli until both produced the same response. Sounds simple, doesn't it? Well, it is simple. Nevertheless, this experiment had a profound influence on practically every branch of psychology. Before examining why, it is helpful to understand the vocabulary associated with the experiment.

Pavlov called the process by which the bell came to elicit salivation in the dog *conditioning*. The neutral stimulus, the bell in the classic experiment, is called the *conditioned stimulus* or CS. Other than arousing curiosity, the CS produces no response in the animal. The other stimulus in the experiment, the food, is called the *unconditioned stimulus* or UCS. The UCS receives its name because, unlike the CS, it produces an innate, reflexive response (salivation, in the classic experiment). This reflexive response is known as the *unconditioned response* or UCR. (The UCS and UCR are *unconditioned* because no training is required to produce their connection.) The CS and UCS are presented sequentially in a series of conditioning trials. The interval between the presentation of the CS and the UCS is known as the *inter-stimulus interval*. After a number of pairings, the CS begins to produce a response on its own. This response is known as the *conditioned response* or CR. The CR and UCR, although similar, are not always identical. For example, the dog in the classic experiment usually produced more saliva at the sight of the food than at the sound of the bell even after many conditioning trials. The important point is that, after conditioning, a previously neutral stimulus produces a response formerly associated only with the UCS.

Pavlov's classic experiment showed how new "reflexes" can be learned by association with innate ones. This demonstration provided empirical support for Sechenov's view that behaviour can be understood as learned reflexes and, at the same time, encouraged Pavlov in his belief that psychology can be studied by objective physiological methods. Pavlov went on to show that conditioning works with practically any neutral stimulus and with a variety of innate reflexes, even unpleasant ones. For example, a mild electric shock to an animal's leg produces an innate reflex — the leg is withdrawn. A neutral CS (say, a bell again) paired with the shock soon begins to produce the same response. What is more, the animal's fear at being shocked (manifested by heavy breathing, barking and so on) also becomes associated with the CS and it shows its fear every time it hears the bell. The conditioning of emotional responses by classical conditioning will be seen to form an important part of the reasoning behind John Watson's classic experiment described later in this chapter.

After conditioning occurs, the CS alone elicits the conditioned response even when the UCS is no longer present. However, if the CS is continually presented alone, the CR gradually disappears. In the classic experiment, repeated presentations of the bell alone produce a little less saliva on each trial. Pavlov called this process *extinction*. Although the gradual nature of extinction makes it seem as if the animal is simply forgetting what was previously learned, matters turn out to be not quite so simple. If, in the classic experiment, an animal who has stopped salivating to the bell is removed from the room and given a rest it will resume salivating to the bell when returned to the conditioning laboratory. This recovery of the CR will occur even though the bell has not been paired again with food. This phenomenon is known as *spontaneous recovery*; it indicates that although the dog has stopped salivating to the CS it has not forgotten what it learned. Further evidence that extinction is not the

same as forgetting comes from *reconditioning* experiments in which animals who show complete extinction of the CR are again given a series of conditioning trials. Such reconditioning always requires fewer pairings of the CS and UCS than the original conditioning, indicating that some memory of the original learning is still present. Pavlov concluded that in many cases of extinction, the CR is temporarily *inhibited* rather than forgotten.

Pavlov spent years exploring the limits of conditioning. He found, among other things, that there are optimum CS-UCS intervals (about one-fourth of a second for the salivary response). Longer intervals lead to less efficient learning. He also showed that presenting the CS after the UCS produces no learning at all. This last finding, by the way, is not one that most "armchair" psychologists of the time predicted. To be sure they believed that learning could occur by "association" but no-one before Pavlov guessed that the order in which stimuli are presented makes any difference.

Although the discovery and exploration of the conditioning process would have been sufficient to earn Pavlov a place in the history of psychology, it is the way he used his discoveries that makes his work im-

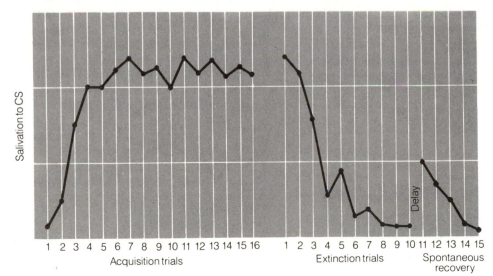

FIG. 5. *The left-hand graph depicts the acquisition of a conditioned salivary response. Drops of salivation produced to the CS (prior to the presentation of the UCS) are plotted on the vertical axis; the number of conditioning trials appears on the horizontal axis. The CR gradually increases until it tops out at about 12 drops of saliva. After 16 conditioning trials, the experimenter switches to extinction. The results appear in the right-hand graph. Note the CR gradually decreases to zero but then recovers when testing begins again after a delay*

Salivation to CS

1 2 3 4 5 6 7 8 9 10 11 12 13 14 15 16
Acquisition trials

1 2 3 4 5 6 7 8 9 10 11 12 13 14 15
Extinction trials

Delay

Spontaneous recovery

portant today. Pavlov showed how conditioning can be used as a substitute for introspection, as an objective way of learning what is happening in a person's or even an animal's mind. His major tools, in this effort, were the related phenomena of *generalisation* and *discrimination*.

Pavlov noticed almost from the beginning of his research that animals conditioned to salivate at the sound of a bell would also salivate (but not quite as much) at the sound of a buzzer or the tick of a metronome. He concluded that the animals were generalising their conditioned response to stimuli similar to the bell. Subsequent experiments showed that the degree of generalisation (measured by the amount of saliva produced) is directly related to the physical similarity of the stimuli. Pavlov immediately realised that stimulus generalisation provided a window into the "mind" of the experimental animal. By presenting a series of stimuli and noting the size of the CR, he could tell how similar the stimuli subjectively appeared to the animal. If the CRs to two stimuli were equal, then Pavlov knew that — to the animal — the two stimuli were identical. If, on the other hand, one stimulus brought forth copious amounts of saliva whereas the other produced only a few drops, Pavlov knew that the two stimuli, although related, appeared subjectively different to the dog. Although the implications of stimulus generalisation were exciting, Pavlov soon found that he could learn even more by requiring animals to make stimulus discriminations.

In a typical discrimination experiment, the animal must learn that one stimulus is reliably associated with the UCS and the other is not. For example, in some trials the bell could be paired with food (as in the classic experiment), while in other trials a buzzer could be presented by itself. In the beginning the animal makes salivary responses to both sounds, but after a while it extinguishes its response to the buzzer and salivates only to the bell. When this happens the animal is said to have learned to discriminate between the two stimuli. Of course, if the two stimuli are very similar the animal will not be able to discriminate between them and it will continue making the CR to both. Thus, by increasing and decreasing stimulus similarity, Pavlov was able to determine the exact point at which an animal could no longer tell two stimuli apart, that is, the point at which, to the animal, the stimuli appeared identical. In this way, Pavlov was able to measure objectively an animal's subjective impressions without engaging in the unsatisfactory enterprise of putting himself in an animal's (or another human's) mind.

Thus Pavlov's simple experiment accomplished several purposes. It showed that reflexes can be learned and that such learning accounts for the way an organism reacts in many situations. In addition, it also provided a way to unite physiology and psychology. Pavlov used his classic experiment to show how the subjective contents of the "mind" can be studied without resorting to introspection. Because the classical conditioning procedure can be applied to questions that are too complex for armchair introspection (whether a dog can discriminate between a bell and a buzzer, for example), Pavlov's classic experiment paved the way for a scientific psychology based on observing objective behaviour.

Pavlov's research was conducted on animals, but conditioning affects human beings as well. Experimenters have demonstrated human conditioning using reflexes such as the knee-jerk or the eye-blink caused by a puff of air. Conditioning in humans has even been shown when the CRs are physiological. For example, a mild electric shock (the UCS) temporarily increases heart rate (UCR). This reflex is innate. If a bell (CS) is rung just before the shock, it will eventually come to produce an increased heart rate (CR) all on its own. It is possible that many of our emotional reactions are learned through conditioning. For example, a baby, who normally looks up at its mother while nursing, learns to associate its mother's face with the pleasures of food. Soon, through conditioning, the mother's face alone evokes the same pleasurable feeling. Negative emotions can also be conditioned. Neutral stimuli paired with a fearful experience may come to produce fear entirely on their own. This hypothesis was the motivation for Watson's classic experiment which is discussed next.

JOHN WATSON: BEHAVIOURIST

John B. Watson was born in 1878 in a small community near Greenville, South Carolina, in southern USA. As a youngster he walked three kilometres each way to attend a small country school and spent a great deal of his own free time doing manual work. He became a fair carpenter while still young and, like Pavlov, maintained a life-long interest in working with his hands. As an adult he built a 10-room house by himself over the course of two summers, and even at the age of 55 he spent his weekends building a barn. Although it is hard to generalise from such a small sample, it is interesting to note that the two men most responsible for the birth of behaviourism were both fond of manual work. In later chapters in this book the lives of antibehaviourists such as Lewis Terman are described. By and large, they turn out to be mechanically inept people who hated working with their hands. It seems psychologists may choose scientific viewpoints that fit comfortably with their own personalities.

Watson was a wild and impulsive youth who got into trouble with the police for fighting and for firing guns on more than one occasion. Although he gave up this reckless behaviour when he reached adulthood, some rebelliousness and resistance to authority remained with him throughout his life. In any event, Watson's troubles were never serious enough to interfere with his school performance. He entered Furman University in Greenville in 1894 when he was 16 years old and emerged five years later with a master's degree. He supported himself during those five years by working as an assistant in the chemical laboratory, a job in which his manual dexterity served him well.

Watson's personality is revealed by his profoundly negative opinions of Furman University and of education in general. He felt that school "leads to a softness and laziness and a prolongation of infancy with a killing of all vocational bents". He looked upon colleges and universities as places "for boys and girls to be penned up in until they reach their majority" at which point the world could "sift them out". Watson reports that he was the only person to pass Greek in his senior year. He accomplished this feat by going to his room at two o'clock in the afternoon before the final exam with one quart of Coca-Cola syrup and sitting in a chair cramming until time for the exam the next day.

In his fourth year, by "some stroke

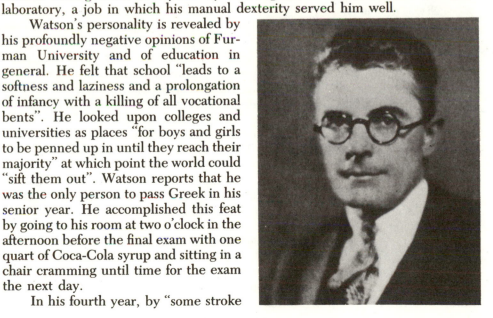

FIG. 6. *John Watson (1878–1958), founder of behaviourism*

of bad luck", Watson handed in a term paper put together "back to front". He failed the course and was kept from graduating. (This is why he was at Furman for five years.) He vowed that he would become a psychologist (the field of the professor who failed him) and so famous that the professor would have to seek him out for help one day. Amazingly, this actually happened. Some years later his former teacher applied to study under Watson, who accepted him. Unfortunately the professor died before he could begin his studies.

After graduating from Furman, Watson attended graduate school at the University of Chicago. Because he arrived in Chicago with only $50 in his pocket, Watson had no choice but to support himself by waiting on tables for $2.50 per week. He sometimes supplemented this income by working as an "assistant janitor". After a few years the load became too much and Watson suffered a sort of nervous collapse. He could not sleep at night, became afraid of the dark and had trouble concentrating. A few weeks' rest, however, and he seemed as good as new. The only remaining trace of his experience was an uncharacteristic (for a behaviourist) interest in Freud's theory of neurosis.

Despite this temporary setback, Watson's research went well and he received his Ph.D. in only three years. At 24 Watson was one of the youngest Ph.D.s ever to graduate from the University of Chicago. He stayed on at Chicago working on psychology and neurophysiology until, in 1907, he was offered the job of Associate Professor of Psychology at Johns Hopkins University in Baltimore at a salary of $2500 per year. Watson hesitated, however, because he wanted more money. Not only did he owe one of his professors $350 (borrowed to publish his doctoral research) but he was also now a married man with a family. In 1908 Johns Hopkins tried again. This time Watson was offered the Chair of Psychology at $3500 per year and he accepted.

In his early years at Johns Hopkins, Watson taught the accepted psychology of the time — examining the contents of the mind through introspection. But, like Pavlov, he soon became disenchanted with this approach, preferring to examine behaviour objectively. These were the years when Pavlov (already famous as a Nobel laureate) was publishing his work on conditioning. Watson was one of the first American psychologists to realise the significance of Pavlov's work for the field. In 1913 he published "Psychology as the Behaviourist Views It", a paper in which he argued vigorously for an objective, non-introspective science of psychology. Watson used the word *behaviourism* to represent his theoretical viewpoint. For him, behaviourism meant a psychological science based solely on observable behavioural phenomena. He did not deny that consciousness exists but believed it could not be studied by introspection. Like Pavlov, he believed that sensations are best studied by observing discriminations and that emotions could be given objective operational definitions as well.

Watson was a vigorous propagandist and his behaviouristic views quickly took hold. He became famous and was elected president of the American Psychological Association in 1915 when he was 37 years old. His career was temporarily interrupted by the First World War, in which he served as an army psychologist on the board responsible for choosing men to be trained as pilots. His military experience was not happy. His rebelliousness and contemptuous attitude toward authority almost got him court martialled or, even worse, sent to the front. Anyway, he got out alive and returned to Johns Hopkins where he continued his research, becoming more and more interested in applying behaviourist techniques to the study of abnormal psychology. He worked closely with Adolph Meyer, the director of the psychiatry clinic at Hopkins. Surprisingly, Meyer, one of Sigmund Freud's students, and Watson, the arch behaviourist, got on very well. It was during these postwar years that Watson's classic experiment on the development of fears in young children was conducted.

CLASSIC EXPERIMENT 2:

LITTLE ALBERT

By far the most important development in modern abnormal psychology was Sigmund Freud's system of psychoanalysis. Before Freud, patients suffering from psychological disorders were viewed with a combination of suspicion and disdain. Suspicion because many symptoms (hysteria, for example) were viewed as signs of malingering, and disdain because psychological disorders were seen as a sign of weakness. Freud spent 10 hours a day for about 40 years listening to patients reveal their most secret inner thoughts and feelings. He used the data gathered in these interviews to form a theory that challenged the traditional view. Because of his work, psychologists and psychiatrists became aware of the importance of unconscious conflicts in creating psychological problems. Freud's background and history are described more fully in Chapter Eleven. For the present, we are concerned only with one of his cases: Little Hans, a boy who feared horses.

Freud published the *Analysis of a Phobia in a Five-year-old Boy* in 1909. As it turns out, the case was to become one of his most famous. The analysis described in the book was carried out almost entirely by mail. Freud met the youngster only once, very briefly. All of his information about the case came from the boy's father. The father would make observations, ask his son questions and relay the answers to Freud, who then wrote back suggesting further questions and observations. Because Freud quoted extensively from this correspondence in his book, Little Hans's phobia is his most completely documented case.

Hans, the five-year-old boy who was the subject of the analysis, was born in Vienna in 1903 to a young doctor and his wife. The doctor was an adherent of Freud's views who attempted to bring up his son with little coercion. He had also got into the habit of writing to Freud about his son's development. In 1906 Hans's sister Hanna was born. Hans showed some jealousy at first but this apparently did not last. There seemed few problems at home until Hans was eight years old. It was then that he developed an unreasonable fear, a phobia, concerning horses. Hans was afraid that a horse might bite him and even refused to leave the house lest he encounter one. He particularly feared white horses with black mouths and blinkers.

Freud examined Hans's father's letters looking for facts that could be of aetiological significance. He noted that Hans often described his father in the same terms he used to describe horses. He referred to both horses and his father as "proud" and "very white" and once asked his father not to "trot" away. Freud also noted that Hans's father had a black beard around his mouth and wore glasses. From these similarities he speculated that there might be a connection between Hans's father and horses. Freud also noted that Hans was fond of crawling into his mother's bed when his father was away.

Freud gathered many such facts from the father's letters and eventually put them together to produce an explanation for Hans's phobia. According to Freud, Hans's fear of horses was intimately related to his attempt to deal with an unconscious

26

conflict. Hans, he felt, was sexually attracted to his mother and jealous of his father, whom he perceived as a rival for his mother's affections. These hostile feelings toward his father were threatening to Hans. After all, his father was much bigger and stronger. Hans could not be comfortable harbouring such feelings about his father, so he tried to get rid of them. One way to do this, according to Freud, is to displace unwanted feelings onto some other object; in Hans's case, it was horses. Hans eventually overcame his fear. In fact, in a later publication, Freud describes a meeting he had with Hans when the boy was 19. Hans, he writes, was a "strapping", well-adjusted youth who was psychologically healthy. (Interestingly, Freud reports that Hans's parents divorced after the analysis of their son's phobia.)

According to Freud, then, Hans's fear of horses was a symbolic representation of his real fear, his father. Freud believed that phobias like Hans's serve a function. They help the individual to redirect unacceptable thoughts into safer channels. Hans was uncomfortable with the feelings he had about his father, so he displaced them onto horses. For Freud, all phobias are ultimately the result of such unconscious conflicts. It was from this case that he developed the concept of the Oedipus complex.

Freud's analysis of Hans's phobia had an enormous impact on psychology. The child, who soon became known as "Little Hans", was his best-known psychoanalytic case. In clinics throughout the world, psychologists began looking for the unconscious conflicts in their phobic patients. There were those, however, who doubted Freud's explanation. One of these doubters was John Watson.

A great part of Watson's discomfort stemmed from Freud's interpretive method which was entirely too subjective for a behaviourist. But it was not only Freud's method that disturbed Watson. He also believed

FIG. 7. *Sigmund Freud (1856–1939), founder of psychoanalysis*

that Freud had ignored some relevant data. In one of his letters, Hans's father mentioned that his son had once witnessed an accident in which large horses pulling a heavily loaded wagon were thrown to the ground and created quite a loud row before things were put right. Watson believed that such an experience by itself could have produced the boy's fear through Pavlovian conditioning. Thus there was no need to look for the cause in unconscious Oedipal conflicts. Watson decided to support his argument with an experiment proving that children's fears could be produced by conditioning. His first attempt to condition fear using artificial thunder and lightning in the laboratory was a failure, but then he hit on another method using a different feared stimulus.

Watson and his graduate student, Rosalie Rayner, chose as their subject an 11-month-old infant named Albert B. Albert's mother was a wet-nurse in a Baltimore hospital for invalid children and Albert had lived in the same hospital most of his life. They described the youngster as stolid and unemotional as well as quite healthy. Although they realised that they were setting out to produce a "phobia" in the child, they were not too worried. They felt that their procedures would do the boy "little harm". And they "comforted" themselves with the knowledge that fears "would arise anyway as soon as the child left the sheltered environment of the nursery for the rough and tumble of the home".

The two experimenters realised that in order to employ Pavlovian conditioning they first had to have an unconditioned stimulus, a UCS, which innately produced fear. They chose for this purpose a loud, unexpected noise created by striking a 120-centimetre-long steel bar with a hammer. They tried out this UCS on Albert who "caught his breath", "puckered his lips" and, after a few such surprises, began to cry. Clearly, the experimenters had found their UCS. As a CS, they used a white laboratory rat. Before the experiment Albert had no fear of the white rat and was willing to touch and play with it.

The experiment began with two conditioning trials in which the rat was presented to Albert followed quickly by the loud noise. Several days later the rat was presented to Albert without the noise and the child was observed to be hesitant about touching it. Albert was then given five more trials during which the rat and the noise were paired. At this point showing him the rat alone (without noise) was enough to make him cry.

The experimenters believed that they had now produced a phobia to rats in Albert by conditioning, and set out to test how widely his fear had generalised. They found no fear of the building blocks Albert habitually played with, but they did find indications of fear of objects related in some way to the rat. For example, Albert now appeared to fear a rabbit and a dog. Watson and Rayner concluded that the child's fear of the rat had generalised to other furry objects. Further evidence of generalisation was Albert's fretting when presented with a seal coat and a Santa Claus mask (with beard). He was also somewhat afraid of cottonwool balls at first, but quickly got over this.

Five days after examining Albert's reaction to these objects, Watson and Rayner noted that his fear of the rat had diminished, so they gave him another conditioning trial. They also banged the bar in the presence of the dog and the rabbit. This latter procedure made fairly meaningless further tests of fear generalisation, which took place about a month later, as Albert had now been conditioned to fear these generalisation stimuli as well. Shortly thereafter Albert went home to live and was never seen again.

This was the entire experiment. There were no control subjects, no careful monitoring of the CR and some confusion introduced by pairing the noise with the rabbit and dog as well as the rat. There is even some doubt about whether Albert's fear of the rat could really be classified as a phobia. According to the experimenters themselves, he showed no fear at all so long as he was permitted to suck his thumb. Watson and Rayner reported: "The moment the hand reached the mouth he became impervious to the stimuli producing fear. Again and again we had to remove the thumb from his mouth before the conditioned response could be obtained." What sort of a phobia is this? And what sort of an experiment?

From an ethical standpoint, it is unlikely that such an experiment could ever be done again. Today's psychologists are bound by ethical rules not to expose subjects to harm and, when harm does occur, they are obliged to do something about it. No-one today would permit Albert to leave the hospital without trying to help him overcome his fear. Watson and Rayner's experiment was also grossly inadequate from a methodological point of view. Their procedure was loose and their measurements were extremely crude. Compare, for example, Pavlov's counting every

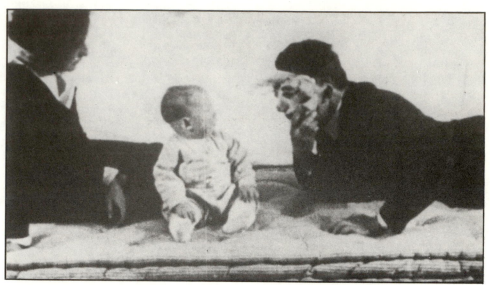

FIG. 8. *John Watson (in mask) and Rosalie Rayner testing the generalisation of Little Albert's phobia*

drop of saliva with Watson and Rayner's description of Albert's response to the fur coat ("he fretted"). Yet the experiment truly is a classic. Not only has it been cited in just about every psychology textbook published since it was performed, it has also convinced many psychologists that there is an alternative to Freudian psychoanalysis. Indeed, this was Watson's main purpose in performing the experiment in the first place. At the end of their paper, Watson and Rayner write:

The Freudians, twenty years from now, unless their hypotheses change, when they come to analyze Albert's fear of a sealskin coat — assuming that he comes to analysis at that age — will probably tease from him the recital of a dream which, upon their analysis, will show that Albert at three years of age attempted to play with the public hair of the mother and was scolded violently for it.

Largely because of this experiment, psychologists came to believe that neurotic symptoms like phobias can be understood in conditioning terms and perhaps even cured by conditioning. Behaviour therapy, a thriving enterprise today, traces its beginning back to this flawed experiment. In this instance, as in others described in this book, an experiment with serious methodological flaws was still able to exert an enormous influence because its findings were so provocative.

AFTERMATH

Pavlov continued to be an active researcher throughout the 1920s and most of the 1930s. He expanded his work on conditioning and became more and more interested in abnormal behaviour. By the time of his death in 1936, he had made major contributions to our understanding not only of conditioning but also abnormal psychology, personality and neurophysiology. Although some of his ideas have inevitably been modified through the years, he is generally considered to have been more right than wrong on most issues and he had much to do with the development of behaviourism. It was Pavlov, more than anyone else, who convinced psychologists to abandon Descartes' dichotomy of mind and soul and to view the mind from "without rather than within".

Watson's classic experiment also attracted a great deal of professional attention. A film he made of Albert's conditioning experiences helped communicate his research to the lay public as well. Despite his experiment's flaws, Watson believed that he had proved his point. Fears could be created by conditioning. But he did not stop at this. All human behaviour, he insisted, was simply a matter of conditioning. This led to his most famous statement:

Give me a dozen healthy infants, well-formed, and my own specialized world to bring them up in, and I'll guarantee to take any one at random and train him to become any type of specialist I might select — doctor, lawyer, artist, merchant chief and yes, even beggarman and thief, regardless of his talents, penchants, tendencies, abilities, vocations and race of his ancestors.

Strong stuff. Unfortunately Watson never got to prove his point. In 1920, just after his classic experiment was published, he became the first scientist to study the physiological aspects of sexual arousal. Anticipating Masters and Johnson by four decades, Watson studied the physiology of sex directly by attaching electrodes to couples and taking recordings while they engaged in intercourse. As a dedicated scientist, Watson decided to become his own experimental subject, but his wife refused to participate. Undaunted, Watson turned elsewhere. His wife soon began to wonder why he was spending so much time in the lab with his young research assistant, Rosalie Rayner. She soon found out. Watson was forced to resign from Johns Hopkins and he never held an academic post again. (A married man's conduct was taken rather more seriously in those days than it is today.) His resignation was followed by a public divorce trial that left him stranded both economically and emotionally. He married Rosalie Rayner and began picking up the pieces of his shattered life by taking a job with the advertising firm J. Walter Thompson. Watson, who had been a professor at age 29, was sent door-to-door canvassing for a rubber boot company and he later sold coffee in Pittsburgh. For a while he was a clerk at Macy's department store in New York. He moved up quickly and by 1924 was a vice-president of J. Walter Thompson. Except for some lectures at the New School for Social Research in New York, Watson never returned to academic life although he did write articles on child-rearing for popular women's magazines like *McCall's*. Watson died in 1958.

Through the years Watson's conditioning of Little Albert (he became known as this in order to contrast him with Freud's Little Hans) became a part of psychological mythology. Like a joke passed on from person to person, Watson's experiment has been transformed through generations of textbooks until it has become distorted beyond all recognition. These distortions go further than mere inaccuracies, although these are common (one textbook even got Albert's name wrong). Some writers have exaggerated the extent of Little Albert's fear generalisation. For example, in one textbook Albert is described as fearing a favourite teddy bear even though there was no mention of such a toy in Watson and Rayner's article. Perhaps most amazing of all is the fabrication, in some textbooks, of Little Albert's "cure". One recent psychology textbook tells in some detail how Albert's phobia was cured by feeding him chocolate in closer and closer proximity with the rat! The authors apparently just could not believe that Watson and Rayner would let Albert go home uncured — but they did.

The mythology that has developed around Little Albert testifies to the strength of Watson's ideas; they are seen as valid despite the weaknesses of his experiment. And, it might be added, despite the failure of others to replicate his findings. In one such attempt, not one out of 15 children learned to fear a wooden toy even when it was repeatedly paired with a loud disagreeable noise. Today most clinical psychologists, even behaviourists, do not conceptualise fear in Pavlovian conditioning terms, preferring instead to follow the *operant* conditioning model developed by Watson's most famous disciple, B. F. Skinner. It is not the aim of this book to explain the difference between these two types of conditioning. It is enough to say that Watson's belief that all phobias are the result of Pavlovian conditioning is almost certainly wrong. Nevertheless, his experiment exerted a great deal of influence on the development of modern psychology. Behaviourism dominated psychological research for decades. Because of Watson's influence it was not until the 1960s that psychologists again turned to studying the "mind" and what goes on in it.

Further Reading

Gray, J. A., *Pavlov*, Harvester Press, Brighton, UK, 1979.

Pavlov, I., *Selected Works* (S. Belsky, trans.), Foreign Languages Publishing House, Moscow, 1955.

Watson, J. B. and Rayner, R., "Conditioned Emotional Reactions", *Journal of Experimental Psychology*, 3, pp. 1–14, 1920.

CHAPTER TWO

THE DIVIDED BRAIN

One of the oldest questions in psychology is: how does the brain affect behaviour? Although there is no universally agreed-upon answer to this question, most of today's psychologists believe that different parts of the brain are specialised for specific psychological functions. This chapter begins with a brief historial review of research into brain–behaviour relationships, aimed at showing how and why psychologists came to adopt this view.

LOCALISATION OF FUNCTION IN THE BRAIN

Faculty Psychology

Speculations about the localisation of function in the brain are as old as anatomy and physiology themselves. The Edwin Smith Surgical Papyrus discovered in Luxor, Egypt, in 1862, and thought to date from about 3000 BC, describes 48 cases of traumatic head injury probably received in battle. Its author makes many attempts to correlate the site of a head injury with subsequent loss of bodily function. The Hippocratic writings of ancient Greece also describe brain–behaviour relationships, including the observation that wounds to one side of the head produce injuries to the other side of the body — a fact, by the way, that appears to have been forgotten for the next 1000 years.

By the fourth century AD the scholars Nemesius and Saint Augustine had developed a theory of brain specialisation that was to remain dominant through-out the Middle Ages. Their theory relegated various psychological functions, called *faculties*, not to the soft tissue of the brain, but to its seemingly empty chambers known as ventricles. In doing so, they were merely following the lead established by the classical anatomist, Galen, who believed that the "psychic gas" that energises behaviour is stored in the brain's ventricles and is transmitted to the various organs of the body through blood vessels and nerve cells (which he thought of as hollow pipes).

Nemesius, Saint Augustine and their students located a different faculty in each chamber. At first the faculties they used were derived from Plato's division of mind into sense and intellect, but the number of faculties was eventually increased to include sensation, perception, memory, imagination, attention, language, judgement and will. Sensation and imagination were located in the front ventricles, reason and thought in the middle ventricles and memory in the rear ones. In case it is not already obvious, it should be noted that these theories were totally speculative. Empirical data were not collected nor relied on. What is more, the faculties, which were derived from everyday life, were used to dictate underlying neuroanatomy. The reasoning went like this: since people have imaginations, there must be a part of the brain devoted to imagination. Since people have memories, another part of the brain must be concerned with memory, and so on.

Although anatomical knowledge increased over the next 1000 years, knowledge of brain function lagged behind (a situation still prevalent today). Faculties remained firmly entrenched although they were eventually moved out of the ventricles and into the tissue of the brain. Much activity was given over to searching for the organ of the "soul". Descartes believed the pineal gland in the middle of the brain to be where the soul lives. He even suggested that the direction in which the pineal gland points (in some people it points up, in others down) affects behaviour.

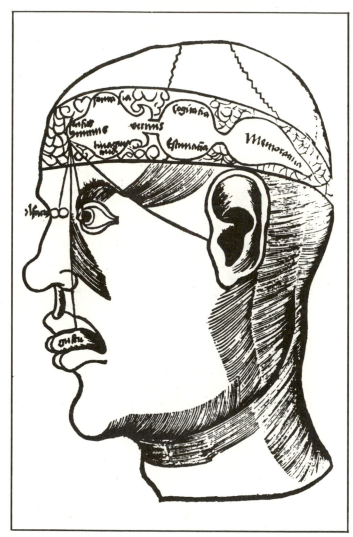

FIG. 9. *A mediaeval woodcut showing the brain's ventricular system. Each ventricle is assigned a faculty: sensation in the front, thinking in the middle, and memory in the rear*

By the eighteenth century, faculty psychology had been going strong for about 1300 years. Yet there was still little consensus about which faculties belong in which brain structures. In addition, few scientists believed the brain to be responsible for all behaviour. Even as late as 1799, Xavier Bichat, the anatomist whose tissue theory initiated modern histology, still thought that the brain was concerned with the intellect but that the heart was the seat of the "passions". Other theorists saw a role for the endocrine glands here as well. This position, however, was soon to become untenable due to the work of Franz Joseph Gall.

The Rise and Fall of Phrenology

Gall was born in Vienna in 1758. He studied medicine and had developed a successful private practice by the time he first began lecturing around 1800. His lectures on the relationship between behaviour and the brain were soon prohibited by the Emperor of Austria on the grounds that they led to materialism and denied the importance of religion. No longer able to lecture, Gall left Austria and with his disciple, Johann Spurzheim, lectured throughout Europe, ending up in France where he became very famous before he died in 1828.

Gall claimed that his interest in the localisation of cerebral functioning began when he was a schoolboy and noticed that a classmate with an extraordinary memory also had protruding eyes. Gall hypothesised that bulging eyes are produced by larger-than-normal brain frontal lobes pushing them outwards. He observed other people to see whether good memory is always correlated with bulging eyes, found that it was, and concluded that the frontal lobes were where the faculty of memory resides. Crude though it may have been, Gall's technique was the first empirical approach to the localisation of brain function. Before him, psychology was a totally theoretical, "armchair" enterprise. Historians generally agree that Gall's most important contribution to psychology was his insistence that brain–behaviour relationships are amenable to empirical observation.

Gall claimed from the beginning that the brain was the organ of the mind. Glands and hearts played no part at all. He also believed that the faculties were innate. Unlike the influential philosopher John Locke, who argued that when we are born our minds are a *tabula rasa* (blank slate), Gall felt that individual differences were too great, even among those growing up in the same environment, to result from anything but heredity. The brain, he felt, was composed of organs, as many as there are faculties; the larger the organ, the stronger the faculty. As a corollary Gall assumed that the skull is a mirror of the underlying brain, so that examining the shape and contours of the skull (a procedure he called *cranioscopy*) can tell the examiner the size of the underlying brain organs. Although the truth or falsity of cranioscopy had no real bearing on the rest of his work, his faith in this method was ultimately to prove Gall's downfall.

Phrenology, a term coined by Gall's student Spurzheim to describe applied cranioscopy, captured the popular fancy, particularly in Great Britain and the United States. Although most scientists ridiculed phrenology, intelligent non-scientists were drawn to it. When Sherlock Holmes deduced from a large-sized hat that its owner was very intelligent, he was merely echoing a popular phrenological belief. Alfred Russell Wallace, co-founder of evolutionary theory, liked to engage in what he called "phreno-mesmerism". He claimed that a hypnotised subject will respond with appropriate facial expressions whenever the hypnotist touches the appropriate parts of a nearby phrenological model head. Walt Whitman even included phrenological terms in his poems.

Phrenological societies and journals sprang up on both sides of the Atlantic and hundreds of books dealing with the new science were published. In one book, called *Heads and What They Tell Us* and published in 1891, W. Pugin Thornton discourses on noses for several pages. "Bonaparte," he says, "chose long-nosed men for his generals, and the opinion prevails that large noses indicate long heads and strong minds." "Sharp noses," on the other hand, "indicate a quick, clear, penetrating, searching, sagacious, knowing mind." Around the same time the following advertisement for an apprentice appeared in the *New York Sun:*

A stout boy not over 15 years of age of German or Scotch parents, to learn a good but difficult trade. N.B. — it will be necessary to bring a recommendation to his abilities from Messrs. Fowlers and Wells, Phrenologists, Nassau Street.

Phrenology had more adherents than the botany and biology of the period. Not only was it a system of brain-

FIG. 10. *Franz Joseph Gall (1758–1828), founder of phrenology*

AN INTELLECTUAL AND VERY AFFECTIONATE BOY
Notice the development of the frontal and occipital regions

I

Observe the differences in the heads of these two boys

II

A BOY WITH DEFICIENT REASONING AND RETENTIVE POWER
AND LITTLE CONTROL OVER HIS PROPENSITIES
Note the depressed forehead

FIG. 11. *An example of phrenology at work from a nineteenth-century phrenology manual. Note how the boys are drawn wearing different clothing and hairstyles*

behavior relationships but also a social philosophy with, according to its adherents, implications for education, social relations and ethics. By examining the external shape of the head, phrenologists told people how to avoid depression, choose careers, select mates, educate children, reform criminals and cure the insane. It did not seem to bother anyone that phrenological statements were completely circular. Saying that someone is a good mother because she has an overdeveloped faculty of "philo-progenitiveness" is little different from explaining that antibiotics cure pneumonia because they have a germ-killing quality. (By the way, philoprogenitiveness is located at the base of the brain.)

Gall's problem was that his theory was not matched with an appropriate scientific method. In correlating personality traits with cerebral landmarks, he relied on evidence supporting his theory and ignored instances where small bumps on the head were associated with extraordinary ability or where large bumps did not signify any special talents. When conflicting evidence could no longer be ignored, he advanced *ad hoc* hypotheses according to which some large bumps could be inhibited by other large bumps or two small bumps could be added together to produce a trait equivalent to that produced by one large one.

The best example of the vacuity of the phrenological approach was Spurzheim's reaction to learning that Descartes' skull was remarkably smaller than average in the forehead region where intelligence is supposed to reside. He merely stated that perhaps Descartes was not so great a thinker as many thought him to be! In other words, the phrenologists tended to accept evidence that supported their point of view and explained away any facts that conflicted with their theory. There were a few attempts to salvage matters by altering the location and even the nature of the faculties. But even this led to conflict. Spurzheim felt "hope" was a faculty whereas Gall did not. Gall felt that "conscience" was part of "benevolence", while Spurzheim thought it was an independent faculty. Phrenology was soon beyond help. The ever-increasing special explanations necessary to deal with counter-examples and the inability to agree on just what a faculty is in the first place proved too heavy a load and phrenology eventually collapsed under its own weight.

The demise of phrenology also saw the demise of faculty psychology. Instead of looking for the brain organ underlying hope, and so on, theorists assumed that simple sensory and motor processes were all that could be localised and that complex social behaviour was somehow constructed from these simple processes. Marie Flourens, the most influential brain scientist in the period following Gall, opposed any but the simplest localisation theories, arguing that the brain is mainly an unspecialised mass. This is a position that was also held in the present century by Karl Lashley. Both Flourens and Lashley experimented by destroying parts of animals' brains and both noted that removing even large amounts of the cerebral cortex had little effect on learning and memory in animals. Lashley spent most of his career searching for the engram, the basic neural unit of memory, but without success. He eventually concluded that memories are not stored in a single brain location but are distributed throughout the brain. This is why, even after a great deal of tissue destruction, many memories still survive.

While Lashley's findings appear to be true for many types of memory, his view of brain functioning was only partly correct; not all brain operations are distributed like memory. Research by Paul Broca, Carl Wernicke and others in the latter part of the last century left little doubt that at least some functions are localised in particular parts of the brain.

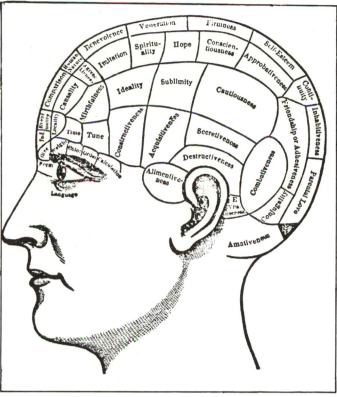

FIG. 12. *The 37 faculties and where to find them according to a phrenological map of the last century*

Localisations and Disconnections

Broca's contribution to our understanding of brain–behaviour relationships began when he first encountered a patient called "Tan". This patient received his name from the hospital staff because, except for the syllable, "tan", he could say nothing else. Today, we would say Tan was suffering from a language disorder known as aphasia. Broca performed an autopsy on Tan's brain after his death, finding damage to the left side of the cerebral cortex. He concluded that the part of the brain specialising in language production was in the left cerebral hemisphere. Subsequent work done by Carl Wernicke confirmed a relationship between brain damage to the left side of the cerebral cortex and language disability. Interestingly, the two scientists found that language disorders result from damage to one of two different brain areas. Although these two language areas are typically found in the left side of the brain, about five per cent of people show the opposite arrangement; for them, language functioning is localised in the right cerebral hemisphere. (There are even some rare individuals who appear to have full language capabilities in both hemispheres.) Today Broca's area (which is located closer to the front of the head than Wernicke's) is characterised as the language motor area, while Wernicke's area is considered the speech understanding centre. Lesions to these areas produce expressive aphasia (difficulties in producing language) and sensory aphasia (problems in understanding language), respectively. The roles of Broca's and Wernicke's areas in language have been confirmed many times since their original identification.

More important than the actual location of the various areas was the theoretical use to which they were put. Wernicke and his colleagues drew

(Left) **FIG. 13.** *Paul Broca (1824–80), the surgeon who discovered the brain's language production area*

(Right) **FIG. 14.** *Carl Wernicke (1848–1905) defined and discovered receptive aphasia and showed how the brain's two language areas interact*

FIG. 15. *When a spoken word is heard, sensations from the ear are received by the auditory cortex but the word is not understood until it is processed by Wernicke's area. A representation of the word is then transmitted through the arcuate fasciculus to Broca's area where it is translated into a motor programme. This programme is supplied to the motor area of the cortex which directs the speech apparatus to pronounce the word. If the arcuate fasciculus is severed, no information travels between Wernicke's and Broca's areas and, therefore, heard words cannot be repeated*

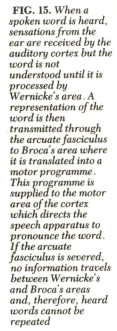

information flow-charts very similar to those drawn by computer programmers today. These charts used boxes and arrows to illustrate how various brain centres communicate with one another. Sometimes syndromes that have not yet been seen in patients were predicted by the flow-chart approach. For example, Wernicke theorised that if the arcuate fasciculus (the main connecting link between Wernicke's and Broca's areas) were severed it would leave the two language centres undamaged, but would cause them to become disconnected. Wernicke predicted that patients with such damage would be unable to repeat what is said to them although they can still speak sensibly and understand language. The reason for this prediction is that disconnecting the two language areas prevents the part of the brain that specialises in understanding incoming language (Wernicke's area) from transmitting any information to the part of the brain concerned with producing language (Broca's area). The usefulness of this approach is underscored by the subsequent discovery of patients suffering from just such a syndrome — today known as conduction aphasia.

The discovery and description of disconnection syndromes marked an important milestone in localisation research. Not only was it now possible to localise at least some functions in the brain, it was also possible to predict new syndromes. For the first time scientists were able to demonstrate that their localisation theories really were capable of predicting behaviour. It is no surprise, therefore, that psychologists became particularly interested in studying an extreme form of disconnection — the split-brain syndrome. One such psychologist was Roger Sperry.

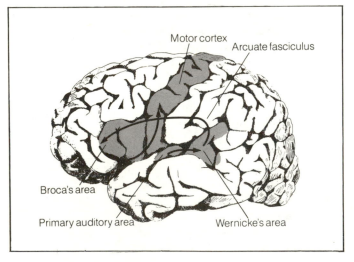

ROGER W. SPERRY AND THE SPLIT BRAIN

Roger Sperry was born in 1913. He graduated from Oberlin College in Ohio but his research career really began in the 1940s at the University of Chicago, where he performed experiments on the genetic mechanisms governing nervous system development. After receiving his doctorate from Chicago, Sperry moved to the Yerkes Laboratories of Primate Biology, where he worked with Karl Lashley. Although he learned a great deal from Lashley (who, by the way, once studied with Watson), Sperry never really accepted Lashley's view that the brain was largely an equipotential mass with little specialisation or localisation of function. During his time at the Yerkes labs, Sperry continued his research into neurological development and also performed experiments concerned with the underlying neurological basis for perception. After leaving the Yerkes labs Sperry returned to the University of Chicago and also spent a brief period at the National Institute of Health. In 1954 he moved to the California Institute of Technology where he became Hixon Professor of Psychobiology, a post he has held ever since.

Sperry's interest in the split brain goes back to his days at the University of Chicago where he and his co-worker, Ronald Myers, severed the optic chiasm (the place where nerve cells from the two eyes cross) of a cat. With its optic chiasm severed, each of the cat's eyes was only connected to one side of its brain in contrast to the normal arrangement in which each eye projects to both sides of the brain. They also cut the cat's corpus callosum, the thick tract of nerve fibres connecting the left and right cerebral hemispheres. For many years it had been believed that these nerve fibres provide the main communication link between the two cerebral hemispheres, but there was no real evidence to support this view. Myers and Sperry provided this evidence, however, when they showed that severing a cat's optic chiasm and corpus callosum appeared to

FIG. 16. *Roger W. Sperry (1913–), discoverer of the dual nature of consciousness*

establish two learning centres, one in each of the cerebral hemispheres. That is, if the cat had its left eye open and its right eye shut while it learned to make a conditioned response, opening its right eye and shutting its left resulted in the cat being unable to make the conditioned response it had just learned. The opposite occurred if conditioning took place with the right eye open and the left eye shut. Thus the cat had to learn the response twice, once for each side of the brain. In this experiment, then, Myers and Sperry showed that — in an animal with a severed corpus callosum — learning stored in one side of the brain does not get across to the other. Or, in Sperry's own words:

It was as though each hemisphere were a separate mental domain operating with a complete disregard — indeed, with a complete lack of awareness — of what went on in the other. The split-brain animal behaved in the test situation as if it had two separate brains.

Although these experimental results seemed to indicate that the corpus callosum is the link through which the hemispheres communicate, there was some conflicting evidence from human research. While no-one would purposely operate on a person's brain solely to find out how it works, there are people who have had their cerebral hemispheres separated for medical reasons. These individuals all suffer from severe forms of epilepsy. Their seizures are not only debilitating, but also uncontrollable by other medical interventions. The rationale for severing the corpus callosum in these patients is that such an operation stops the spread of seizures from one hemisphere to the other. Psychological studies, conducted in the 1940s by A. J. Akelaitis and his colleagues, of 26 patients who had undergone this operation revealed no specific disabilities in learning or any other behaviour. As a consequence, Akelaitis questioned the whole notion of disconnection syndromes. (Early researchers also claimed that the operation did not help control the seizures.)

There the matter rested, the discrepancy between the animal and human research unresolved, until the early 1960s when Joseph Bogen and Philip Vogel, both neurosurgeons, proposed trying the operation on a 48-year-old war veteran, known as "W.J.", whose epilepsy was not controllable in any other way. Bogen was aware of Sperry's animal research and invited him to study W.J. (and other patients who later received the same operation). Vogel severed W.J.'s corpus callosum and also most of the other, smaller, connections between his two cerebral hemispheres. Medically, the operation was an immediate success: W.J.'s seizures were markedly reduced. The favourable outcome of W.J.'s surgery led the surgeons to operate on a second patient. This time the patient was a housewife in her thirties. Once again, the surgery produced marked improvement. Over the years similar beneficial results have been obtained with other patients who could not be helped in any other way. Clearly the pessimistic findings reported by earlier researchers were incorrect. The operation is beneficial in helping severe epileptics to live more normal lives. While Akelaitis's pessimistic conclusions about the usefulness of the surgery seemed incorrect, observations that the operation had little effect on a patient's behaviour seemed quite accurate. Superficially, at least, the surgery appeared to have little or no effect on W.J.'s behaviour. He could still perform intellectual tasks, carry on intelligent conversations and perform normal work. But the appearance of normality was deceptive. Careful testing showed that W.J. and the other split-brain patients behave in rather peculiar ways. In fact, their peculiar behaviour constitutes the most interesting disconnection syndrome yet discovered.

CLASSIC EXPERIMENT 3:

SPLITTING THE MIND

Although the surgeons knew they were splitting the brain, it was Sperry who demonstrated that by doing so they split the mind as well. Sperry's basic testing arrangement is shown in Figure 17. This apparatus permits the experimenter to project visual stimuli to the right or left half of the screen and to place objects in the patient's right or left hand outside his field of vision. Because of the anatomy of the visual system (Figure 18), material presented to one side of the screen (to one visual field) goes to only one hemisphere. Of course, the patient could always move his eyes and the material would then enter both cerebral hemispheres. To prevent this, the patient is directed to fixate on the centre of the visual display and stimuli are presented very briefly (for one-tenth of a second or less), faster than an eye movement can be made.

In the test shown in Figure 17 the experimental subject fixates on the centre of the visual display while words are flashed simultaneously in both visual fields. The words appear and disappear so quickly that there is no time for an eye or head movement. In this way, the word "key" reaches only the right hemisphere and the word "ring" only the left hemisphere. Using this experimental set-up, Sperry and his colleague, Michael Gazzaniga, were able to show an extraordinary difference in performance between subjects who had not had surgery and those who had undergone the split-brain operation.[1]

If subjects with intact corpus cal-

losums are required to say what they saw flashed on the screen, they report seeing the word "keyring". Split-brain patients, on the other hand, invariably report only the word "ring" which was projected to the left hemisphere, seemingly unaware of the word "key". If pressed, split-brain patients may admit to seeing a "flash of light" on the left side of the screen, but they deny seeing another word projected there. The explanation for this curious difference between split-brain patients and intact subjects hinges on the localisation of function in the brain. Most people have language ability localised in the left hemisphere. Thus, when the word "ring" is projected to the right visual field, it goes straight to the part of the brain that can talk. When the word

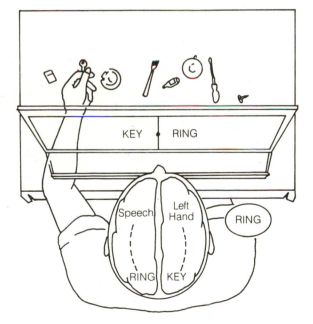

FIG. 17. *Apparatus used in the split-brain experiment. Provided the patient fixates on the centre of the screen, the word "key" presented on the left is registered only in the right cerebral hemisphere. This hemisphere directs the left hand to pick up the key. But the patient's verbal report is "ring" because this is the only word "seen" by the speaking left hemisphere*

---

1. The term "subjects" is used throughout this book to denote the participants in psychological research. "Subjects" may have negative connotations for some readers (and some psychologists). It is used here instead of "participants" or other similar words because it is the term most commonly used in the literature.

"key" is projected to the left visual field, however, it goes to the right hemisphere, which is mute and unable to identify the word verbally. Thus, split-brain patients can only verbalise words projected to the left (speaking) hemisphere and deny even seeing words projected to the right hemisphere. In contrast, intact subjects can verbalise both words because those projected to the (mute) right hemisphere are transmitted across their intact corpus callosum to the (talking) left hemisphere. Such information transfer between hemispheres is impossible for the split-brain patients who have had the communication link between their cerebral hemispheres severed.

Although the right hemisphere is mute and cannot verbally identify words projected in the left visual

field, it is nevertheless aware of what is going on. Sperry and Gazzaniga showed this by taking advantage of the fact that each hemisphere controls the muscles of the opposite side of the body. More specifically, the left hemisphere controls the right hand and the right hemisphere controls the left. The experimenters simply asked the split-brain patients to search out and touch the object whose name they just saw projected on the screen. If directed to use their *left* hand (held out of sight as shown in Figure 17), split-brain subjects search out the key even though they had just denied seeing the word! Thus, switching to a non-verbal response allowed the right hemisphere (which controls the left hand) to reveal what it saw, something it could not do verbally.

Interestingly, when asked to name the object they have just touched with their left hand, the split-brain patients respond "ring". If pressed further to describe the "kind of ring" seen, patients answer "wedding *ring*" or "circus *ring*". It is as if the speaking left hemisphere is merely hunting in its memory for associations to the word "ring". Any reference to "keyring" would be pure luck.

This experiment not only demonstrated that the corpus callosum is the main communication link between the two hemispheres in humans (just as Sperry showed it was in the cat), it also reveals that severing the corpus callosum produces two conscious "minds". The mind of the left hemisphere, the one capable of talking, stores information independently of the mind of the right hemisphere, which can communicate only by gestures. Also, with the corpus callosum severed, neither hemisphere knows what the other has seen.

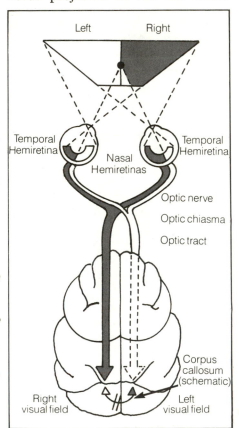

FIG. 18. *The human visual system: the anatomical relationship that must be understood in considering split-brain studies. Half of each eye is connected to opposite sides of the brain. Specifically, the temporal half of the right eye projects to the left hemisphere and vice versa. Provided the subject fixates on a central point, information projected to the right visual field goes only to the left hemisphere and anything projected to the left visual field goes only to the right hemisphere. In normal subjects, information could still be shared by the hemispheres simply by sending it across the corpus callosum. In split-brain patients, such sharing is impossible*

AFTERMATH

The dramatic nature of these experimental findings led Sperry and his co-workers to conduct many additional experimental studies of split-brain patients. Most of these studies used the same experimental apparatus just described.

For example, one experiment required patients to indicate, by lifting a finger, whether an object briefly projected to the left visual field was one that they had seen earlier in the test. Subjects with intact corpus callosums have no difficulty in performing this task. The experimenters found that split-brain patients also have little difficulty provided that the object had previously been presented in the left visual field. If, however, the picture had previously been presented to the right visual field, the patients claim no recollection of having seen it earlier. In other words, unlike subjects whose hemispheres share information, items presented to the left visual field (to the right hemisphere) are stored and recalled separately from items presented to the left hemisphere in subjects who have undergone the operation. This is additional evidence that split-brain patients no longer have a single visual world, but two, one in each hemisphere.

Further tests revealed even more about how the two cerebral hemispheres work. For example, if two different figures are flashed simultaneously in the two visual fields (say "$" on the left and a "?" on the right) and the patient is asked to draw what he saw using his left hand out of sight, he reproduces the figure seen on the left half of the screen (the "$"). However, if asked to say what he has drawn, the patient says it was a "?" which appeared in the right half of the visual field. Clearly, one hemisphere had no idea what the other was doing.

Tests based on touch also revealed how mental awareness is separated between the two hemispheres in split-brain patients. For instance, objects placed in their right hands can be verbally identified because touch cues are going to the speaking left hemisphere. Items placed in their left hands, however, cannot be verbally identified but can be picked out of a dozen or more other items simply by examining these by hand. Touch identification, however, works only when the same hand that originally held the item is making the choice. The patients cannot identify with one hand an object held only moments before by the other hand. Interestingly, since they are unable to name objects held by their left hands, the split-brain patients claim also to be unable to pick out previously

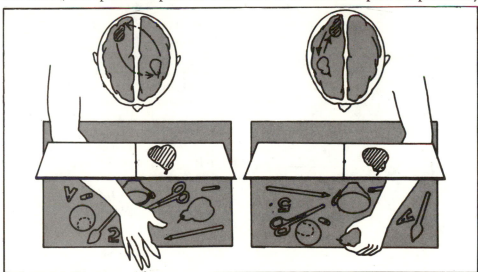

FIG. 19. *When a picture of a pear is projected to the left side of the screen it is registered in the right hemisphere. Since this hemisphere controls only the left hand, the patient can pick out the pear only with this hand and not with the right*

held objects from a mixed group of objects with their left hands. When told that they have, in fact, been doing this successfully, they are surprised, and claim that their success must have been due to luck.

If different objects are placed in each hand and then removed and hidden among other objects, the patients will hunt for each object separately with each hand. The left hand may even pick up the object held by the right, examine it and reject it. The two hands act as if they belong to two different people.

Even hand placement reveals important differences between split-brain and intact subjects. In one test, subjects are told to hold both hands out of sight, straight in front of them but not touching. One hand is then placed into a position by the experimenter (say, made into a fist). The subject is then asked to assume the same position with the other hand. Anyone with an intact corpus callosum can do this quite easily but the split-brain subject cannot do it because the two hemispheres fail to communicate.

These experiments clearly show that patients who have had the connections between their cerebral hemispheres severed have severe difficulties in integrating information obtained separately by each hemisphere. Yet the earlier observations failed to notice these disabilities. One possible explanation is that the patients studied by Akelaitis and his colleagues did not have their cerebral hemispheres completely disconnected. This would also explain why their epilepsy failed to improve. However, there is another reason why these cognitive difficulties may have failed to be noted: they are easily compensated for under uncontrolled conditions. For example, if visual stimuli are presented for longer than one-tenth of a second (as they normally are outside the laboratory), the patients can move their eyes and the stimuli will enter both hemispheres rather than one. Similarly, if patients are permitted to see their hands, they have little trouble using visual cues to guide them.

FIG. 20. *Claimed specialisations and modes of thought of the two hemispheres. Many psychologists believe these claims are over-exaggerated and that there are many tasks that can be accomplished by both hemispheres*

Sperry and his colleagues reported several additional ways in which the disconnected hemispheres of the split-brain patients try to "help" one another perform a task. For example, patients may transfer knowledge possessed by the left hemisphere to the right hemisphere by saying it aloud. In other words, since the patients cannot transfer information internally across the corpus callosum, they use an external route, saying out loud what they wish the other hemisphere to know so that it enters the right hemisphere through the hearing mechanism. Similarly, the right hemisphere can signal the left by pointing or using other nonverbal signals. Thus it was only by holding constant the opportunities for such "cheating" that Sperry and his colleagues were able to show that split-brain patients were, indeed, of "two minds".

Sperry's experiments clearly indicated that the corpus callosum serves as communication channel for combining and integrating the perceptions and knowledge of the two hemispheres. Later research also revealed that although the left hemisphere is specialised for language, the right specialises in nonverbal tasks such as recognising faces.

Sperry's research captured the public's imagination as well as the interest of other psychologists. Sometimes this enthusiasm has gone well beyond the experimental data. For example,

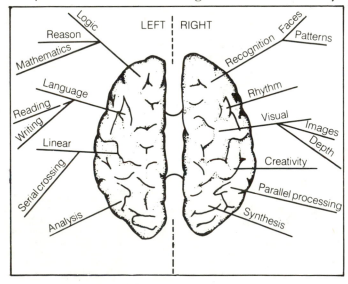

some have claimed that social groups differ in the way their hemispheres are organised. In the years since Sperry's split-brain research, such speculations have increased steadily. Different patterns of brain organisation have been said to distinguish right-wing from left-wing political groups, psychiatric patients from non-patients, autistic from other children, language students, psychology students, engineering students and architecture students from one another as well as from other students, easily hypnotised subjects from those difficult to hypnotise, musicians from non-musicians, Japanese from Americans, American Indians from other Americans, males from females, stutterers from fluent speakers, the deaf from those that can hear, Chinese readers from those who cannot read Chinese, Jews from Catholics and both Jews and Catholics from Protestants, and literates from illiterates. The great diversity of these claims presents some logical problems, particularly when several studies are considered jointly. For instance, are Jews and Protestants, who according to one researcher rely more on their left than right hemispheres, unlikely to become architects? The logic, you see, becomes a bit hard to swallow.

Educational writers have also jumped on the bandwagon, recommending that curricula be developed to teach both hemispheres. In fact, a method of developing the right hemisphere based on Shakespeare's *Hamlet* has been published and a book called *Drawing on the Right Side of the Brain* has made best-seller lists. Educational methods for modifying "hemisphericity" have appeared along with questionnaires designed to assess the relative balance of the hemispheres in an individual's cognitive strategies. There is even a new "science" of neurolinguistic sociology which traces the development of social groups to differences in hemispheric specialisation. Poetry and ancient mythology, too, have been given "split-brain" interpretations — in a popular book Princeton psychologist Julian Jaynes argues that the "voice of the gods" so often referred to in Greek epic poems is really an example of right-hemisphere speech.

Psychologist Oliver Zangwill of Cambridge University has correctly characterised many of these claims as "... an updated phrenology that seeks to provide a scientific justification for some ... irrational and disturbing trends in modern thought".

Despite the overgeneralisation of some of his original findings, Sperry's research remains a landmark in the study of brain–behaviour relationships. Research with split-brain patients continues today with much of the modern emphasis on the implications of the split-brain research for the theory of mind. The finding that within a split-brain individual one hemisphere is not aware of the activities of the other implies that whatever the mind may be, it is closely tied to the brain. Splitting the latter also splits the former. Sperry has been awarded many honours for his work, including the Nobel Prize in physiology and medicine in 1981. In awarding the prize, the Nobel committee noted that Sperry had "brilliantly succeeded in extracting the secrets of the hemispheres".

Further Reading

Fodor, J. A., "The Mind–Body Problem", *Scientific American, 244*, pp. 124–33, 1981.

Gazzaniga, M. S. and LeDoux, J. E., *The Integrated Mind*, Plenum, New York, 1978.

Sperry, R. W., "Hemisphere Deconnection and Unity in Conscious Awareness", *American Psychologist, 23*, pp. 723–33, 1968.

Sperry, R.W., *Science and Moral Priority: The Merging of Mind, Brain and Values*, Columbia University Press, New York, 1982.

CHAPTER THREE

PSYCHOPHYSICS

When the first experimental psychologists began studying behaviour scientific-ally, they modelled their efforts on the activities of physicists. Physicists, after all, were the most respected of all scientists and much of their work was of obvious relevance to the new science of psychology. Newton, for example, had dis-covered the spectral quality of white light, and other physicists had done research into the detection of sounds. Because much of nineteenth-century physics was given over to measuring things (the speed of light, the distance to the planets), it is probably no surprise that the early experimental psychologists also devoted most of their efforts to developing measures — mental measures. The individual whose name is most closely connected with mental measurement in the last century is Gustav Fechner, the founder of a psychological subspecialty known as *psychophysics*.

GUSTAV FECHNER AND THE
BIRTH OF PSYCHOPHYSICS

Fechner was born in 1801 in a small town in southern Germany. His father, the town's pastor, was known as a "progressive" thinker who saw no difficulty in combining deep religious feelings with an appreciation for science. In later life Fechner came to share the same interests as his father, but the two had very little time to interact. The senior Fechner died when Gustav was only five, and for the next nine years the youngster, his mother and brother were cared for by an uncle who was also a preacher. Fechner entered the University of Leipzig when he was 16, enrolling in the faculty of medicine. In those years Leipzig was one of the world's most famous universities and home to many influential scientists. Fechner remained at the University of Leipzig for the rest of his life.

Fechner completed his medical studies when he was 21; but he was not a typical doctor. For one thing, while still a medical student, he began publishing articles satirising what he saw as some of the nonscientific aspects of medical practice. These satires appeared periodically in the years following his graduation under the pen name "Dr Mises". As things turned out, Fechner did not practise medicine for very long. Instead, soon after completing his medical studies, Fechner began to study physics and mathematics, supporting himself financially by translating scientific books into German.

In 1824 Fechner began to lecture in physics at the university while also conducting his own research. In the next six years he published several original research papers in physics and developed a following among both students and other physicists. At the relatively young age of 33, the newly married Fechner was appointed Professor of Physics. He seemed to have a splendid career ahead

FIG. 21. *Gustav T. Fechner (1801–87), founder of psychophysics*

of him, but within six years his physics career was over.

Fechner suffered what today would probably be called a nervous break-down; the strain of overwork had taken its toll. He resigned his chair, took to his bed and for many years cut himself off from everyone. Then, suddenly, he began to improve. His recovery, which he and his family considered miraculous, led him to renew his interest in religion. Thus it was that in his forties Fechner turned away from physics and toward philosophy and religion.

In 1848 Fechner published a book on the "mental life" of plants and in 1851 he published a strange book called *Zend-Avesta* which was concerned with, among other things, the "true" nature of heaven. The *Zend-Avesta* also contained Fechner's first attempt to convince the intellectual world that the soul (or consciousness) exists in everything. Mind and matter, he argued, are really only two ways of looking at the same thing; they are identical but appear different depending on one's viewpoint.

In the middle of the last century objectivity in science was held in high esteem and no vague philosophy based purely on armchair speculations was taken very seriously. Thus Fechner's philosophical views did not cause much of a stir among intellectuals or anyone else. Fechner pondered the problem of how to convince others that there is no difference between mind and matter and claimed that while lying in bed on the morning of 22 October 1850 the solution came to him. He could demonstrate the identity of mind and body (indeed of everything in the universe) if he could show that there is a definite mathematical relationship between the physical and mental worlds. Fechner realised, of course, that subjective sensory experiences cannot be measured directly, so he set out to measure them indirectly. The result of Fechner's early-morning inspiration was a book called *Elements of Psychophysics*, which was published in 1860. Fechner called his new science *psychophysics* because he believed that he had tied together the mental and physical worlds. In Fechner's own words, psychophysics is the "exact science of the functional relations ... between body and mind". After a quiet start the book began to claim the attention of physiologists, physicists and psychologists. Before long, its author was famous and the science of psychophysics was well established.

In order to appreciate what Fechner thought he was doing, it is necessary to understand his view of the relationship between mind and body. Thus, before the precise nature of Fechner's psychophysics is described, we must take another look at the mind–body problem, and Fechner's attempt to resolve it.

FECHNER'S SOLUTION TO THE MIND–BODY PROBLEM

Traditionally there have been two philosophical approaches to the mind–body problem: dualist theories and monist (or materialist) theories. The dualist considers mind and body to be separate things. Although the mind may arise from the workings of the nervous system, dualists believe it is not actually part of the body but a separate, non-physical substance. Materialists, on the other hand, view the mind as identical with the physical state of the nervous system. For them, all mental processes are ultimately identical with nervous system activity. Materialist and dualist theories both have their strong and weak points.

The main strength of the dualist view is that it coincides with everyday thinking. Behaviour is commonly explained by reference to internal causes — causes that originate in the mind. For example, when we say that an office worker carried an umbrella to work because he *believed* it was likely to rain, we are implying that his state of mind when he set out for work that morning caused him to take along an umbrella. If this same worker habitually stays late at the office, takes work home and devotes himself to advancing his career, these behaviours might be explained as the result of a strong *motive to achieve*. Achievement motives, like beliefs, exist only in the mind.

Dualism's weaknesses stem largely from the non-physical nature of the mind. If it occupies no physical location, where does the mind store its memories and carry out its thinking? If the mind is really separate from the brain, why does brain damage affect its operations? Finally, if the mind is non-physical, how can it produce behaviour (which is clearly physical) without violating Newton's laws of conservation (matter and energy can neither be created nor destroyed)?

Materialism's strength lies in its rejection of metaphysical entities in favour of measurable, observable, objective, physical matter. But materialism, as a philosophy of mind, has some serious problems of its own. For example, if no "mind" exists outside the workings of the nervous system, how is it possible for the brain to be aware of itself? Who or what observes our thoughts when we think to ourselves? And what determines our behavioural choices? If we decide to read a book rather than go to the cinema, who made the choice? Materialists have tried to answer these questions by postulating that one part of the brain serves as an "executive" (a kind of managing director). This executive is said to control the activities of the rest of the nervous system. But this is not really a satisfactory answer because it is not clear who or what controls the executive. Materialists can invent a higher executive (a chairman of the board who gives orders to the managing director) but this solves nothing because we do not know who controls him. A philosopher once described the elusive executive that determines the actions of the nervous system as the "ghost in the machine" — a ghost that no materialist philosopher has yet been able to completely exorcise.

Religion, of course, has always distinguished between the body and the soul. Philosophical distinctions, however, have been rather different. Plato, for example, divided thoughts and objects into two "worlds". The superior world contains timeless abstract ideas such as freedom, liberty and beauty; the inferior world consists of everyday physical reality. For Plato, beauty as an abstract ideal is present innately in the mind and lasts forever independently of any particular beautiful object or person. Ultimately, Plato came to identify the mind with the timeless ideals that it contained and differentiated it from the physical world whose existence was fleeting.

Plato's distinction, in one form or another, lasted for thousands of years. Even during the seventeenth and eighteenth centuries when modern science was born, European philosophers like René Descartes and Immanuel Kant still distinguished between the physical world and a non-corporeal mind. However, this dualistic philosophy was eventually challenged by English empiricist philosophers like John Locke who argued quite strongly against the notions of innate ideas and a non-corporeal mind. For Locke, all knowledge comes from experience and is stored in a materialist brain. Locke's philosophy was particularly welcome among scientists who tended to be suspicious of metaphysics in general and non-observable entities (like the mind) in particular.

By the nineteenth century the success of physics had all but eliminated the dualist view among physical scientists. As already noted, the early experimental psychologists tended to apply the methods of physics to the study of consciousness. And along with its scientific methods, psychologists adopted physics' materialist philosophy as well. By the time Fechner became involved in psychological research, almost all scientists were materialists.

Fechner's recovery after years of debilitating illness rekindled religious feelings that had long lain dormant. Materialism, with its denial not only of a non-physical mind but also of a non-corporeal soul, was anathema to his new-found beliefs. A former Professor of Physics, he did not abandon his scientific training in favour of metaphysics but, like his father, tried to combine science and religion. Instead of adopting dualism, Fechner argued for *pan-psychism*, a form of *pantheism*.

Pantheistic religions can be traced back to classical civilisations. Even among the ancient Greeks with their human-like gods, there were those who argued that the physical universe, and all that it contains, are merely reflections of God. For pantheists, God exists in everything and everything is God. Pantheism still exists today among some Buddhists and among many tribal people such as Australian Aborigines. Fechner argued that dualism was really an illusion which stemmed from the way in which observations were made. Internal, introspective observations lead one to believe the mind and body are separate, whereas objective, external observations favour materialism. In actuality, argued Fechner, both internal and external observers are studying the same thing. The mind and the body are really two sides of the same reality; everything contains the mind because everything contains God.

Fechner thought he could prove the essential "oneness" of mind and body if he could demonstrate a mathematical relationship between subjective sensations and external stimuli. As we shall see, Fechner's success in this endeavour actually gave more support to the dualist position than to panpsychism. Before we get to Fechner's psychophysics, however, it is necessary to review the work of another nineteenth-century scientist whose research laid the foundation for Fechner's creation.

WEBER'S CONSTANT

Although Fechner claimed that his original conception for psychophysics came to him fully formed and uninfluenced by earlier research, he acknowledged the importance of measurements made in the 1830s by the physiologist Ernst Weber on his thinking. Weber, like Fechner, was the son of a preacher who first set out to study medicine and later switched to physics and physiology. Although he performed research in a variety of areas, Weber's main interest was in the sense of touch. His monograph on the subject, *De Tactu* (published in Latin, a common practice in those times), not only made him famous but won him the Chair of Physiology at Leipzig University, the same university where Fechner occupied the Chair of Physics.

As a physiologist, Weber was interested in the operation of the various sensory systems. His focus was on what psychologists call *sensation*. Hardness, warmth, redness and pain are all sensations. It is important to differentiate between sensations and *perceptions*, which are really interpretations of sensations. The difference between sensation and perception can be made clear by reference to ordinary experience. Let us say you are driving quickly along a highway and notice a moving blur some way ahead. The blur constitutes a visual sensation. If you begin to slow down because you believe the blur to be an animal crossing the road, you have interpreted your sensation to form a perception — you have perceived an animal in the road. Your perception may be incorrect; as you get closer you may find that the blur is merely some roadside litter blowing in the wind. Sensations, on the other hand, are never right or wrong; they are merely the raw data upon which perceptual judgements are based. This does not mean that sensations are perfectly accurate representations of the physical world. There is often a mismatch between external stimuli and internal sensation. For example, two tones of slightly different pitch may sound identical to us because our auditory apparatus is not sensitive enough to pick up the small difference.

The resolving power of the senses, the smallest difference between two stimuli that can be detected, was Weber's main research interest. His technique was to ask people to compare two stimuli. For example, he would have a subject hold a 100-gram weight (called the standard or referent) in one hand and a 101-gram weight in the other. The subject would then be asked whether the two weights were equal. If the subject answered yes (and most did), Weber had him continue to hold the standard weight while the 101-gram comparison weight was increased to 102. Once again the subject was asked if the two weights were equal. The procedure was repeated, each time slightly increasing the comparison weight, until the subject indicated he could discriminate between the two weights. Clearly Weber's comparison procedure is not applicable only to weights. The ability to discriminate between the brightness of two lights, the loudness of two sounds, the temperature of two samples of water, even the taste of two salt solutions may all be determined in more or less the same fashion. Weber, in fact, used this procedure to evaluate the sensitivity of several different senses, coming up with a rather curious finding.

Consider the weight example again. When a 100-gram weight served as the standard, Weber found that subjects required a 102-gram comparison weight in order to detect any difference between the two. If, however, subjects were given a 200-gram standard weight, they were unable to discriminate it from a 202-gram weight. In fact, the comparison weight had to be at least 204 grams in order for a difference to be detected. Similarly, when subjects were given a 400-gram standard, they only noticed a difference if the comparison weight was

Vision (Brightness)	1/60
Weights	1/50
Temperature	1/30
Pressure on skin	1/7
Smell	1/4
Taste (Salt)	1/3

FIG. 22. *Values of Weber's Constant for different senses*

at least 408 grams. That is, the size of the difference required for discrimination increased as the standard weight got heavier. In itself this is not especially surprising. In every sensory modality the importance of a particular level of stimulation is determined by the "background" in which it occurs. Lighting a match appears to produce a great deal of light in a dark room and hardly any at all in daylight. Similarly, sounds that can be heard in a quiet room in the middle of the night may go undetected in broad daylight. What is curious about Weber's results is that in every instance the amount of change necessary to be detected was always a *constant* proportion of the standard weight. The arithmetic was quite clear. For a 100-gram standard, the difference required was two grams; for a 200-gram standard, a four-gram difference was needed and for a 400-gram standard, the "just noticeable difference" was eight grams. In each case the difference required for discrimination was one-fiftieth of the standard weight.

Weber did not only study weight discrimination. He also experimented with visual and tone discrimination. In both cases he obtained similar results. The difference necessary for discrimination was always a constant proportion of the standard stimulus (although, as shown in Figure 22, the proportion is not the same for every stimulus). The fraction describing the just noticeable difference in each sensory modality is today known as *Weber's Constant*. However, Weber himself never actually stated his findings mathematically. This was left to Fechner who devised the following equation:

$$\frac{\Delta I}{I} = k$$

In this equation, I is the intensity of the standard stimulus, ΔI is the extra intensity required for a second stimulus to be just noticeably different from the standard and k is Weber's Constant. Fechner called this equation Weber's law, acknowledging the physiologist's measurements; Weber himself never seemed to realise he had discovered a law. He certainly never anticipated the use to which Fechner would put his observations.

MEASURING MENTAL SENSATIONS

The discovery of Weber's law solved Fechner's most pressing problem — how to measure the mind. Recall that his goal was to mathematically relate external physical stimuli to internal mental states. To do this he had to be able to measure, in numbers, both physical stimuli and mental states. Physical stimuli presented no problem; there were balance scales, thermometers and yardsticks suitable for measuring them. But measuring mental states was another matter altogether. What Fechner needed was a measurement device similar to a thermometer or yardstick but divided into mental rather than physical units. He used the relationship described by Weber's law to develop this scale.

Fechner's reasoning went something like this. Rulers are used to measure length, but length is an abstract property; it does not really exist by itself. Length is made concrete by adopting some measurement unit. Since all measurement units are equally arbitrary, the precise unit chosen is immaterial. Whether rulers are divided into inches or centimetres, the result is the same — a scale that is directly related to length. Similarly, a mental scale can be in any unit so long as it is directly related to the abstract quality being measured.

Based on Weber's findings, Fechner defined the measurement unit for mental sensations as the *just noticeable difference* (JND). Each JND is the increase in stimulus intensity required before a subject can report a "just noticeable difference". Since JNDs are directly related to stimulus intensity (Weber's law again), mental sensations can be measured simply by measuring the stimuli giving rise to them. Also, since all good physical measures have some sort of zero point (zero centimetres, zero kilograms, and so on), Fechner gave his mental sensation scale a zero point too. This was defined as the *absolute threshold*. The absolute threshold for any sensory system is the lowest level of stimulus intensity necessary for a subject to detect its presence 50 per cent of the time. The absolute threshold for loudness, for instance, is the softest sound a subject can reliably detect on half the occasions it is presented.

Vision	A candle flame at 50 kilometres on a clear night
Hearing	Tick of a wristwatch at 6 metres in a quiet room
Taste	One teaspoon of sugar in 2 litres of water
Smell	One drop of perfume diffused in an average house
Touch	An insect falling on your cheek from a height of 1 centimetre

FIG. 23. *Approximate absolute thresholds*

Having worked out a scale for measuring mental sensations, Fechner set out to show that these sensations have a direct relationship to external stimuli. He hoped that such a demonstration would help to convince people that mind and matter were really only two sides of the same thing. But he found considerable variability in the measurement of both absolute thresholds and JNDs. Different observations yielded different values. Fechner saw this variability as primarily a methodological problem; he blamed the use of nonstandardised experimental procedures for the inconsistent findings. For this reason he set out to devise experimental techniques that would yield reliable measures of mental sensations. He based these "psychophysical" techniques on the work of other scientists; so, in one sense they were not original. However, it was Fechner who tied the methods together and showed how they relate to his ultimate purpose, the measurement of mental sensations.

CLASSIC EXPERIMENT 4:

FECHNER'S PSYCHOPHYSICS

Fechner called his experimental procedures "psychophysics" because he believed they represented an amalgamation of physical measurement with psychological measurement. In his book *Elements of Psychophysics* Fechner describes three psychophysical methods. Each is both an experimental procedure and a mathematical treatment. Although all three can justifiably be called classics, only the first of his methods is described in detail here because it is the method most closely associated with psychophysics.

Just Noticeable Differences

Fechner called the first of his psychophysical techniques the method of *just noticeable differences*. Today, this approach is generally known as the *method of limits*. Fechner described the use of this method for determining the sensitivity of weight estimation as follows:

In the application of the method of just noticeable differences, a person compares the weight of two containers, A and B, by lifting them, after they have been given slightly different loads. The difference in weight will be felt if it is large enough; otherwise it will not be noticed. The method of just noticeable differences consists in determining how much the weights have to differ so that they can just be discriminated . . .

Although the procedure sounds similar to Weber's and simple in theory, Fechner found that it is not quite so straightforward in actual practice. Unless great care is taken, the threshold determined by the method of just noticeable differences can be biased in several ways. For example, after a number of trials in which the comparison weight is heavier than the standard, the subject may get in the habit of always responding "heavier" even when this response is no longer correct. Psychophysicists call the tendency to continue making the same response the *error of habituation*. Jumping the gun and changing a response from "heavier" to "lighter" before actually sensing any change is another possible response bias. Psychophysicists call this tendency the *error of anticipation*. To avoid such potential biases, Fechner advocated frequent changes of sequence. Again, in his own words:

If, for example, experiments are to be conducted with a series of standard weights, one could proceed by first taking an ascending series [beginning with a comparison smaller than the standard and slowly adjusting upwards], then a descending series, on the same day, and repeating on the next day with a descending series followed by an ascending series. One could also run through the series with only ascending trials on one day and descending the following, keeping to this alternation methodically through the whole series of days necessary to complete the experimental run.

Alternating the ascending and descending series, while necessary, does not control all possible sources of bias. Fechner also took great pains to control any biasing influences that could arise from the experimental materials. For example, in his weight-lifting experiments he used an apparatus designed to eliminate any possible clues to the size of the weights involved. The apparatus consisted of four vertical brass bars connected at the bottom by cross bars. Weights made of lead or zinc were fitted solidly into the frame. Each of these frames was covered on all sides by wood to form hollow boxes. The external appearance of the boxes held no clue to the weight they contained. Each box (one was designated the standard, the other the comparison) was lifted once using a wooden handle fitted into its top. Although the containers looked alike Fechner still alternated the box used as the standard in order to be sure that small, unnoticed differences between the boxes did not contaminate his findings. Fechner made sure that the weights would always be lifted to the same height by placing a horizontal board above the laboratory bench; he also controlled the amount of time each weight spent in the air by lifting the weights in time with the clicks of a metronome. Finally, Fechner shifted the standard weight from the right to the left hand periodically in order to control for any differences in sensitivity between the two hands. Fechner's careful experimental techniques not only minimised unwanted biasing of the experimental results, they also set the standard for careful psychological research for many decades.

The method of just noticeable differences can be applied to tasks other than weight estimation. It can be used to determine both absolute thresholds and JNDs for every sense modality. For example, Figure 24 depicts an experiment designed to determine the absolute threshold of audible pitch. Subjects in the experiment were merely asked whether they heard a sound. The first column of the table, reading downwards, records one subject's responses ("Y" for yes and "N" for no) in a descending

Frequency (Hz)	Alternate descending and ascending series									
24	Y									
23	Y									
22	Y		Y							
21	Y		Y							
20	Y		Y						Y	
19	Y		Y				Y		Y	
18	Y		Y		Y		Y		Y	
17	Y		Y		Y		Y		Y	
16	Y	Y	Y		Y		Y		Y	
15	Y	N	Y	Y	Y	Y	Y		Y	Y
14	N	N	N	N	a?	N	?	Y	?	N
13		N		N		N		N		N
12		N		N		N		N		N
11		N		N		N		N		
10		N		N				N		
9				N				N		
8				N				N		
7				N				N		

(1) T = 14.5 15.5 14.5 14.5 14.5 14.5 14.5 13.5 14.5 14.5
M = 14.5;   SD = .45

(2) AvT = 15.0   14.5   14.5   14.0   14.5
M = 14.5;   SD = .32

FIG. 24. *Determining the threshold by the method of limits. See text for explanation*

a? = "Doubtful", and counts as a shift in sign from the previous judgment.

series. Using a set of precision tuning forks, the experimenter began by presenting a 24-hertz (24 cycles per second) tone which the subject had no difficulty in detecting. The experimenter lowered this tone by one hertz and tried again. Once again, the subject responded yes. The experimenter continued to lower the tone by one hertz and at 14 hertz the subject responded no. The experimenter concluded that the threshold must be somewhere between 14 and 15 hertz. Since no finer discriminations were tested, the experimenter estimated the threshold as 14.5 hertz and entered this amount under T.

The experimenter then began an ascending series of tones starting at 10 hertz — well below the subject's threshold. The tone was increased until the subject responded yes. Since this time the change in response (from no to yes) occurred at 16 hertz, the threshold was assumed to lie between 15 and 16 and it was recorded as 15.5 hertz. The experimenter continued these ascending and descending series until he was satisfied that the threshold values were not fluctuating very much. He also varied the starting point each time in order to minimise any tendency toward the errors of habituation or anticipation.

When the experiment was completed the absolute threshold for pitch was determined by averaging the various T values, a procedure which yielded an absolute threshold of 14.5 hertz. For Fechner, this value then becomes the zero point of a scale for measuring the mental sensations produced by pitch. Finding the zero point, however, is only just the beginning. Now he must determine the measurement units, the just noticeable differences between stimuli which comprise the scale.

The method of just noticeable differences can also be used to determine JND units. To do this, the experimenter must use two stimuli, a standard and a comparison. In addition, three rather than two response categories are necessary. In the experiment depicted in Figure 25 the experimenter is attempting to determine the increase necessary for a change in pitch to be discriminated when the standard tone is set at 50 hertz. The subject is asked to respond higher (the comparison stimulus is higher than the standard), lower (the comparison is lower than the standard), or equal (the two are the same). The experimenter begins by presenting a comparison stimulus well above the standard in pitch and adjusts downward until the subject reports that the two sounds are equal. The point at which the response changes from higher to equal (T+) is noted but the experimenter does not stop here. He continues to adjust downward until the subject responds lower. This point (T−) is also recorded. The experimenter then presents an ascending series of stimuli beginning with a tone much lower than the standard and adjusting upwards until the subject reports that the comparison and standard tones are equal in pitch. This point (T−) is recorded but the experimenter continues to adjust upwards until the subject responds higher (T+). These ascending and descending trials are repeated until the experimenter is confident that the judgements he has recorded are stable.

The just noticeable difference is calculated by first subtracting the average T− value from the average T+ value. The difference between these numbers is called the *interval of uncertainty*. All pitches falling in this interval are subjectively equivalent for the subject. The centre of the interval of uncertainty represents the *point of subjective equality*, the point at which a sensation is perceived to be equal to the external stimulus. So, one-half the interval of uncertainty represents the amount that must be added or subtracted from the standard for the observer to notice a

Values of comparison	Responses in alternate descending and ascending series							
80	+	+		+	+	+		
70	+	+	+	+	+	+	+	+
60	+	+	+	=	=	=	+	+
Standard =50	=	=	−	+	+	+	=	=
40	=	−	−	−	−	=	+	+
30	−	−	−	−	−	=	=	
20	−	−					−	−
10	−						−	−
T(+)=	55	55	55	45	65	45	55	35 Mean T(+)= 51.25
T(−)=	35	45	55	45	45	35	25	25 Mean T(−)=38.75

IU = Interval of Uncertainty = $T(+) - T(-) = 51.25 - 38.75 = 12.5$

DL = Difference Threshold = 1/2 Interval of Uncertainty = 0.625

PSE = Point of Subjective Equality = $\dfrac{T(+) + T(-)}{2} = \dfrac{51.25 + 38.75}{2} = 45$

CE = Constant Error = $PSE - ST = 45 - 50 = -5$

FIG. 25. *Determining the just noticeable difference by the method of limits. See text for explanation*

change — one JND. Repeating the experiment with different standard tones permits the experimenter to build a scale of JNDs for pitch sensitivity with a starting point at the absolute threshold and each unit representing an increase of one JND.

The method of just noticeable differences is the psychophysical method most directly related to the concept of threshold. But it is not perfect. For one thing, there are the response biases already mentioned. In addition, fatigue can also affect the results. Fechner was aware of these potential problems and suggested that other psychophysical methods should be used to check the validity of any results obtained using the method of just noticeable differences.

Additional Psychophysical Methods

Fechner's second psychophysical method, the *method of average error* is better known today as the *method of adjustment*. The new name describes the technique very well. In this method the subject is required to manipulate (adjust) a continuously variable stimulus until it is equal to some standard. For example, the sub-ject may be shown a standard lamp and asked to adjust a variable lamp until it is just as bright as the standard. Sometimes the subject adjusts the variable lamp to be brighter than the standard, sometimes he makes it dimmer than the standard. The brightness difference between the variable lamp and the standard represents the subject's error. The smaller this error, the better the subject's sensitivity. If the comparison is repeated many times the size of the subject's error will vary slightly from trial to trial. Both the average error and the variability of the subject's errors can be used to measure brightness sensitivity. Although subjects enjoy the method of average error more than the method of just noticeable differences (because they get to participate more actively in the experiment), it is not possible to use this psychophysical method with all stimuli. For example, sounds are difficult to compare this way because they have to be presented successively rather than simultaneously. This is not a problem for Fechner's third psychophysical technique, the *method of right and wrong cases*.

Known today as the *method of constant stimuli*, this psychophysical technique consists of presenting comparison and standard stimuli and asking the subject to determine the direction in which the comparison stimulus differs from the standard. For example, suppose a psychophysicist is interested in judging the length of lines. A standard line of 70 millimetres is presented, say, by projecting it on a screen. This standard line is followed by one of five comparison lines. These comparison lines measure 68, 69, 70, 71 and 72 millimetres respectively. The subject must say whether the comparison (only one comparison is projected in any one trial) is longer or shorter than the standard line. Sometimes the comparison is presented first and the standard second in order to minimise response biases. Using mathematical formulae developed by Fechner, data gathered by this method can be used to determine JNDs for hearing, vision and all the other senses.

AFTERMATH

From the beginning Fechner's work was controversial. Critics attacked his belief that he was actually measuring mental sensation and questioned his assumption that all JNDs are equal. But by far the most important criticism of Fechner's work concerned the zero point of his scale — the absolute threshold. As noted earlier, the absolute threshold is defined not in terms of zero physical energy but as the level of stimulus energy required to arouse a response 50 per cent of the time. Since the threshold is defined arbitrarily in statistical terms, some other statistical definition (say, the level of stimulus energy that produces a response 25 per cent of the time) could always be adopted. Unfortunately, this new definition would yield a different threshold and thereby change the zero point of Fechner's scale.

The statistical definition of the absolute threshold also means that there is a class of "negative" sensations. These sensations are too weak to produce a response 50 per cent of the time, but they do sometimes produce responses. On those occasions when such stimuli fail to arouse a response, they may still be detected unconsciously. In fact, Sigmund Freud used Fechner's statistical notion of the absolute threshold when developing his theory of the unconscious. Despite the peculiar notion of negative sensations, Fechner believed that absolute thresholds (although hard to measure) really exist. Others argued that the existence of negative sensations proved that there are no absolute thresholds. Instead, they believed that sensations increase in a smooth continuous manner and do not abruptly change from "no sensation" to "sensation". Numerous experimental studies conducted in the years since Fechner's original work have failed to find support for the notion of a fixed

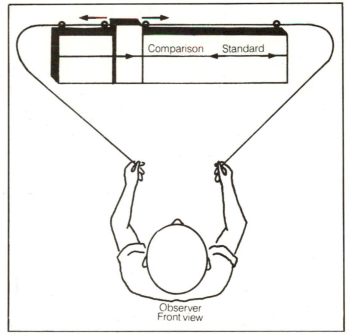

FIG. 26. *The method of adjustment. The subject manipulates the comparison until it is subjectively equal in length to the standard*

Comparison   Standard

Observer
Front view

threshold. A subject's attitude, motivation, fatigue, interest and level of attention can all affect where the threshold falls. Today the most commonly accepted approach to studying sensation, the theory of signal detection, does not even include the notion of an absolute threshold.

Fechner's techniques and theoretical assumptions may have been criticised but his philosophy, his main reason for inventing psychophysics in the first place, was almost completely ignored. The publication of *Elements of Psychophysics* did nothing to advance the cause of panpsychism. In fact, since physical stimuli and sensations had to be regarded as separate in order to be measured (and the relationship between them determined), Fechner's research did more to foster dualism than any other contemporary theory about the relationship between the body and the mind.

Even though Fechner's philosophy never really gained many adherents and his belief in absolute thresholds and equal JNDs did not withstand searching experimentation, he is one of the greats of experimental psychology. His importance does not lie in his philosophy of mind or even in his delineation of the psychophysical methods. It derives from his attempt to develop measurement methods suitable to the new scientific psychology. Fechner set experimental psychology on a quantitative course that it was to follow for many decades. It also convinced the scientists of the time that a mathematical and truly scientific psychology was possible.

Further Reading

Fechner, G., *Elements of Psychophysics*, (Vol. 1), Holt, Rinehart & Winston, New York, 1966 (original published in 1860).

Fodor, J. A., "The Mind–Body Problem", *Scientific American*, *244*, pp. 124–33, 1981.

Jones, F.N., "History of Psychophysics and Judgement", in E. C. Carterette and M. P. Friedman (eds), *Handbook of Perception*, (Vol. 1), Academic Press, New York, 1974.

PART 2

Perceiving, Remembering and Feeling

The first experimental psychologists were the structuralists whose goal was to uncover the basic elements (the atoms) of thoughts and sensations through introspection. Although it took many years, by the early part of the present century most experimental psychologists had reached the conclusion that the structuralist research programme had failed. Instead of commonly agreed upon facts, introspection had produced sterile arguments about such matters as whether the sensation of *purple* is more *reddish* than *bluish*. The structuralists were replaced by the functionalists, who were more interested in the interaction of psychic events than in their physical nature. That is, they were less concerned with what thoughts and sensations are than with why they occur.

In a way the functionalist approach to psychology is similar to the method used by classical geneticists. Before the identification of genes and DNA, geneticists approached their subject entirely from the "outside". They would crossbreed plants and animals, observe their offspring, and try to infer the biological mechanisms that produced them. The functionalists adopted a similar approach to the study of psychological phenomena; they attempted to infer mental mechanisms by observing how organisms behave in different situations. Like the seventeenth-century dualists, the functionalists, too, assumed that a man who looks at a cloudy sky and reaches for an umbrella has formed a *belief* that it may rain. This belief cannot be seen, of course; it is a hypothetical mental entity inferred from observing the subject's behaviour in a particular situation. Except for the few remaining radical behaviourists who argue that psychology has no business inferring mental entities — for them the connection between the cloudy weather (the stimulus) and reaching for the umbrella (the response) is sufficient — most of today's experimental psychologists have adopted an essentially functionalist stance.

The following three chapters describe functionalist approaches to several important psychological phenomena: the mechanisms controlling human memory (Chapter Four), how we perceive the world around us (Chapter Five), and the psychological basis of emotion (Chapter Six).

MEMORY

Without memory we could not learn, we could not carry on intelligent conversations (because we could not remember the thoughts we wished to express) and life would lack any continuity. Each day would consist of a string of momentary experiences unrelated to one another and without any links to our past. Without memory we would not even realise that we have a "self" because the very notion of a self depends on a continuous memory. In this chapter two classic memory experiments are described. The first, performed by Hermann Ebbinghaus, began what is known today as the *verbal learning* tradition. The second experiment, conducted by Frederic Bartlett, started a rather different tradition — the treatment of memory as a dynamic *cognitive* information system.

THE WAX TABLET

According to Plato, who had a lot to say about psychological matters, memory can be considered similar to a block of wax: "When we wish to remember anything which we have seen or heard ... we hold the wax up to the perceptions and thoughts and in that material receive the impressions of them." For Plato, poor or indistinct memories are similar to poorly formed wax impressions. Although the outlines may be seen, the details are hard to make out.

At one level Plato must be correct — the brain has to be changed in some way when we commit information to memory. But as an explanation for everyday memory experiences Plato's "visual" analogy is quite misleading. For example, if memory is similar to wax impressions, then we should expect those who visualise memory images most vividly to have the best recall. About 100 years ago the English scientist Francis Galton performed an experiment dealing with precisely this question. He wrote to a large number of eminent men and asked them to imagine their breakfast table on the morning they received his letter. Each subject was asked to comment on the vividness and detail of their mental image. Galton found marked differences among his respondents. Some reported that their image was as clear as if they were still sitting at their breakfast table, others reported that they could not conjure up any image at all. Galton concluded, quite justifiably, that there are individual differences in imagery ability.

Unfortunately, Galton's experiment did not really test Plato's hypothesis because he did not show that clear images contain more faithful representations of breakfast tables than indistinct images. Some years later Frederic Bartlett, whose classic research is described later in this chapter, repeated Galton's experiment but also performed an independent check on his subjects' accuracy. He found that although subjects who claim to have vivid images are more confident about their memories than those with poor images, they are, in fact, no more accurate in their recall.

There are two possible interpretations of Bartlett's result. Either Plato's analogy is wrong — there is no relationship between the vividness of a memory and its accuracy — or subjective reports of vividness are inaccurate. It is impossible to choose between these two explanations simply by asking people about their images. Instead, memory experiments are required. The first person to perform such experiments was Hermann Ebbinghaus.

HERMANN EBBINGHAUS: FATHER OF MEMORY RESEARCH

Hermann Ebbinghaus was born in 1850 in a small town near Bonn, Germany. His father was a middle-class merchant and, by all reports, Ebbinghaus had a comfortable childhood. He studied at the local *gymnasium* and at the age of 17 entered the University of Bonn, where he intended to study history. Ebbinghaus did not stay at Bonn long, however. In fact, he did not stay at any university for long. By the time he was 20 he had also attended the universities of Halle and Berlin, where he became more interested in philosophy than history.

Ebbinghaus's peripatetic academic career was briefly interrupted by the Franco-Prussian War, during which he served in the German army. This experience seemed to have satisfied his wanderlust because he returned to Bonn after the war and remained there until he received his doctorate in philosophy in 1873. Ebbinghaus's doctoral research dealt with the psychological problem of the unconscious, though from a philosophical rather than a psychological viewpoint.

Ebbinghaus spent the next seven years in what he preferred to call "independent study". He travelled around Germany, England and France visiting universities, reading books and living off an income provided largely by his family. It was during this period, while browsing through a secondhand book shop in Paris, that Ebbinghaus came across Gustav Fechner's book *Elements of Psychophysics* (see Chapter Three for more on Fechner). Ebbinghaus was impressed by Fechner's book, particularly his demonstration that rigorous, empirical methods could be applied to psychological problems. But he felt that Fechner had not gone far enough. Fechner had applied his methodology solely to simple mental sensations; he had not examined the "higher mental processes" involved in more complex forms of human cognition. Ebbinghaus decided to redress this imbalance. Alone, without colleagues or a university position, Ebbinghaus set out to adapt Fechner's psychophysical methods to the study of memory. As it turned out his approach was rather different from Fechner's, but Ebbinghaus always felt indebted to the older psychologist and, many years later, dedicated his famous psychology text-book to him.

In 1880 Ebbinghaus took his first university position as *dozent* (tutor) at the University of Berlin. His first task was to repeat all of his memory experiments in order to verify his results. Five years later, satisfied that his findings were indeed reliable, Ebbinghaus published his first book, *Über das Gedächtnis (On Memory)*. In this book Ebbinghaus described experiments dealing with the effect of repetition on retention, the strength of associations in memory and the relationship between

FIG. 27. *Hermann Ebbinghaus (1850–1909), first memory experimenter*

time and forgetting. The book made quite a stir among experimental psychologists as it showed how "higher mental processes" could be studied by careful experimentation. In 1886, largely as a result of his book, Ebbinghaus was given a low-level professorial post at the university. He held this post for eight years, but did not pursue memory research any further. This was fairly typical behaviour for Ebbinghaus. He had the kind of mind that always requires new challenges. For the rest of his career he made a habit of performing innovative research in areas neglected by other psychologists, but he always left the follow-up work to others. A few years after his memory book Ebbinghaus published a seminal work on colour vision, followed shortly by a description of how to go about measuring the mental capacity of children. The latter work was published several years *before* Binet's more famous effort (see Chapter Eleven for more on Binet).

In 1890 Ebbinghaus and a colleague, Arthur Konig, founded the journal *Zeitschrift für Psychologie und Physiologie der Sinnesorgane* which, under a shorter name, remains one of the premier psychological journals today. In 1894 Ebbinghaus left Berlin for the University of Breslau, where he took up the Chair of Psychology. He was an extremely popular lecturer and, after his psychology textbook appeared in 1897, a successful author as well. His textbook was so well received that it went into several large editions, making him a sought-after speaker. Ebbinghaus was also well liked as a person. He was friendly and sympathetic to younger colleagues and he enjoyed both the professional and social aspects of psychology meetings.

Compared with psychologists like Piaget, who published hundreds of scientific papers and books, Ebbinghaus's publication output was small. What he lacked in quantity, however, he more than made up for in quality. His originality, clarity and humanity were responsible for starting many people along research careers. His influence is all the more impressive given that he had no teachers (all of his research ideas and methods were self-generated) and he founded no school. Although there were (and are) Piagetians and Freudians, there were never Ebbinghausians. Ebbinghaus's contribution was mainly to provide experimental psychology with a set of methods. These methods became so much a part of the science, they were often used without citing their source — it was as if they had always been available. The most famous of his methods were the ones he used in the classic experiments described in the next section.

CLASSIC EXPERIMENT 5:

REMEMBERING AND FORGETTING

When Ebbinghaus decided to study memory experimentally, he was breaking with a 2000-year-old philosophical tradition. Instead of the armchair philosophical analyses of the past, Ebbinghaus, like Fechner, felt that objective research methods were required. He also followed Fechner in believing that psychological problems must be simplified in order to be studied. Simplification, he maintained, is particularly important when studying memory because we do not all have the same knowledge and experiences. (It is no good testing people's memory of famous historical events if they have not been taught these events in the first place.) In order to study memory processes uninfluenced by prior knowledge and experience, Ebbinghaus invented an entirely new memory device — the nonsense syllable.

Nonsense syllables are combinations of three letters — two consonants surrounding a randomly chosen vowel — that can be pronounced but have no meaning. Some examples of English nonsense syllables are CAZ, KIB, and KUX. Ebbinghaus believed that since nonsense syllables have no meaning they make ideal stimuli for memory experiments; they permit investigators to study "pure" memory phenomena (the effect of the amount of practice on recall, for instance) uncontaminated by the influence of prior learning and experience. The nonsense syllable was Ebbinghaus's invention; noone had ever used one before but hundreds of memory experimenters have used them since.

Ebbinghaus created 2300 nonsense syllables and then began to teach them to a willing and dedicated experimental subject — himself. Testing oneself was an unusual experimental approach even in those days, but remember Ebbinghaus had no university position at the time he began these experiments and no access to other subjects. What is more, it is unlikely that he could have persuaded many others to do what he required; for the next two years he learned and relearned more than 1000 lists each containing 12 to 16 nonsense syllables.

Ebbinghaus would begin by rapidly reading each syllable in the list aloud once through. He would then try to repeat the entire list from memory. If he failed he would run through the same "read-test" procedure again and again until he could recite the entire list once through without error. After reaching this criterion Ebbinghaus would wait a while and then try to recall the list again. If he failed he would repeat his earlier procedure, reading the list aloud and testing his memory until he once again could recall every syllable perfectly. In order to have some measure by which to compare his performance on different occasions, Ebbinghaus devised a memory retention measure he called *memory savings*.

Memory savings is calculated by subtracting the number of recitations required to relearn a list from the number required to learn the list in the first place. This difference is known as the number of repetitions

62

saved. (Because relearning is faster than original learning, the number of repetitions saved is always a positive number.) The savings score can be used to express memory retention in percentage form. This percentage is calculated by dividing the number of repetitions saved by the number required for original learning (multiplied by 100 to get rid of the decimals). Thus, a list of nonsense syllables that required 100 repetitions originally and 50 upon relearning represents a savings score of 50 per cent (50/100 × 100 = 50).

Ebbinghaus was a compulsively careful experimenter. He recited the nonsense syllables aloud at a set rate keeping time with a metronome. He made certain to test himself at the same time each day to control for the effects of fatigue and he never tested himself when something other than the experiment was on his mind (or, as he put it: "... whenever great changes in the inner or outer life occurred"). In two years of experimentation, using just the methods described, Ebbinghaus performed experiments that answered many fundamental questions about how memory works. His most famous experiment involved the relationship between study time and memory and the relationship between the time elapsed since learning and the amount of material forgotten.

FIG. 28. The relationship between the amount retained and the time devoted to learning is a simple straight line. Ebbinghaus's finding is known today as the "total time hypothesis"

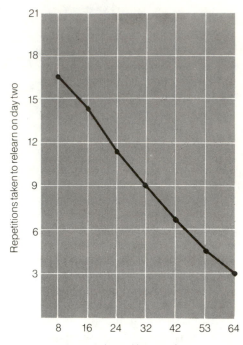

Study Time and Memory

Ebbinghaus's experiment on study time was designed to answer the following question: is the amount of time spent learning directly related to recall? Or, put another way, does more time spent learning always translate into better retention or is there some point at which additional learning no longer improves memory? Ebbinghaus answered this question by learning a series of 16-syllable lists. On a single day he would choose one of these lists and attempt to learn it by reading the syllables aloud at a fairly brisk pace. He would not do this just once, however, but many times. Some lists were repeated eight times, others 16 and still others 24, 32, 42, 50 or even 64 times.

The next day Ebbinghaus would try to reproduce the list perfectly. If he could not he would repeat the list aloud as many times as necessary until he could recite it by heart. Ebbinghaus calculated memory retention scores as a function of the number of repetitions involved in the original learning; his findings appear in graphic form in Figure 28. As can be seen, the relationship between the number of repetitions on the first day and the number of repetitions required on the second day is a decreasing straight line. The amount of material retained in memory is directly affected by the time spent in original learning; double the original learning time and you double recall. There was no evidence at all that the value of practice begins to taper off. The notion that the amount of time devoted to study determines the amount of material recalled is today known as the *total time hypothesis*, and has been confirmed many times since Ebbinghaus's original experiment.

Forgetting

Ebbinghaus's second classic experiment was almost the inverse of his first. This time, instead of the relationship between time spent studying and recall he was interested in determining the relationship between time since learning and forgetting. He wanted to know whether this relationship is a straight-line one as in the previous demonstration or whether forgetting follows a different time course from learning. Once again Ebbinghaus began by learning lists of nonsense syllables. His procedure was to practise each list until he could recite it once through perfectly and then to relearn the same list after a delay. The period between original learning and relearning varied from 20 minutes to 31 days. Once again the percentage memory retention score was his main dependent variable. The results of this experiment are shown in Figure 29.

These results are rather different from the earlier ones. Forgetting does not follow a steady, straight-line course like learning. Instead, forgetting is very rapid at first and then slows down. About half the material in the list is lost in the first hour, but between the fifth and thirty-first days after learning only five per cent of the syllables are forgotten. Eventually forgetting appears to stop altogether. It is as if once a memory has reached a certain point it becomes permanent and is not forgotten. Ebbinghaus himself put it this way:

It is reasonable to be surprised at this initial rapidity and late slowness. One hour after the end of learning, forgetting had already progressed so far that one-half the amount

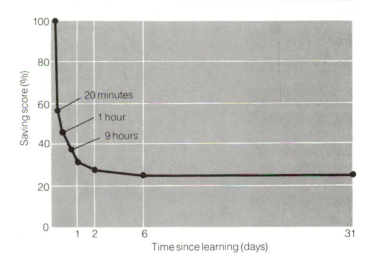

of original work had to be expended before the series of syllables could be reproduced again; after 8 hours the work to be made up amounted to two thirds of the first effort. Gradually, however, the process became slower, so that even for rather long periods the additional losses could be ascertained only with difficulty.

There seems to be no point at which memory actually reaches zero and no more is recalled. Ebbinghaus demonstrated this by studying some stanzas from the poem "Don Juan" until he could recite them perfectly, and then testing himself on them 20 years later. Despite the long time period he found that it took less time to relearn the stanzas on the second occasion than it did to learn them 20 years earlier.

Of course, the exact amount forgotten in any time period is not always the same as that shown in the graph in Figure 29. Ebbinghaus has already shown that memory is better if more time is devoted to original learning. However, it is only the values on the vertical axis of the graph that change with more learning time, not the shape of the forgetting curve. The same-shaped *forgetting curve* has been reproduced on many occasions by experimenters using materials other than nonsense syllables and subjects other than Ebbinghaus. Today the forgetting curve is taken

FIG. 29. *Ebbinghaus's classic forgetting curve. Each point on the graph represents the percentage of items recalled from the original list. As can be seen, more forgetting occurs during the first 20 minutes than in the remaining 31 days*

as representing a basic psychological law.

Ebbinghaus's memory research is often described as one of the greatest advances made by experimental psychology. Not only have his findings withstood the test of time (and replication) but his techniques have been adopted by psychologists to study many disparate memory and learning phenomena.

AFTERMATH

One aspect of Ebbinghaus's method that was particularly influential was his invention of the nonsense syllable. Following Ebbinghaus's lead, psychologists interested in studying memory routinely designed experiments using meaningless stimuli. In this way they believed they were studying pure memory uninfluenced by prior experience. Before long, memory study was a flourishing field of psychological research. Psychologists performed hundreds of experiments examining how recall is affected by changes in the type of material to be remembered (nonsense syllables, numbers, sometimes words), the order in which material is presented, the number of repetitions required to learn, the time since learning occurred and whether the original material is read aloud or silently. As a whole, this field of research came to be known as *verbal learning* since it is concerned with the conditions facilitating the learning of verbal materials. The results of these experiments can be summarised fairly succinctly: when it comes to learning meaningless stimuli, success is determined by how well the materials are impressed on the mind (number of repetitions, and so on).

Although few early psychologists seemed aware of them, there are serious problems with Ebbinghaus's simplified approach to memory research. One problem stems from his assumption that nonsense syllables are meaningless. As it turns out, they are not. Many seemingly meaningless nonsense syllables do produce strong associations affecting the ease with which they are recalled by some persons. For example, the syllable BON may be meaningless for some people but create certain associations for those who know French. Individuals in the latter group have an easier time remembering BON than those in the former.

An even more important problem with Ebbinghaus's method is that in trying to eliminate the effects of prior knowledge and subjective associations on memory he also eliminated an important aspect of how memory operates. Ebbinghaus's approach creates a highly artificial laboratory situation in which a memory is established by repetition rather than by its connection with other memories already present in a subject's mind. There is strong evidence that in the "real world" the connections among memories are more important determinants of what and how well we recall than merely the number of times an item is repeated. This evidence comes not from verbal learning experiments but from clinical observation.

One of the most sensitive clinical observers of memory was Sigmund Freud. His method was to infer mental processes from his patients' words and behaviours. Although his method was less controlled than laboratory-based experiments, his findings were often quite dramatic. For example, in his book *The Psychopathology of Everyday Life*, Freud describes an incident that occurred when he struck up a conversation with a young man on a train. The two men were talking about the current rise of European anti-Semitism when the young man quoted, in Latin, a verse from the *Aeneid*. The quotation alluded to future generations righting their fathers' wrongs; but he got the quote wrong. As Freud pointed out, the word *aliquis* (someone) was omitted. In his writings Freud had often claimed that such errors are not accidents. On the contrary, he maintained that memory lapses and even everyday slips of the tongue (Freudian slips) are motivated by unconscious forces. The young man knew this and challenged Freud to explain why he had forgotten the crucial word.

Freud agreed to the challenge and instructed the young traveller to free-associate to the word *aliquis*. After producing associations like liquid and fluid, Freud's companion then produced the names of several Roman Catholic saints, including Saint Simon who had been murdered as a child and Saint Januarius, whose dried blood, he had heard, was preserved in a bottle in Italy and mysteriously turned to liquid each year on the same day. The young man hesitated after this because he did not want to say what next popped into his mind, but Freud encouraged him and he admitted that he was expecting a message from a woman that could prove annoying. Much to the young man's shock, Freud immediately guessed that the message was that she had missed her menstrual period and was pregnant. Freud went on to explain that all of the young man's associations were related to this theme. First there was the *liquid*, then the calendar-like name Saint Januarius, the saint murdered as a child and the blood that "miraculously" liquefies. The original memory lapse, said Freud, can now be understood. The quotation was concerned with posterity — something the young man could do without.

Freud's conception of memory is obviously different from Ebbinghaus's. Ebbinghaus looked upon memory as an orderly warehouse full of merchandise. When we want to recall a particular memory we merely go to the proper part of the warehouse and lift it off the shelf. In contrast to this "static" view, Freud believed that memory is "dynamic". Instead of an orderly mental warehouse full of facts, dates and incidents, Freud saw memory as a constantly changing set of interconnections held together by unconscious themes. Of the two points of view, Freud's seems to coincide with everyday experience. Take names, for example. Everyone has had the experience of meeting a familiar person but not being able to recall the person's name. Other names spring to mind, and often these are related to the target name in some way. For example, you may recall that the name begins with the letter R, but you know it is not Roberta or Rosemary. Then you remember that it has something to do with birds and finally recall that it is Robyn. William James, the famous American philosopher and psychologist, described this common experience in his 1890 psychology textbook:

Suppose we try to recall a forgotten name. The state of our consciousness is peculiar. There is a gap therein; but no mere gap. It is a gap that is intensely active. A sort of wraith of the name is in it, beckoning us in a given direction, making us at moments tingle with the sense of their closeness and then letting us sink back without the longed-for term. If wrong names are proposed to us, this singular definite gap acts immediately so as to negate them. They do not fit into its mold. And the gap of one word does not feel like the gap of another, all empty of content as both might seem necessarily to be when described as gaps.

This "tip-of-the-tongue" phenomenon (and our ability to do crossword puzzles, for that matter) strongly suggests that Freud's view of memory is more realistic than Ebbinghaus's. There is more to recall than merely fetching a memory off a warehouse shelf; memory is dynamic and highly individualistic. The experimental psychologist who did most to uncover the dynamic nature of memory is Frederic Bartlett whose work is described next.

FREDERIC C. BARTLETT: PIONEER BRITISH PSYCHOLOGIST

Frederic Bartlett was a product of the best education nineteenth-century England could offer. He was born in 1886 and received his BA and MA in London before entering Saint John's College at Cambridge University in 1912. At that time psychology was very much a poor relation at Cambridge, indeed in

England. There was no Chair of Psychology at any university in the country, and few lectureships. Cambridge did have a psychology laboratory, however. It had been founded several years earlier by C. S. Myers, a physician, physiologist and anthropologist, mainly with his own money and gifts from relatives. In 1914 Bartlett became assistant director of the laboratory, working under Myers who was director. Neither position carried any salary. Except for a break during the First World War, when he worked on applying psychology to practical military problems, Bartlett remained at Cambridge for the rest of his career. His military experience stayed with him, however, in the form of a life-long belief that psychology should concentrate on practical problems wherever possible.

FIG. 30. *Sir Frederic C. Bartlett (1886–1969), first Professor of Psychology at Cambridge University*

In 1922, when Myers retired, Bartlett became director of the psychology laboratory. He was also given the post of Reader in Psychology. At that stage no higher position in psychology was available in England. Nine years later, when Cambridge eventually established a Chair of Experimental Psychology, Bartlett became the university's first Professor of Psychology. At the time the only other psychology professor in England was Cyril Burt at the University of London. The establishment of these two chairs should not be taken as signifying a trend, however. Oxford University did not get around to appointing a professor of psychology until 1947.

The 1920s and 1930s were productive years for Bartlett. He published several books on various topics, including *Psychology and Primitive Culture*, *Psychology and the Soldier* and his most famous book, *Remembering*. He also took over the editorship of the *British Journal of Psychology*, a post he held until 1948. During this period he also found time to visit Africa, where he gathered important data on how different social experiences affect memory. Throughout his career Bartlett insisted on the importance of culture and social context in determining behaviour.

Although Bartlett's research made him well known among psychologists, his students also knew him as a stimulating teacher. He preferred group discussions to formal lectures and encouraged students to think analytically about the problems they were studying. His style attracted many students to Cambridge, quite a few of whom now hold important positions in psychology themselves. Bartlett was also an efficient administrator who presided over explosive growth in his department with seemingly little effort. In 1922, when he took over the psychology laboratory, its staff consisted of the director and one assistant. In 1952, when he retired, Bartlett was overseeing a research and technical staff of 70. In recognition of his scientific and educational accomplishments, he was elected to the Royal Society in 1932 and knighted in 1948. Bartlett died in 1969 at the age of 82. Of all his contributions to psychology the one that has become a classic is his experiment on the dynamic nature of memory.

CLASSIC EXPERIMENT 6:

THE WAR
OF THE GHOSTS

Bartlett, like all experimentalists, believed that psychology should employ rigorous scientific methods but, unlike many psychologists, he did not believe that these methods should be identical to those used by physicists. Physicists approach their subject matter by simplifying the phenomena they wish to study in order to reduce them to their essence. Psychologists like Ebbinghaus tried to do the same. The advantages of this approach to memory research are obvious. It reduces a complex system — human memory — to a series of simple ones, each of which can be studied under carefully defined laboratory conditions. Bartlett understood this but argued that this advantage is far outweighed by an important disadvantage — simplifying memory this way eliminates many of its most interesting aspects. Bartlett argued that by using relatively meaningless nonsense syllables, Ebbinghaus had failed to study how experience and knowledge are used to store and retrieve memories. Even if we knew everything there is to know about the mastery and recall of lists of nonsense syllables, Bartlett said, we would still know very little about how memory operates in the real world. The same point may be made rather differently: psychologists who study nonsense syllables are like the man who searches under a bright streetlamp for the wallet he dropped in the dark bushes across the street. Both give as their reason: "There is more light here."

Like Freud, Bartlett did not believe that memory is simply a matter of picking episodes off hypothetical mental shelves. Nor did Bartlett believe that memories just reappear like images in Plato's wax tablet. According to Bartlett, memories must be constructed. He put it this way:

. . . the description of memories as "fixed and lifeless" is merely an unpleasant fiction . . . memory is itself constructive . . . I have regarded it rather as one achievement in the line of the ceaseless struggle to master and enjoy a world full of variety and rapid change. Memory, and all the life of images and words which goes with it, is one with the age-old acquisition of the distance senses, and with that development of constructive imagination and constructive thought wherein at length we find the most complete release from the narrowness of presented time and place.

In order to illustrate this point, Bartlett conducted experiments using meaningful materials recalled in naturalistic (rather than artificial) situations. His main technique was to ask subjects to memorise and recall stories. One story has become particularly famous. It comes from a North American Indian folktale called *The War of the Ghosts*. Bartlett chose this story because, although it is certainly meaningful, it deals with matters quite foreign to any of his British subjects. Bartlett's procedure was very simple. Subjects merely read the story to themselves and then tried to recall it. To see what it was like, why not try being a subject yourself? The story is reprinted below. Read it twice through at your normal reading rate (Bartlett's usual instructions) and then close the book, wait fifteen minutes and see what you remember.

THE WAR OF THE GHOSTS

One night two young men from Egulac went down to the river to hunt seals, and while they were there it became foggy and calm. Then they heard war cries, and they thought: 'Maybe this is a war party.' They escaped to the shore, and hid behind a log. Now canoes came up, and they heard the noise of paddles, and saw one canoe coming up to them. There were five men in the canoe, and they said:

'What do you think? We wish to take you along. We are going up the river to make war on the people.'

One of the young men said: 'I have no arrows.'

'Arrows are in the canoe,' they said.

'I will not go along. I might be killed. My relatives do not know where I have gone. But you,' he said, turning to the other, 'may go with them.'

So one of the young men went, but the other returned home.

And the warriors went up the river to a town on the other side of Kalama. The people came down to the water, and they began to fight, and many were killed. But presently the young man heard one of the warriors say: 'Quick, let us go home: that Indian has been hit.' Now he thought: 'Oh, they are ghosts.' He did not feel sick, but they said he had been shot.

So the canoes went back to Egulac, and the young man went ashore to his house, and made a fire. And he told everybody and said: 'Behold I accompanied the ghosts, and we went to fight. Many of our fellows were killed, and many of those who attacked us were killed. They said I was hit, and I did not feel sick.'

He told it all, and then he became quiet. When the sun rose he fell down. Something black came out of his mouth. His face became contorted. The people jumped up and cried.

He was dead.

The End

How did you do? If you are anything like the 20 subjects Bartlett tested, the story you remembered is shorter and more concise than the original. You have also probably forgotten the exact spelling of some of the proper names (Egulac, Kalama). By themselves, these errors indicate that memory is fallible, not that it is constructive. But there were other

types of errors made by Bartlett's subjects that indicate quite clearly the dynamic nature of memory. Consider the following version of the story produced by one of Bartlett's subjects some time after first reading it:

I have no idea of the title.

There were two men in a boat, sailing towards an island. When they approached the island, some natives came rushing towards them, and informed them that there was fighting going on on the island, and invited them to join. One said to the other: 'You had better go. I cannot very well, because I have relatives expecting me, and they will not know what has become of me. But you have no one to expect you.' So one accompanied the natives, but the other returned.

Here there is a part that I can't remember. What I don't know is how the man got to the fight. However, anyhow the man was in the midst of the fighting, and was wounded. The natives endeavoured to persuade the man to return, but he assured them that he had not been wounded.

I have an idea that his fighting won the admiration of the natives.

The wounded man ultimately fell unconscious. He was taken from the fighting by the natives.

Then, I think it is, the natives describe what happened, and they seem to have imagined seeing a ghost coming out of his mouth. Really it was a kind of materialisation of his breath. I know this phrase was not in the story, but that is the idea I have. Ultimately, the man died at dawn the next day.

The supernatural aspects of this story appear to have been difficult for this subject (being European) to comprehend (particularly the business about ghosts and the Indian's death). So, in order to make sense of the story, he changed them. In his version the Indian did not ride up the river with ghosts but with real warriors. There still is a ghost in the story but it is now an imaginary one coming out of the mouth of the unconscious Indian. Note also that one of the Indian's excuses for not fighting, "I have no arrows", is omitted, and the other excuse, "worried relatives" (a theme more familiar to the subject) is emphasised. Every subject rationalised the story to some degree although the precise nature of their rationalisations depended on each individual's interests and experiences.

Although most subjects produced stories that were more concise than the original, some added material to the story in order to bring it into closer agreement with their prior knowledge and beliefs. For instance, one subject ended the story with the following scene:

The next morning, when the neighbours came round to see how he was, they found him in a fever. And when he came out into the open sunrise he fell down. The neighbours shrieked. He became livid and writhed upon the ground. Something black came out of his mouth, and he died. So, the neighbours decided that he must have been to war with the ghosts.

Bartlett argued that this subject added the fever to the story in order to make the Indian's peculiar behaviour more understandable to someone with a European outlook.

Bartlett analysed his subjects' stories and looked for common errors. One interesting one was the tendency of most male subjects to forget the Indian's "no arrows" excuse for not joining the war party. Females rarely made this error. Bartlett reasoned that this was because the males had all been or were about to leave for war. The Indian's other excuse ("relatives would miss him") recalled the male subjects' own feelings and was, therefore, uppermost in their minds. It is easy to see that for Bartlett, like Freud, memory may be organised and motivated by unconscious needs and feelings.

In summary, Bartlett found that in addition to omitting details, subjects tend to alter their memories in order to make the story more coherent. These alterations are constructed from each subject's individual viewpoint, but there were some common themes. Most subjects played down the supernatural ele-

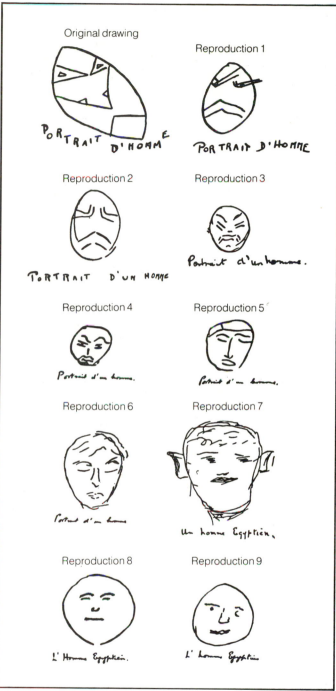

ments in the story and almost all subjects rationalised the stories in order to provide a coherent explanation for facts they did not understand. "Something black came out of his mouth", for example, became "a ghost came out of his mouth", or, in one story, "he foamed at the mouth". In a similar manner many subjects

FIG. 31. *Bartlett found that verbal materials were not the only things transformed in memory. The picture* Portrait d'homme *was also transformed in the direction of a more human-looking face when subjects tried to draw it from memory*

altered the story in ways consonant with their own experience and vocabulary. Canoes became boats and paddling became rowing, for example.

Bartlett concluded that subjects in his experiment were not simply "reading back" a copy of the story when they recalled it — they were actively constructing a story of their own. Subjects recall the story's main theme (their interpretation of the main theme, to be precise) and then fill in the details in a way that substantiates their interpretation. Discrepant details are either transformed or forgotten in the process. In short, for Bartlett memory is just one aspect of active, creative thought. In this regard his views on memory are similar to Gibson's ideas about perception described in Chapter Five. Both believe that psychological functions cannot be divorced from one another and that all cognition (including perception and memory) involves "making sense" of information being received from the environment. Bartlett's research began a field of memory research much different from Ebbinghaus's verbal learning. Bartlett's followers emphasised the cognitive and constructive aspects of memory.

AFTERMATH

Bartlett's research, first described in the 1930s, did not have an immediate affect on experimental psychology. Ebbinghaus's verbal learning approach was much more in tune with the behaviourist influence predominant in those days. Slowly, however, Bartlett's views took hold and with the cognitive revolution in psychology in the 1960s his constructive approach has become predominant. Today virtually all memory experiments are concerned with how information is transformed in memory.

One of Bartlett's ideas has become especially influential in recent years; this is the notion of *schemas*. Bartlett described a *schema* as a body of organised knowledge in memory. For instance, we have schemas for dining out (wait to be seated, receive a menu, order food and wine, and so on) and a schema for taking an airplane trip (check luggage in, receive seat allocation, proceed to gate, and so on). When we are faced with new information to learn, we try whenever possible to incorporate it into an already existing schema. Memory distortions can occur during this process. For example, in one experiment in which subjects read and then recalled a story about someone going to a restaurant, some remembered a description of the person eating and paying the bill even though neither event was actually mentioned in the story.

Although schemas can sometimes distort recall, they can also help it. This is because they permit us to use information already resident in memory to help organise new knowledge. Schemas may be quite elaborate. Bartlett, for example, described an incident that occurred on his visit to Africa. A white cattle farmer suggested that Bartlett interview one of his herdsmen who had a phenomenal memory for cattle. Bartlett asked the herdsman to give him details of cattle purchases made by his former boss more than a year before. The man immediately reeled off a list of transactions of the form, "From Ndoda Kedeli, one young red heifer, the calf of a red cow, and with a white belly for one pound". The various transactions the herdsman recalled were all checked against official records and found to be almost perfectly accurate, even though none of the purchases was actually made by the herdsman himself. Bartlett explained this remarkable performance as the result of the importance of cattle to the local culture. On any other topic the herdsman's memory was no better than average.

Much the same point was made by the Dutch psychologist Adriaan de Groot who studied chess masters. In one experiment he found that after a brief exposure (five seconds), chess masters could reproduce a chess board with all pieces in their correct position 90 per cent of the time. By comparison, ordinary players achieved only 40 per cent accuracy under the same conditions. Interestingly, this difference only turned up when the boards were actually taken from chess games. When the pieces were randomly distributed across the board the masters were no more accurate than the average players. De Groot concluded that chess masters have developed elaborate schemas for chess games; these schemas help them assimilate board information rapidly and reproduce it accurately. When they are faced with a memory task that does not fit in with their schema (a random board) their memory, like the African herdsman's, is no better than average.

"About how fast were the cars going when they crashed into each other?"

The constructive nature of memory, emphasised by Bartlett, has important implications for our criminal justice system in which considerable credence is placed on eyewitness testimony. Elizabeth Loftus, an American psychologist, highlighted these implications in an experiment in which subjects were shown a film of an automobile accident. Immediately after viewing the film, subjects were asked questions about what they had seen. One group of subjects was asked: "About how fast were the cars going when they *crashed* into one another?" Another group was asked: "How fast were the cars going when they *hit* one another?" A week later subjects returned to the laboratory to answer questions about the film. On this occasion all subjects were asked: "Did you see any broken glass?" Although there was no broken glass in the film, subjects given the *crashed* question a week earlier remembered seeing broken glass twice as often as those given the *hit* question.

Loftus's results have obvious implications for eyewitness identifications, particularly identification parades. The importance of identification parades to the criminal justice system cannot be overestimated. In one British study 45 per cent of identification parades were found to have led to a suspect being identified and 82 per cent of those

FIG. 32. *The top illustration represents the accident actually seen by subjects in Loftus's experiment. Then comes the "crashed" question which leads to the altered memory pictured in the bottom illustration*

72

identified were convicted. Even in cases where eyewitness identification was the only evidence against them, 74 per cent of defendants were convicted. The vast majority of eyewitness identifications are undoubtedly accurate; but mistakes do happen. In recent years several people have been released from prisons in America and the UK after the real perpetrators have been captured. In each case the innocent person was convicted on the basis of eyewitness testimony.

It really is not very surprising that eyewitness testimony is sometimes in error. Our memories even for objects we see every day are a good deal less than perfect. Try to draw a picture of a common coin (one cent or one pence or whatever coin you see every day) then compare your picture with a real coin. How close did you get? Do not worry about how good your picture is; this is not a drawing experiment. Just count the number of details you included. If you are like most people you will accurately recall no more than half the details on the coin. And this is an object you see practically every day. Crimes often occur in less than ideal perceptual circumstances (at night, for example) when witnesses and victims are in an excited emotional state, which makes memory even more difficult.

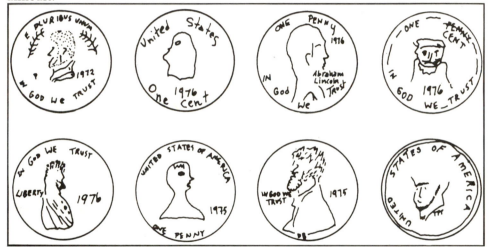

FIG. 33. *Eight attempts at drawing a US penny piece from memory. It is very difficult to reproduce accurately even common objects like coins we see every day*

The fallibility of eyewitness identification is particularly striking in an incident that occurred in Australia. A psychologist who appeared on a television show (along with a police official) to discuss the constructive nature of memory was arrested some time later and identified, in an identification parade, by a woman as the man who raped her. The alleged rape took place exactly at the time that the psychologist was on television discussing eyewitness testimony with the police official. It turned out that the woman was watching the show when the rape occurred and had registered the psychologist's face, which she now recalled as the rapist's.

Even so-called cases of exceptional memory often turn out to be largely constructed. During the American Watergate hearings in the early 1970s, John Dean, the man who was responsible for President Nixon's eventual downfall was known as the man with the "tape-recorder" memory because of his ability to recall what appeared to be verbatim conservations held in the Oval Office. When the actual transcripts of tape-recordings secretly made of those conversations were released, however, it became clear that Dean had not recalled the conversations verbatim. He often recalled things that were not said and placed remarks into the wrong speakers' mouths. It was general themes and not specific remarks that he recalled.

All psychologists today recognise the dynamic nature of memory. In a way, then, it is fair to say that Freud's views on memory, rather than Ebbinghaus's, have prevailed. But there is a difference between Freud's approach to psychology and the one advocated by Bartlett. Bartlett insisted on careful measurement and objective scientific methods. In this he agreed with Ebbinghaus. Thus, the two classic experimenters described in this chapter have each left psychology with a lasting legacy. Ebbinghaus gave researchers a rigorous methodology while Bartlett convinced psychologists of the notion that memory is constructive.

Further Reading

Bartlett, F. C., *Remembering*, Cambridge University Press, Cambridge, 1950 (original published in 1932).

Ebbinghaus, H., *Memory*, (H. Ruyer and C. E. Bussenius, trans.), Teachers College Press, New York, 1913.

Freud, S., "The Psychopathology of Everyday Life", in A. A. Brill (ed.), *The Basic Writings of Sigmund Freud*, Modern Library, New York, 1938 (original published in 1904).

Loftus, E., *Eyewitness Testimony*, Harvard University Press, Cambridge, Massachusetts, 1979.

CHAPTER FIVE

SENSATION VERSUS PERCEPTION

Perceptual psychologists study how people make sense of the world. The major question they try to answer is: why do things appear as they do? At first glance this question appears simple, but the answer turns out to be quite complicated. Complications arise because the sense organs — eyes, ears, nose, tongue, skin — are not really perceptual organs. Animals or humans who have their optic or auditory nerves severed (the nerves connecting these organs to the brain) can no longer see or hear even though their eyes and ears continue to work perfectly. This means that although perceptual organs register environmental information in the form of sensory sensations (light, sounds, smells, tastes, touch), it is the brain that decides what these sensations represent. In a very literal sense, then, beauty is not in the eye of the beholder; the brain is the organ of perception.

Perception is the oldest area in experimental psychology. In fact, until fairly recently psychology's other branches — social, abnormal, physiological, developmental — were viewed as merely subspecialties of perception. In the early part of this century psychologists studying perception (the Gestalt psychologists mainly), concentrated on how sensory sensations produce subjective experiences. These psychologists believed that sounds, tastes or light patterns constitute the "raw data" of perception. According to the Gestaltists, these patterns of sensation represent nothing by themselves. They are given meaning by the brain which interprets them in the light of past experience. This view of perception was challenged by psychologist James J. Gibson, whose classic experiment is described in this chapter.

The chapter begins with a brief review of some of the problems faced by the Gestalt approach to perception, followed by a description of Gibson's alternative. Since most perceptual research has involved vision rather than hearing, touch, taste or smell, many of the examples given in this chapter deal with visual perception. However, as we shall see, the principles and problems of visual perception apply to the other senses, too.

EYES AND CAMERAS, EARS AND MICROPHONES

It is very common, particularly in high-school science textbooks, to see the eye described as a camera and (somewhat less frequently) the ear described as a microphone. From the standpoint of anatomy, these are not unreasonable descriptions. The eye, like the camera, has an adjustable opening that controls the amount of entering light, a lens that serves to focus the light and a retina on which (like film) an image is formed. Ears, like microphones, have vibrating membranes that transform sound energy into mechanical energy and ultimately into information concerning pitch, timbre and volume.

The Gestalt psychologists of the early twentieth century extended the camera and microphone analogies beyond sensation to perception by assuming that the eye sends pictures to the brain while the ear sends sounds. According to the Gestaltists these brain "pictures" and brain "sounds" give rise to perceptions of the external environment. Although they did not seriously pursue the microphone analogy, Gestalt psychologists often wrote about pictures in the brain.

Their notion was that light entering the eye through the iris is focused by the lens on the retina, where it produces an image of the external world. This retinal image constitutes the raw sensory data that the brain uses to construct perceptions. Gestalt psychologists believed that a copy of the retinal image is transmitted along the optic nerves to the visual area of the brain. They viewed this brain area as a sort of organic movie screen upon which an image of the external world is projected in the form of electrical impulses. Of course, the Gestaltists knew that there is no movie screen in the brain. What they had in mind was a pattern of brain cells that mimicked a screen. Different brain cells

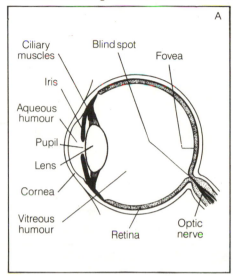

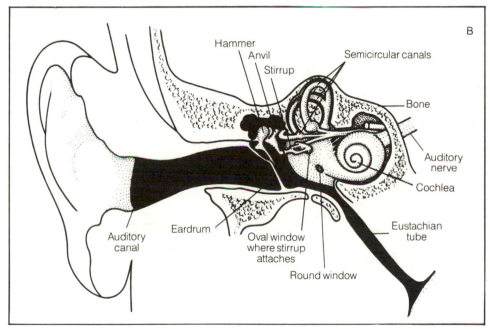

FIG. 34. The eye (A) and the ear (B) have often been compared with the camera and the microphone. The eye has a lens which can change shape in order to focus objects at different distances. It can also adjust the pupil to change the amount of light admitted through the iris. The sound waves entering the ear reverberate against the eardrum which produces vibrations in the bones of the middle ear. The result is a series of nerve impulses that carry sound information to the brain via the auditory nerve

represent different points in space. Nevertheless, the end result is still some sort of picture in the brain.

Although Gestalt psychologists were certain that visual perception involves forming brain pictures, they did not believe these pictures were necessarily identical to what actually exists in the external world. Newspaper photographs, for example, are comprised of hundreds of small dots, yet at viewing distance they are seen as tonal pictures. For Gestalt psychologists, discovering the principles by which sensations produced in the eye are organised into pictures in

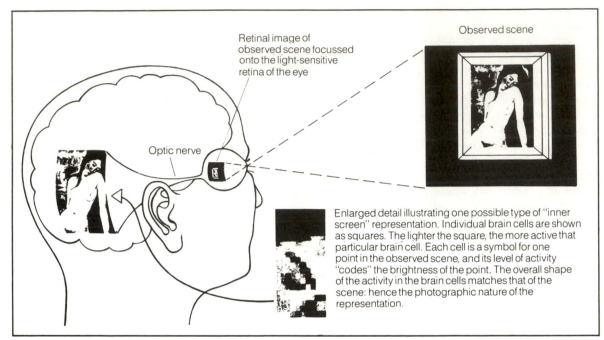

Retinal image of observed scene focussed onto the light-sensitive retina of the eye

Observed scene

Optic nerve

Enlarged detail illustrating one possible type of "inner screen" representation. Individual brain cells are shown as squares. The lighter the square, the more active that particular brain cell. Each cell is a symbol for one point in the observed scene, and its level of activity "codes" the brightness of the point. The overall shape of the activity in the brain cells matches that of the scene: hence the photographic nature of the representation.

FIG. 35. *Gestalt psychologists viewed the perceptual system as a kind of organic television set with pictures coded in the brain in the form of electric impulses*

the brain was the main task facing psychology. They emphasised that perception involves more than adding up a series of visual sensations. "The whole," they said, "is more than the sum of its parts."

Gestalt Organisational Principles

Some of the Gestalt "laws of perceptual organisation" are illustrated in Figure 36. The first illustration (36A) demonstrates the law of *proximity*. Items close together in space tend to be seen as belonging together. In 36B we see the law of *similarity* at work. Similar items tend to be grouped together. The law of *continuation* is illustrated in Figure 37. Although two separate lines can easily be distinguished in 37A and 37B, combining them produces a perception of two rather different lines. According to the law of continuation this is because we tend to see straight lines as continuing straight and curved or angled ones as continuing curved. It takes great effort to see a line that alternates between curved and straight. Figure 38 illustrates the law of *closure*. Incomplete figures tend to be seen as complete; we fill in environmental gaps to form our perceptions.

Gestalt organisational principles are not only applicable to visual stimuli. The Gestaltists also identified organisational principles for the senses of touch and hearing. Although they did not write about "sounds" in the head, Gestalt psychologists were interested in how the separate notes of a musical

(Top) FIG. 36. *A. According to the gestalt law of proximity, items close to one another are seen to go together B. Because of the gestalt law of similarity, this figure is seen as two triangles; one with its point at the top, the other with a point at the bottom*

(Middle) FIG. 37. *The gestalt principle of continuation. We can perceive the figure in A as being composed of the two lines in B but not of the two lines in C*

(Bottom) FIG. 38. *Example of the gestalt law of closure which states that we tend to see a complete object even when some parts are missing*

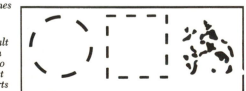

score are organised into patterns or melodies. For them, a melody is an excellent example of a "whole" that is more than the sum of its parts. The national anthem is easily recognisable no matter what key it is played in or on what instrument. According to Gestaltists this is because the pattern produced by individual sounds — the melody — has properties of its own which exist independently of the particular notes that comprise it. As we shall see later in this chapter, the existence of patterns that remain constant while the sensations that produce them change was an important aspect of Gibson's research.

Visual Illusions and Ambiguous Figures

The Gestalt psychologists devoted a great deal of research effort to explaining *visual illusions*. Figure 39 shows an illusion known as Fraser's spiral. In reality there is no spiral here at all. If you trace the outline of one spiral carefully with your finger, you will find that the picture actually consists of concentric circles. What you have perceived is different from the physical reality.

Elaborate drawings are not required to produce visual illusions. Compelling illusions can be produced by a few simple lines. For example, the illusion in Figure 40 involves only straight lines and arrow heads. Although the line with outgoing fins appears longer than the line with ingoing fins, the truth is that the two lines are identical. Measure them and see. The "railroad" illusion in Figure 41 is also simple yet powerful. The upper horizontal line looks longer, but in fact the two are the same length. Several additional illusions are depicted in Figure 42.

Gestalt psychologists tried (not always successfully) to explain these illusions using the various laws of perceptual organisation. They also tried to apply their organising principles to a class of visual stimuli known as *ambiguous figures*. Figure 43A is the work of the Danish psychologist Edgar

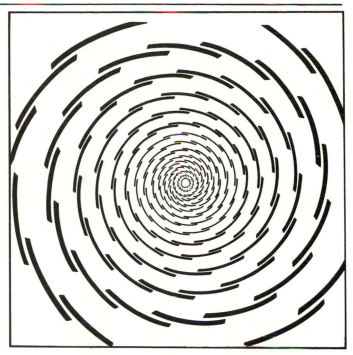

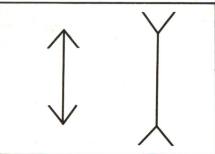

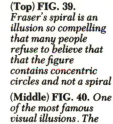

(Top) FIG. 39.
Fraser's spiral is an illusion so compelling that many people refuse to believe that that the figure contains concentric circles and not a spiral

(Middle) FIG. 40. *One of the most famous visual illusions. The vertical lines are actually the same length*

(Bottom) FIG. 41. *Although the upper horizontal line appears longer, both lines are equal in length*

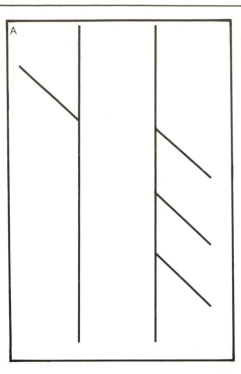

Rubin. The figure, which can be seen as either two faces or a vase, is an example of what is known as *figure-ground reversal*. Sometimes the white vase is the figure and the black faces are the background; at other times the figure is perceived the other way around. Figure 43B was first described by the American psychologist E. G. Boring. The picture may be seen as a pretty young woman or a frightening old witch; two completely different perceptions in the same picture. The young lady is in profile with long eyelashes showing at her cheek and a black ribbon around her neck. When the picture is seen as a hideous old woman, the young girl's chin becomes an ugly nose and the ribbon around her neck becomes the old hag's mouth. The change in appearance is generally not immediate, so look at the picture for a while. If you have some trouble, let your eyes roam over the

FIG. 42. *Three more common illusions:*
A. The line on the left is actually a continuation of the centre line on the right
B. The three figures are all the same height
C. The slanted lines are all parallel

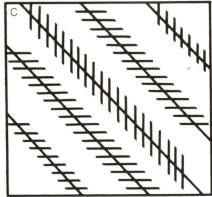

area that forms the cheek-nose, and eventually you will see the whole face change shape. Figure 43C is known as the Necker cube after the Swiss scientist L. A. Necker. Stare at the diamond and do not be impatient, something extraordinary will happen.

Since ambiguous figures can be seen as more than one thing even though the actual image on the retina does not change, the Gestalt psychologists had some difficulty explaining them. The best theory they could offer is that ambiguous figures are the result of two or more organisational principles competing against one another with neither principle having the strength to prevail.

Visual illusions and ambiguous pictures show that perception involves more than merely registering the sensations falling on the retina — and more than just transmitting the retinal image to the brain. The Gestalt theorists realised this, so they searched for the organising principles that determine how retinal images are transformed to produce brain pictures. Unfortunately, there were two fundamental problems in their approach. First, there is the matter of brain pictures themselves. The Gestalt psychologists assumed that brain pictures produce perception, but they never bothered to say how. That is, they did not explain how we recognise what is in the brain's pictures. Imagine, for example, that you are looking across the table at Christmas dinner. An image of the person seated opposite you falls on your retina and is transmitted to your brain. How do you know that the individual in the picture in your brain is your grandmother? Is there a little man in your brain that looks at the picture and lets you know who it is? But then, wouldn't he require a little man of his own to recognise his brain picture and so on for an infinity of little men?

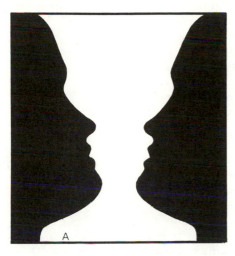

FIG. 43. A. Rubin's "Peter–Paul goblet". The ambiguous figure can be seen in two distinctly different ways
B. Boring's "wife–mother-in-law" figure can be seen as a pretty girl or an old witch
C. Stare at the diamond in the Necker cube and see what happens

The second problem with the Gestalt approach is that it views the organism as basically a passive receiver of sensations. There are patterns in the sensory world — but the organism does not actually search for them — they just appear. While they were able to explain some perceptual phenomena this way, Gestalt psychologists had difficulty accounting for stable perceptions in the constantly changing natural world. That is, they could not easily account for the phenomenon known as *perceptual constancy*.

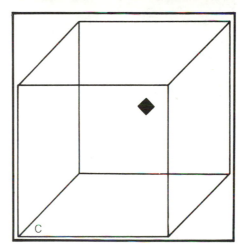

Perceptual Constancy

Although the input to our senses changes as we move about in the environment, we still perceive a stable world. If we stand directly in front of a window, the image of the window on our retinas is rectangular. If we move to one side, the image on our retinas takes on the appearance of a trapezoid. Despite this change in retinal image, however, we still perceive the window as a rectangle. Our perception has not changed although the image on the retina most certainly has. Similarly, as we walk through a room, the walls do not appear to change shape and the objects in a room do not appear to change location although the image on our retinas is continuously changing.

Perceptual psychologists have identified several different types of perceptual constancy. *Size constancy*, for example, is a term used to describe the fact that the perceived size of an object does not vary with the size of the image the object produces on the retina. If you see someone you know across the street and decide to walk over and say hello, the individual does not appear to grow taller as you approach although his image on your retina gets bigger as you get closer.

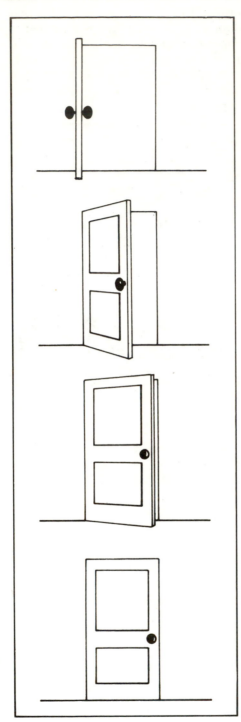

FIG. 44. *As the door closes, the image it casts on the retina changes dramatically yet it is still easily recognised as a door. This is what psychologists call "shape constancy"*

Brightness constancy is similar to size constancy. It refers to the common finding that objects do not change in whiteness even when the amount of light hitting the retina changes dramatically. Coal that looks black in dim light continues to look black in bright light; snow that appears white during the day still appears white at night. This is true despite the large brightness changes in the image falling on the retina.

Movement and Perception

Perceptual constancy is an everyday fact of life. As we move about in the environment, the light hitting our retinas continuously changes and so does our retinal image of the external world. Nevertheless, we still perceive the world as stable. Even more interesting is what happens when the world is in motion. Suppose you are looking out your window at cars driving by in the street. As a car passes across your visual field, it casts an image on the retinas of your eyes. As the car moves, so does the image on your retinas. Now suppose you are looking out your window at a parked car. If you move your head from left to right, the car's image will also move across the retinas of your eyes. In fact, if the only information available to you is the image falling on your retinas, you would be unable to tell whether it is you or the car that is moving. Nevertheless, in reality no-one ever has trouble telling the difference.

The ability to distinguish between one's own motion and external motion (along with the various kinds of perceptual constancy) constitutes clear evidence that perception is not based solely on what is happening to retinal images. Contrary to what the Gestaltists believed, perception does not involve transmitting retinal images (or tunes, or smells, or any other sensations) to the brain in literal form.

But what is the alternative? If the sense organs are not sending sensations to the brain, what are they transmitting? The answer is environmental information. The sense organs most certainly communicate with the brain, but what they transmit is not meaningless patterns of sensations but *information* about the stable characteristics of the environment. Just as we are able to abstract melodies from music played in various keys and on different instruments, we also seem to be able to extract stable visual patterns from the ever-changing flux of visual stimulation. It is information about these patterns, not retinal images, that constitutes the raw data of visual perception. The only way we can abstract such patterns is to actively look for them. We are not simply passive receivers of sensory stimulation but active explorers of our environment. This active view of perception was the insight of James Gibson.

JAMES J. GIBSON AND MODERN PERCEPTUAL PSYCHOLOGY

Gibson was born in 1904 in a small town in Ohio, heart of the American midwest. His family was strict Presbyterian and he was brought up in that faith. Gibson's father was a railroad surveyor and the youth spent a good deal of his formative years riding on trains. In his autobiography Gibson notes that these rail trips let him know "what the world looked like from a railroad train and how it seemed to flow inward when seen from the rear platform and expand outward when seen from the locomotive". The family eventually settled in Chicago, where Gibson began his education at Northwestern University. He later shifted to Princeton University where he received his Ph.D. in 1928. His first university teaching job was at Smith College, at that time a girls' school. He met and married Eleanor Jack there in 1932. Eleanor Gibson was also to become a celebrated experimental psychologist, collaborating on many occasions with her husband. While at Smith, Gibson also met and interacted with Kurt Koffka, one of the leading figures of Gestalt psychology. Although not himself a Gestalt psychologist, Gibson, like everyone else who knew him, was much influenced by Koffka's thought. Gibson was particularly interested in Koffka's search for the organisational principles of perception.

When the Second World War broke out Gibson joined the military, where he conducted research on the selection and training of pilots. During his war years Gibson's interest in perception deepened. After the war the Gibsons moved to Cornell University where, except for sabbaticals, James Gibson spent the rest of his life. Gibson remained an active researcher and theorist throughout his academic career and into retirement. He died in 1979.

FIG. 45. *James J. Gibson (1904–79) investigated the active nature of perception*

CLASSIC EXPERIMENT 7:

PERCEPTION THROUGH ACTIVE TOUCH

Gibson's research into perception was guided by his belief that human beings are not passive receivers of sensory sensations but active seekers of information. He was concerned with explaining how individuals extract patterns (such as melodies) from environmental stimuli. Gibson called these patterns *invariants* because they do not change with changes in the sensations that give rise to them. In fact, invariants are actually *produced* by a stream of changing sensations in much the same way that a melody is produced by a pattern of musical notes. Thus, for Gibson, perception requires active exploration. This is the reason he saw nothing unusual or amazing about perceptual constancy in the face of changing retinal images. For Gibson, it was precisely such changes in sensations that make perception possible.

Gibson performed many experiments demonstrating the role of active exploration in perception, but by far the simplest and most convincing was a classic experiment concerned with the sense of touch. The object of

this experiment was to show that perception does not depend on passively receiving stimulation but rather on actively exploring the environment. The materials he used in the experiment were bent strips of metal fitted with handles and shaped into the six forms depicted in Figure 46. In fact, the forms were actually biscuit or cookie cutters, moulds used to cut dough into fancy shapes. The six shapes were chosen because they were all different. No two had the same number of curves or corners.

Each subject was seated at a table across from the experimenter. The two were separated by a curtain that hung across the centre of the table. Before the experiment began the subjects were shown the metal shapes. In addition a numbered drawing of each shape was hung on the curtain in front of them. During the experiment subjects slid one hand out of sight under the curtain. This hand was allowed to rest palm up on the table.

There were two experimental conditions. In one, subjects were told to open and relax their hands and one

FIG. 46. *Gibson's experimental apparatus: common kitchen biscuit cutters*

of the forms was pressed into their palms by means of a mechanical device. In the other condition, subjects were asked to cup their fingers upward and be prepared to feel the edges of the shape by running their fingers around it. In both conditions, the subjects' task was to pick out from the six pictures hanging on the curtain the form they were currently touching.

Since there were six forms, the subject could be expected to pick the correct one simply by chance one-sixth of the time (16.7 per cent). When the subjects passively held their hands out and were touched by the shape, they identified it correctly 29 per cent of the time. Better than chance, but not much. On the other hand, when subjects were permitted to actively explore the objects, they correctly identified them 95 per cent of the time. The main difference between the two conditions is that in the passive condition there was no motion between the skin and the biscuit cutter, whereas in the active condition subjects moved their fingers around the object. Some traced the outline with one finger, others used all of their fingers. Some subjects always traced in one direction, others moved their fingers back and forth. It did not matter how they did it; those subjects who actively explored the form rarely missed identifying it.

Although the result of this simple experiment was clear — active touch led to considerably better accuracy than passive touch — it was always possible that the result was merely a function of sensitivity differences between the palm, where passive touch took place, and the fingertips, which were involved in active touch. Perhaps the fingertips are just more sensitive than the palms. In order to rule out this possibility Gibson ran a third experimental condition. This time the metal shapes were not just pressed into the palm of the hand, they were also continuously

rotated clockwise and counterclockwise with a twisting motion. The same skin regions were stimulated in this condition as in the passive condition. The only difference was that, as the biscuit cutter twisted, the sensations received by the subject were constantly changing. This condition was not equivalent to having the subjects explore the shapes themselves. For one thing, their fingers and the muscles of their arm and hand were not engaged. But rotating the shape was clearly different from just pressing it into the palm. The subjects in this third condition correctly identified the shape 72 per cent of the time.

This simple experiment, using kitchen biscuit cutters, demonstrates quite clearly that perception does not involve transmitting a literal facsimile of sensory sensations to the brain. If the form of the sensations on the skin is really the raw data of perception (as the Gestaltists would have it), then the condition in which the shapes were pressed into the palm should have produced the best recognition. This is because subjects in this condition were the only ones to actually feel the form of the object. In the active touch condition, especially when subjects ran their fingers around the edges of the shapes, no sensations corresponding to the form of the biscuit cutter were ever present on the skin. At any one time the subject was receiving sensations corresponding to a straight edge or a curve, but at no time was the whole object being touched simultaneously. Yet active touch produced the most accurate perception. This finding is only explainable if we assume that the changing sensations the subject receives give rise to the perception of shape. This interpretation of the results is supported by the subjective reports of some of the subjects. Gibson asked subjects in the third condition why having the shape twisted made it easier to identify. Several reported that the shapes tended to stand out more when they were twisted.

As subjects who traced the form with their finger were most accurate, Gibson concluded that form perception is best when sensations (from a moving finger) are changing most. This result fitted in nicely with his perceptual theory. That is, continuous changes in sensory stimulation as the finger moves around the edge of the form results in the isolation of sensory invariants. These invariants, not the form of the object pressing on the skin, produce perception.

AFTERMATH

The demonstration that active rather than passive stimulation produces perception has been repeated in the other senses. For example, Gibson's view of perception helped to explain an important but confusing visual phenomenon. Scientists have known for many years that the eyes are never entirely still. They vibrate around 50 times per second. This visual tremor ensures that an image is never fixed on one retinal spot but actually moves about as the eyes vibrate. Early in this century, a means of stabilising an image on the retina by attaching a special lens directly to the eye was devised.

Since the lens moves along with the eyeball, images can be projected onto a fixed retinal location. When this is done subjects report that whatever they are looking at quickly disappears. An image is still projected onto the retina, but they no longer see it. This is just what would be expected if, as Gibson said, perception derives from active exploration and change. When the eye is no longer actively exploring the object — because its image is fixed on the retina — it is not perceived. Constant motion is necessary for perception to take place.

Gibson argued that environmental invariants are also responsible for phenomena such as size constancy. As we all know, if we see a girl we know across the street and walk over to greet her, she does not appear to change size even though her image on our retina gets much larger. According to Gibson this phenomenon is the result of certain invariants in the scene. For example, as we move closer to someone, their size relative to the background constantly changes. But since the person and the background are changing together, the relationships between them remain unaltered. These relationships provide information for the perception of size. Similarly, brightness constancy can be seen as the result of unchanged ratios of brightness. It is true that snow appears white at night even though it is producing much less light, but since everything else is also dimmer, the relative brightness ratio in the scene has not changed.

Gibson also applied his ideas to the movement perception problem noted previously. According to Gibson it is wrong to think that the image moving on the retina is the data from which movement is inferred, any more than that the pressure of the biscuit cutter on the palm is the data which gives rise to shape. It is the changes that occur as the organism interacts with the environment that contain the crucial data for the perception of movement. Thus there really is no paradox in our ability to differentiate between movement in the world and the movement of our head; the information reaching the brain is different in each case.

Gibson devoted the last years of his life to studying how environmental invariants are identified by the organism interacting with its environment. His students have carried on this work in a field they now call *ecological optics*. This is the study of how we extract information from the constantly changing flux of sensory sensations. Gibson's research led to a fundamental change in the way scientists view perception. The Gestalt psychologists thought that sensations (retinal images, smells, sound vibrations and so on) were meaningless by themselves and needed to be interpreted by the brain. All of their research efforts were devoted to explaining why perceptions often differed from the form of the raw data (in visual illusions, for example). Gibson turned the whole issue around. In his biscuit cutter experiment, he showed that perception does not involve transmitting a facsimile of the biscuit cutter to the brain, but rather an active search for information about its shape. Perception, he discovered, involves isolating information about the form of objects, not the form of sensory sensations.

Further Reading

Gibson, J. J., "Observations on Active Touch", *Psychological Bulletin*, *69*, pp. 477–91, 1962.

Gibson, J. J., *The Senses Considered as Perceptual Systems*, Houghton Mifflin, Boston, 1966.

Gregory, R., *Eye and Brain* (second edition), McGraw-Hill, New York, 1973.

CHAPTER SIX:

EMOTIONS

Admirers of the defunct (but frequently rerun) television series *Star Trek* will recall the Starship Enterprise's Vulcan officer, Mr Spock. Spock differed from earthlings in two important ways: he had odd, pointy ears and he was always eminently logical and unemotional. Unlike Captain Kirk, Spock was never tempted by the seductive outer-space sirens who regularly tried to lure the space mariners to destruction. And even when the murderous Romulans seemed certain to destroy their starship, Spock never panicked. On such occasions the rest of the crew would accuse him of being "inhuman" since, to them, the essential characteristic of a human being is the ability to feel emotions.

The importance of emotions in our lives is apparent in our language. There are over 400 English words to describe feelings (joy, passion, sorrow, ecstasy, anger, fear, lust, love, grief, awe and so on), each with a slightly different meaning. From a psychological point of view it is important to note that these "emotional" words are not only used to describe how someone feels at a particular moment; emotions are also commonly believed to be the motivating force behind human behaviour. We believe that bank robbers are "driven by greed", sex criminals "maddened by lust" and lovers "smitten by passion". Anyone who has watched a cat bare its teeth and arch its back when faced with an intruder to its territory knows that animal behaviour, too, can be driven by emotion. Yet, despite the importance attached to emotions by novelists, poets and almost everyone else, experimental psychologists have tended to neglect them. Only one in 100 psychology experiments is concerned with emotion; the remainder deal with aspects of perception or cognition.

One of the reasons why emotions have not received much experimental attention is their complexity. They have physiological components (our hearts beat faster when we are afraid, for example), cognitive components (we must determine whether the situation in which we find ourselves is threatening before we know whether fear is appropriate) and social components (there are occasions when we find it useful to hide our emotions). Overwhelmed by the complex interactions among these components, psychologists interested in studying emotions have found it necessary to simplify their work by isolating one component from the others. Thus some researchers study only emotions' physiological aspects, others only their social expression. As will be seen in this chapter, this research strategy has not succeeded in clarifying how emotions operate in the real world. This is because studying the various components in isolation produces a distorted picture of how emotions really work. The experiment described in this chapter is considered a classic because it was the first to show how emotions, in all their complexity, could be studied experimentally.

PSYCHOBIOLOGY OF EMOTIONS

Recognising Emotions in Others

The modern study of emotion begins, like so many other advances in biology, with Charles Darwin. In his book *The Expression of Emotions in Man and Animals* Darwin developed the idea that emotions evolved because they have survival value. Take *fear*, for instance. Fear helps the organism to survive because those who become afraid run away and thereby avoid harm. Although they originally evolved to preserve life, Darwin believed that over the centuries emotions acquired uses and meanings in addition to their original protective ones. For example, *disgust*, according to Darwin, originated in attempts to rid oneself of poisonous food. But today the same emotion occurs when no food is involved. As Darwin put it:

The term 'disgust', in its simplest sense, means something offensive to the taste ... But as disgust also causes annoyance, it is generally accompanied by a frown, and often by gestures as if to push away or to guard oneself against the offensive object ... Extreme disgust is expressed by movements around the mouth identical with those preparatory to the act of vomiting. The mouth is opened widely, with the upper lip strongly retracted ... The partial closure of the eyelids, or the turning away of the eyes or of the whole body, are likewise highly expressive of disdain. These actions seem to declare that the despised person is not worth looking at, or is disagreeable to behold ... Spitting seems an almost universal sign of contempt or disgust; and spitting obviously represents the rejection of anything offensive from the mouth.

Not only did Darwin believe that emotions motivate an organism's behaviour, he also felt that the ability to recognise what others are feeling is also important for survival. His point seems self-evident: an organism that can tell when a potential enemy is angry and about to strike has a better chance to survive (by escaping) than one that cannot. After giving some thought to how we recognise someone else's emotions, Darwin concluded that facial expressions are the key. In other words, we know what others are feeling because their emotions are "written all over their face".

In order to test this hypothesis, Darwin performed the first psychological experiment on emotions. He collected a series of photographs; each contained the face of a person displaying a different emotion. He showed these pictures to 20 people and asked them to judge the emotion expressed in each picture. For most of the pictures he found universal agreement among his 20 judges. There were some photographs, however, that his subjects had difficulty in classifying. Although before the experiment Darwin felt that all of the pictures were good examples of specific emotions, he concluded that those pictures that failed to produce agreement must have been poor examples of the emotions they were meant to represent. In this way, Darwin's hypothesis was able to emerge unscathed from its contact with negative data.

Darwin's experiment has been repeated many times in the past 100 years. Figure 48 depicts the results of one such experiment conducted in five different countries. As can be seen, there is considerable agreement among people from different cultures about the emotions expressed by different facial expressions. Even when these photographs were shown to Papua New Guinean tribesmen — jungle dwellers who had little or no contact with western civilisation or white people — the results were the same. Thus there is some support for Darwin's notion that emotions are expressed in facial expressions. The ability to recognise these emotions appears to be a universal human accomplishment.

Although most of the pictures in Figure 48 produced substantial agreement among judges, we can see traces of what happened in Darwin's original experiment: not all pictures produced the same level of agreement. There was less

PRIMARY EMOTION	FUNCTION	FUNCTIONAL DESCRIPTION
Fear	Protection	Behaviour designed to avoid danger or harm, such as running away or any action that puts distance between an organism and the source of danger.
Anger	Destruction	Behaviour designed to eliminate a barrier to satisfaction of an important need. This includes biting, striking, or various symbolic acts of destruction, such as cursing or threatening.
Joy	Incorporation	Behaviour that involves accepting a beneficial stimulus from the outside world, as in eating, grooming, mating, or affiliation with members of one's own social group. Such actions have the effect of nurturing the individual.
Disgust	Rejection	Behaviour designed to expel something harmful that has been ingested, such as vomiting or, at times, defecation. This behaviour is believed to be associated with feelings of contempt and hostility and with sarcasm, all of which are essentially a rejection of other people or their ideas.
Acceptance	Reproduction	Behaviour designed to provide contact with the opposite sex for the purpose of perpetuating one's gene pool. Expressions of this function include sexual signalling, courtship rituals, and sexual intercourse.
Sadness	Reintegration	Behaviour associated with the loss of someone who has provided important nurturance in the past. In such circumstances, the individual sends signals that serve to encourage the return of the lost individual or to attract a substitute. Expressions of this function include crying, emission of distress signals, and "babyish" behaviour.
Surprise	Orientation	Behavioural reactions to contact with a new, unfamiliar stimulus; a loud noise, a strange animal, or a new territory, for example. The organism must quickly reorient the body and stop what it is doing so that the sense organs can take in information about the novel stimulus.
Anticipation	Exploration	Behaviour designed to bring the organism into contact with many aspects of its environment. Getting to know one's neighbourhood permits a form of mental mapping that enables the animal to anticipate and deal with future challenges to its survival.

FIG. 47. *Functional aspects of the primary emotions from an evolutionary standpoint*

agreement about the photograph meant to express *fear*, for example, than the picture representing *happiness*. If facial expression is really all we have to go by in judging another's emotions, the ambiguity of some of the pictures suggests that we should make a fair number of mistakes, frequently attributing the wrong emotions to others in everyday life. But we do not. We rarely have any difficulty telling when someone is afraid, happy, grief-stricken and so on. Our accuracy at guessing one another's emotions — even though facial expressions are sometimes unclear — means that Darwin's hypothesis is not complete. We must use cues other than facial expression to decide what people are feeling.

Several additional cues to emotion have been identified. One potent source of information is the non-verbal cues transmitted by parts of the body other than

	United States (N=99)	Brazil (N=40)	Chile (N=119)	Argentina (N=168)	Japan (N=29)
	97% Happiness	95%	95%	98%	100%
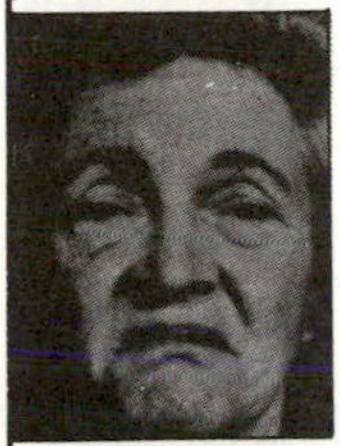	92% Disgust	97%	92%	92%	90%
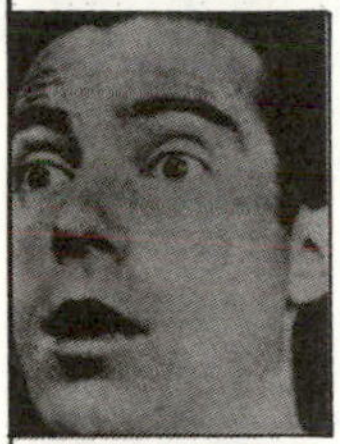	95% Surprise	87%	93%	95%	100%
	84% Sadness	59%	88%	78%	62%
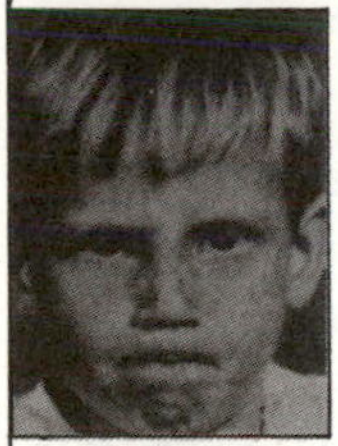	67% Anger	90%	94%	90%	90%
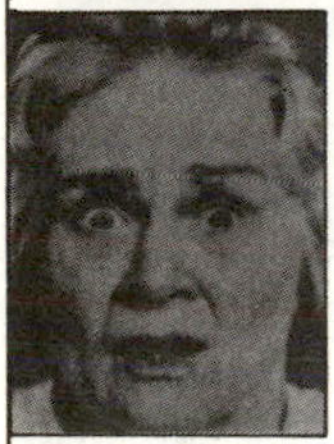	85% Fear	67%	68%	54%	66%

Percentage agreement in how photograph was judged across cultures

FIG. 48. *Judgement of the emotions in faces by the members of five different cultures*

the face. Wringing hands, hanging head, arms wrapped around the chest, even a person's posture can tell us as much about what they are feeling as their facial expression. And then, of course, there is their voice. Soothing, shrieking, trembling, sobbing — there is probably no stronger cue to someone's emotional state than voice quality. Indeed, as radio plays have shown, voice quality is probably the most potent cue we have about what someone is feeling.

Even when faces are obscured and voices silent, it is still possible to infer someone's emotional state from observing his overt behaviour. For example, if from a distance we see a young child begin to run away when approached by a dog, we can infer that the child is afraid even though we cannot see its face or hear its cries.

As can be seen there is much more information available about another's emotional state than just their facial expression. Body language and coping behaviours can also help us to infer how someone else is feeling. By integrating information from all of these sources (none of which is perfect by itself), our judgements become more accurate than they would be if they were based on facial expression alone. The existence of different types of cues to emotion explains why we are so accurate in guessing how someone is feeling.

It may seem surprising that Darwin, who was such a meticulous observer, failed to realise that emotions are expressed in many ways, not just by facial expression. Darwin's oversight appears traceable to the problem already mentioned — the tendency to simplify emotional phenomena in order to study them. Darwin chose one aspect of how emotions are recognised, facial expressions, and looked at it in isolation. By doing so he missed the obvious evidence that emotions can be recognised in many different ways. Other researchers, coming later, "discovered" these additional cues to emotions; cues that should have been obvious all along. In the next section you will see how this sequence — isolating one aspect of emotion and then finding that we cannot understand it without considering other aspects — was repeated by scientists studying a related question. These researchers were not interested in how we recognised another's emotional state but in how we recognise our own.

Recognising Our Own Emotions

Theories about how we recognise our own emotions were put forth simultaneously by American psychologist William James and Danish psychologist Carl Lange around the turn of the century. Because both men proposed essentially the same hypothesis, their theory is known today as the James–Lange theory of emotions. This theory states that emotions are secondary reactions to physiological events. In other words, instead of saying: "I smile because I'm happy", the James–Lange theory maintains that the correct phrasing should be: "I'm happy because I smile". The theory appears to deny commonsense. To most people, statements like: "I'm sad because I cry" and "I'm afraid because I run" put the horse before the cart. Nevertheless, we have all had experiences that are consistent with the James–Lange theory.

Think about what happens when you narrowly miss hitting someone who has darted out in front of your moving car. Chances are your first act is to slam on the brakes and screech to a halt. After the car is safely stopped you notice that your heart is beating rapidly and your face is flushed with sweat; and then you begin to feel fear. As the James–Lange theory predicts, only after the car is stopped and the accident averted does the emotion occur. On a smaller scale the same thing happens whenever you slip on a stairway and recover your balance by grabbing the railing — fear is felt after, not before, your physiological reaction.

Although most of the examples given by James and Lange describe emotions as responses to overt actions (smiling, running and so on), both psychologists realised that overt actions do not always occur. Sometimes emotions and the physiological events that trigger them are hidden. In such cases the James–Lange theory asserts that emotions are produced by reaction to internal, physiological changes. Thus just because someone appears overtly unmoved by tragic news does not mean no emotions are present. According to the James–Lange theory the tragic news produces an internal physiological reaction — increased heart rate, sweat, a knot in the stomach — which, in turn, produces the hidden emotion of grief.

During Combat Missions Did You Feel	Often	Sometimes
A pounding heart and rapid pulse	30%	56%
That your muscles were very tense	30	53
Easily irritated, angry, or "sore"	22	58
Dryness of the throat or mouth	30	50
"Nervous perspiration" or "cold sweat"	26	53
"Butterflies" in the stomach	23	53
A sense of unreality — that this could not be happening to you	20	49
A need to urinate very frequently	25	40
Trembling	11	53
Confused or rattled	3	50
Weak or faint	4	37
That right after a mission you were unable to remember the details of what had happened	5	34
Sick to the stomach	5	33
Unable to concentrate	3	32
That you had wet or soiled your pants	1	4

FIG. 49. *Symptoms of fear reported by Second World War combat pilots*

There is no doubt that internal physiological changes do occur in emotional situations. We have all experienced the symptoms — dry mouth, heavy breathing, rapid heartbeat, perspiration, trembling, hot flushes, a sinking feeling in the pit of the stomach — that are caused by strong emotions. These physiological symptoms are produced by the sympathetic division of the autonomic nervous system and appear to have evolved to mobilise the body's defences in situations requiring physical exertion. Any threatening or highly emotional situation can give rise to similar physiological changes. In addition to the symptoms already described the "autonomic arousal" syndrome includes: the release of the hormone adrenalin which produces alertness, an increase in blood sugar to provide extra energy, and speeded heart and respiration rates to provide more oxygen to the muscles. At the same time blood supply is reduced to vessels near the skin in order to reduce bleeding in case of injury and proteins that cause blood clotting are manufactured in order to prevent excessive blood loss should injury occur.

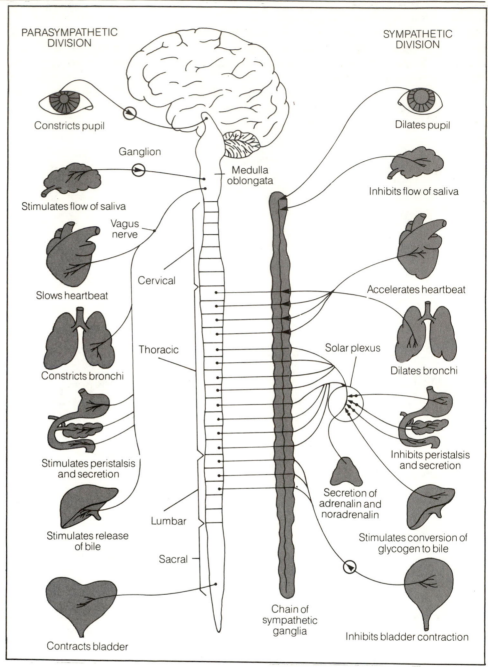

PARASYMPATHETIC
DIVISION

SYMPATHETIC
DIVISION

Constricts pupil

Dilates pupil

Ganglion

Medulla
oblongata

Stimulates flow of saliva

Inhibits flow of saliva

Vagus
nerve

Slows heartbeat

Cervical

Accelerates heartbeat

Constricts bronchi

Thoracic

Solar plexus

Dilates bronchi

Stimulates peristalsis
and secretion

Inhibits peristalsis
and secretion

Lumbar

Secretion of
adrenalin and
noradrenalin

Stimulates release
of bile

Sacral

Stimulates conversion of
glycogen to bile

Chain of
sympathetic
ganglia

Contracts bladder

Inhibits bladder contraction

FIG. 50. *The autonomic nervous system. The sympathetic division produces arousal and the parasympathetic division reduces it*

Autonomic arousal in emotional situations has been carefully studied by medical researchers because chronic arousal has been found to be related to a class of illnesses called *psychosomatic disorders*. Psychosomatic disorders such as peptic ulcer, hypertension and dermatitis, to name but three, received their names because emotionality has been found to be a factor in their aetiology. In a way the relationship between physiological responses to emotion and psychosomatic illness is somewhat ironic. Physiological responses originally evolved in order to help threatened organisms protect themselves. But today, when some people (busy executives, soldiers, air-traffic controllers, police officers) are placed under almost constant stress, the same physiological mechanisms can be quite harmful.

Autonomic arousal in emotion-generating situations also underlies the rationale for lie detectors. Lie-detector machines (called polygraphs because they produce graphic records of several physiological variables) record heart rate, respiration rate and changes in skin electrical activity. In the typical lie-detection interview the polygraph operator asks the subject two kinds of questions: neutral and critical. The neutral questions are routine ones like "Where were you born?" or "Where did you attend school?". Since these questions do not produce emotional responses, the polygraph record made during the neutral questions provides a sort of baseline; it shows how the subject responds when not aroused.

After a baseline has been established, the operator asks the critical questions that concern the subject of interest. For instance: "Were you present at the bank on the day of the robbery?" The polygraph record made during answers to the critical questions is compared with the record made during the neutral questions and differences between the two are taken as indicating emotional arousal and, therefore, lies. Although seemingly based on objective observations of physiological reactions, lie detectors are far from perfectly accurate. Unemotional people, subjects on certain tranquilliser drugs and conscious faking can distort the lie detector's results. For this reason lie-detector evidence is rarely permitted in criminal trials.

Although the James–Lange theory of emotions appears to be supported by everyday experience as well as by scientific evidence that emotions do produce internal physiological reactions, it does have some serious drawbacks. For one thing, many autonomic reactions take place too slowly to affect emotional responding. For instance, some of the autonomic changes accompanying emotions are produced by the secretion of hormones like adrenalin — a slow process. People often feel their emotions well before adrenalin has had a chance to produce its physiological effect.

A second, and more important, problem for the James–Lange theory is the requirement that every emotion produce its own characteristic pattern of autonomic arousal. If the physiological concomitants of emotional arousal were always the same we would be unable to distinguish one emotion from another. Over the years since the James–Lange theory was first proposed, physiologists have tried to identify different patterns of autonomic arousal corresponding to the different emotions, but they have largely failed. Physiological arousal turns out to be non-specific. The same arousal pattern is produced during fear as during sexual excitement and even during anger. Yet, despite the James–Lange theory's predictions, we have no trouble telling these various emotions apart.

Since the James–Lange theory depends on the existence of characteristic physiological states corresponding to the different emotions, and since no such states could be identified, by the 1920s psychologists began to look around for alternative theories. One theory, proposed by psychologist Walter Cannon, stated that emotions are not produced by physiological reactions to emotional situations nor are physiological reactions produced by emotions. Instead Cannon argued that both are produced by a third agent, a lower brain centre called the *thalamus*. According to Cannon's theory an emotionally arousing situation (say, a threatening man in a dark alley) produces a reaction in the thalamus which, in turn, sends a message to both the autonomic system and the higher brain cortex simultaneously. This message is interpreted by the cortex as an emotion and by the autonomic nervous system as a signal to produce the physiological arousal associated with emotion (increased heart rate and so on). In other words, according to Cannon the physiological correlates of emotions and their cognitive interpretation (in this case fear) are not directly connected. Both are produced by the lower brain's reaction to an emotional situation.

Subsequent physiological investigations have revealed that the thalamus is not involved in emotional behaviour but the *hypothalamus* and parts of the brain's *limbic system* are. The hypothalamus is a small structure lying just above the brain stem. It has centres governing biological drives such as hunger, thirst and sex and also controls hormonal activities. Electrical stimulation of different parts of the hypothalamus in animals has been shown to produce clear indications of emotional behaviour, especially fear and anger. The limbic system is a set of brain structures ringing the mid-brain and involved in waking, sleeping and excitement. It appears to be able to modulate the organism's arousal level.

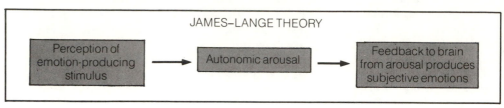

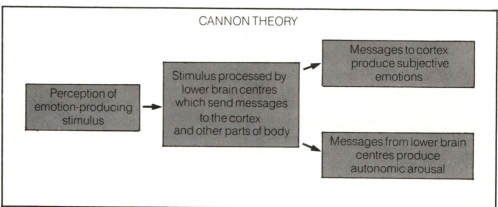

FIG. 51. *The James–Lange theory of emotions views the subjective emotional response as being due to feedback from bodily responses to threat. According to Cannon, emotions occur as soon as the cortex of the brain receives a message from lower brain centres and does not depend on feedback from other body organs*

Dramatic evidence of the limbic system's role in emotional behaviour came from an incident that occurred some years ago. A man went to the top of a tower at the University of Texas and began shooting at passers-by with a high-powered rifle. Before he was finished more than a dozen people were dead and many more were injured. An autopsy on the gunman (who was finally killed by police) revealed that he had a large tumour in his limbic system.

It has also been shown that mild stimulation of the hypothalamus and the limbic system results in increased autonomic activity such as that associated with emotions. Thus, although Cannon was wrong about the thalamus, he was correct about lower brain centres being involved in emotions. It also seems he was correct about there being no direct connection between autonomic activity and specific emotions. This evidence comes from a French physician named Maranon who injected adrenalin into 210 patients. The adrenalin produced autonomic arousal almost identical to that experienced during emotions. When he asked his patients to describe how they felt, over 70 per cent reported just their physical reactions without attributing any emotional feelings to them. The remainder reported emotional-type feelings, but even these patients realised that no emotions were really present. Instead of saying they felt happy or afraid, they reported feeling *as if* they were afraid or *as if* they were happy. This result is contrary to the predictions of the James–Lange theory but consistent with Cannon's. That is, Maranon's subjects did not experience emotions as a result of their physiological arousal; they could divorce the physiological effects produced by the drug from the subjective feelings produced by real emotions.

Maranon's finding made it clear that the James–Lange theory was wrong and that Cannon's theory was closer to the truth. But it still did not show how, if autonomic responses are non-specific, we are able to feel specific emotions. How do we know when we are sad or happy if the physiological arousal accompanying both emotions is identical? This was the question that the classic experiment described next was designed to answer.

STANLEY SCHACHTER: COGNITIVE SOCIAL PSYCHOLOGIST

Stanley Schachter was born in New York City in 1922. He was educated in state schools until he entered Yale University. He received a bachelor's degree from Yale in 1942 and a master's degree in 1944. Schachter's education was interrupted by the Second World War in which he served as a sergeant in the US air force. His military duties involved psychological research on the visual problems faced by pilots during battle. After the war Schachter entered the Massachusetts Institute of Technology where he spent two years before transferring to the University of Michigan, the institution from which he received his doctorate in 1950.

Schachter's first academic position was as Assistant Professor at the University of Minnesota in Minneapolis. By the time he left Minnesota for Columbia University in 1958 he was a Professor of Psychology. Except for visiting positions at other universities, Schachter has remained at Columbia University where he served as chairman of the department of psychology for several years. Schachter has been an important influence on many students and colleagues during his years at Columbia. One person he influenced is Bibb Latané who followed him to Columbia from Minnesota. Latané's classic research on bystander intervention is described in Chapter Eight.

Schachter has been a Fulbright Fellow and has won the Sociopsychological Prize of the American Association for the Advancement of Science. In 1969 he won the Distinguished Scientific Achievement Award from the American Psychological Association "for consistent, coherent and creative work that has materially advanced our understanding of behaviour in social contexts".

As his award notes, Schachter has performed important research on several topics, but his most commonly cited research is his classic experiment on emotions. This experiment was conducted in the early 1960s in collaboration with Jerome Singer.

FIG. 52. *Stanley Schachter (1922–) demonstrated how the social context interacts with autonomic arousal to produce emotions*

COGNITIONS AND EMOTIONS

Although Schachter and Singer agreed with Cannon's claim that autonomic responses are not specific enough to produce different emotions, they did not believe the James–Lange theory to be entirely wrong. So they came up with a theory of emotions that incorporated the best parts of both earlier theories. According to Schachter and Singer there is a connection between autonomic responses and emotions, but this connection is mediated by the social context. Put simply, their theory was that an individual who experiences physiological arousal tries to account for this arousal on the basis of the social context in which it occurs. For example, autonomic arousal while watching a movie love scene is interpreted as sexual excitement, while the very same autonomic arousal ex-

FIG. 53. According to Schachter's theory, the subjective experience of an emotion is the result of integrating information from current social context, past experiences and autonomic arousal

perienced during a horror movie is interpreted as fear. Schachter and Singer put it like this:

Imagine a man walking down a dark alley; a figure with a gun suddenly appears. The perception-cognition 'figure-with-a-gun' in some fashion initiates a state of physiological arousal; this state of arousal is interpreted in terms of knowledge about dark alleys and guns and the state of arousal is labelled 'fear'.

Schachter and Singer set out to design an experiment to demonstrate how the social context interacts with autonomic arousal to produce emotions. The experiment they performed was a more sophisticated version of the one performed by Maranon 20 years earlier. Schachter and Singer maintained that Maranon's study (in which most patients injected with adrenalin did not associate autonomic arousal with emotions) was not an adequate test of either Cannon's or the James–Lange theory of emotions. They argued that since all Maranon's patients knew they were receiving adrenalin, it was only natural that they would attribute their autonomic arousal to the drug rather than to emotions. When their heartbeats speeded up and their mouths became dry, Maranon's patients concluded that these symptoms were not cues to emotion (as they normally are) but simply drug effects. Even those patients who felt something like emotions assumed that these feelings were produced by the drug and therefore reported their feelings "as if" they were emotions.

Schachter and Singer wondered what would have happened if Maranon

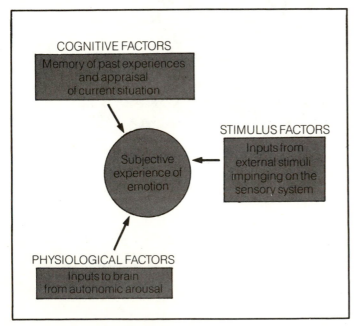

COGNITIVE FACTORS

Memory of past experiences and appraisal of current situation

STIMULUS FACTORS

Inputs from external stimuli impinging on the sensory system

Subjective experience of emotion

PHYSIOLOGICAL FACTORS

Inputs to brain from autonomic arousal

had somehow been able to give the drug to his patients without their being aware of it (surreptitiously slipped into their coffee or sprayed in the air so they could breathe it in). Under these circumstances the patients could not have attributed their autonomic symptoms to the drug; they would not have even known they had received it. Would they then have looked for a cause for their arousal in their present situation? If something funny was happening, would they have labelled themselves as happy? If something threatening was going on, would they have reported feeling frightened?

This was the experiment that Schachter and Singer would have liked to perform, but ethical considerations intervened. Very few psychological questions are important enough to justify exposing subjects to drugs without their consent. The experiment they finally carried out was, therefore, something of a compromise. But, as will be shown, the results were intriguing.

Schachter and Singer recruited subjects for an experiment they claimed was concerned with the effects of a vitamin supplement on vision. The vitamin supplement was called Suproxin and was administered by injection. In reality subjects either received an inert placebo (saline) or a small dose of the same drug used by Maranon — adrenalin. Subjects who received the placebo were told not to expect any side effects. The remaining subjects, those who received adrenalin, were divided into three conditions.

Subjects in the *informed* condition were told that Suproxin produces side effects and they should not be surprised to experience heart palpitations, hand tremors and warm flushes. The experimenters reasoned that subjects in this condition were in a position similar to Maranon's patients. They should attribute their autonomic arousal to the drug and so experience little or no emotion.

Subjects in the second group were told that Suproxin is a mild drug without side effects. Although this instruction was meant to keep them from attributing their arousal to the drug, it is not without its problems. After all, members of the informed group were told to expect side effects and just the anticipation of symptoms could have made them tense and nervous, particularly when compared with members of the second group who were told not to expect any side effects. For this reason, the experimenters included a third group in their study — the *misinformed* group. These subjects were told to expect side effects (so they should be as apprehensive as the *informed* group) but the side effects they were warned about were not those the drug actually produces. Instead of warm flushes and palpitations, members of the misinformed group were told to expect numb feet, itching and a slight headache. Schachter and Singer reasoned that the *misinformed* group could serve as a control for any fear produced simply by expecting side effects.

To summarise thus far, the experimenters created a situation in which all subjects (except those who received the placebo) would feel the same pattern of physiological arousal. One group would know that their physiological symptoms were produced by the drug they received, whereas the others would not attribute their autonomic arousal to the drug either because they were told the drug did not produce side effects or because they were told to expect a different pattern of side effects from the one the drug actually produced. Schachter and Singer believed that subjects who were not expecting the drug to produce arousal could not attribute their autonomic responses to the drug and would, therefore, experience an emotion. The exact nature of this emotion would depend on the social context. Subjects placed in different social situations would produce different interpretations, and different emotions.

Schachter manipulated the social context with the help of a confederate. After receiving the drug subjects were told they had to wait 20 minutes before further testing because that was the time required for the drug to take effect. During this waiting period subjects were asked to sit in a room along with another person who ostensibly was also a subject, but was really the experimenter's confederate. After the experimenter left to test other subjects, the confederate went into a rehearsed routine. For half the subjects the confederate doodled on a notepad, threw crumpled paper "balls" into a cup (in what he pretended was a basketball game), flew paper airplanes, played with a hula hoop and otherwise tried to create an air of levity. For the other half of the subjects, the confederate acted angry and behaved in a disagreeable manner about a questionnaire they were asked to complete during their 20-minute wait. The questionnaire was certainly anger-provoking. For example, it contained the question: With how many men (other than your father) has your mother had extra-marital relationships? Four and under ____; five to nine ____; 10 and over ____. The confederate became progressively more annoyed by such questions and eventually tore up his questionnaire and threw it on the floor saying: "I'm not wasting any more time. I'm . . . leaving."

According to Schachter and Singer subjects in the informed condition should feel little emotion as they would attribute their autonomic arousal to the drug rather than to the behaviour of the confederate. The groups given adrenalin but led to expect either no symptoms or different ones from those they actually experienced are another matter. These subjects should respond differentially to the two social contexts established by the confederate.

Specifically, they should behave like the confederate and report themselves as experiencing the mood (elated or angry) he tried to create.

Schachter and Singer observed their subjects through a one-way mirror; they also obtained a mood description by having each subject complete a questionnaire. The outcome was fairly close to what they predicted. *Misinformed* subjects were more likely to behave like the confederate and to report their mood as similar to his than correctly informed subjects. The experimenters concluded that their hypothesis was supported. Individuals who find themselves in a state of physiological arousal give this state an emotional label by interpreting it within their current social context. Change the context and you change the emotion even though the physiological state remains unchanged.

But then we come to the placebo subjects. They were expected to show little emotion in this experiment because they did not receive an arousal-producing drug. Nevertheless, they were found to display emotions and to behave like the confederate. Schachter and Singer hypothesised that perhaps these placebo subjects were autonomically aroused simply by observing the confederate's behaviour. They performed a further experiment in which the effect of adrenalin was compared not with a placebo but with a tranquilliser which made subjects *less* autonomically aroused than previously. All subjects in this experiment watched a comic film. Reactions to the movie were monitored by noting the number of smiles and laughs made by the members of the audience. As expected, those subjects who received adrenalin found the film funnier than those who received the tranquilliser. Thus, as Schachter and Singer predicted, subjects who are autonomically aroused looked for an explanation for their feelings in the social context in which they found themselves. Since

		SUBJECT'S EXPECTATIONS	
		Expects symptoms	Does not expect symptoms
ACTOR'S PERFORMANCE	Angry	Subject unaffected by actor	Subject becomes angry
	Happy	Subject unaffected by actor	Subject becomes happy

FIG. 54. *The design of Schachter's experiment. Subjects were placed in one of four conditions depending on what they were told about the drug's side effects and the behaviour of the experimenter's confederate*

nothing else was present to cause their arousal, they concluded it must have been the film that was producing their arousal and they reported feeling happy.

The results of Schachter and Singer's classic experiment and this supplemental finding support their theory of emotions. The physiological changes produced by autonomic activation are, indeed, non-specific. The emotion an individual feels (if any) depends on the context in which autonomic arousal takes place.

AFTERMATH

Another psychologist, George Mandler, compared Schachter and Singer's theory of emotions to a jukebox. To operate a jukebox you must first insert a coin and then make a selection. Either one can be done alone, but both are necessary to produce music. The coin you insert energises the machine, but it has no specific tune it favours. You must read the titles and decide which tune to play. By analogy, autonomic arousal is like the coin. It can energise a wide variety of emotions, but has no distinctive pattern signifying any one. Similarly, cognitive appraisal of the social context is like making a music selection: it determines the emotion we feel (or the song we hear).

Over the years additional evidence has been provided favouring Schachter's theory of emotions. One source of support comes from studies of paraplegics and quadriplegics who have severe injuries to their spinal cords. Damage to the spinal cord produces a lack of feeling and, therefore, the inability to experience physiological arousal. According to Schachter's theory spinal injury patients should not experience emotions and this prediction appears to be largely correct.

In one study, army veterans with spinal cord injuries were divided into five groups on the basis of where in the spinal cord their injury occurred. In one group, injuries were near the base of the spine only partly blocking their ability to experience autonomic arousal. In another group, the injury was located near the neck. These patients experienced almost no feelings of arousal. The other patients had lesions between these two extremes. All were asked about their feelings when placed in fearful situations. They were also asked to compare the intensity of the emotions they experience, in similar situations, both before and after their injury. The experimenters found that as the site of the injury moved up the spine, emotionality decreased. Compared with their reactions before they were injured, those with the highest injuries reported the largest decrease in emotionality; those with injuries at the base of the spine reported the smallest. Comments from the patients also showed that their emotional lives had changed. Some said they could act angry when required but their anger is "cold", more like a "mental anger" than a true emotion. One subject told the experimenters: "I say I'm afraid, like when I'm going into a real stiff exam at school, but I don't really feel afraid, not all tense and shaky with the hollow feeling in my stomach, like I used to."

Richard Lazarus, an American psychologist, has provided data which seem to indicate that how one interprets a situation can determine not only one's emotions but also whether autonomic arousal even occurs. In his experiment (conducted with several colleagues), student subjects were shown an emotion-generating film depicting the initiation rites of a tribe of Australian Aborigines. The film showed a primitive operation being performed on the sex organs of adolescent boys. Three soundtracks accompanied the film. In the *trauma* sound-track, the gory parts of the rite were emphasised. In the *denial* soundtrack, these aspects were ignored or downplayed. In the *intellectualisation* soundtrack, the rite was described entirely from the viewpoint of its anthropological significance. Different groups of subjects viewed the film with different soundtracks and one group saw the film accompanied by no soundtrack at all. The experimenters measured subjects' heart rates and skin electrical activity (two indicators of autonomic arousal) while the film was in progress. They found higher heart rate and larger skin responses among subjects in the trauma condition than among those who viewed the silent picture. However, the denial and intellectualisation soundtracks produced hardly any arousal at all. The experimenters concluded that these latter soundtracks led the subjects to interpretations of the film that minimised its emotion-producing aspects. Thus it appears that the interpretation one makes of a situation can affect autonomic responding.

Some studies suggest that physiological arousal may not be as important a part of emotions as Schachter believes. One such study was performed by psychologist Stuart Valins. Valins had subjects sit in a chair in a darkened room with a microphone strapped to their chests. A wire from the microphone ran to a tape-recorder. Subjects were told that the microphone would pick up their heartbeats while they watched slides of *Playboy* centrefolds appear on a screen. These heartbeats would be amplified so that the subjects could hear them as they were recorded. Actually the microphone was a fake. The heartbeat the subjects heard was not their own but a tape controlled by the experimenter. Several times during the experiment, when randomly selected slides appeared on the screen, the experimenter speeded up the tape so that subjects heard "their" heart beating faster. At the conclusion of the experiment each subject was told he could keep his favourite photo. The experimenter showed subjects the photographs and watched to see which one they picked. Most often, the subjects chose those that were accompanied by fast heartbeats. They appear to have taken the false heartbeat as evidence of their own physiological arousal and, therefore, interpreted the photos presented at the time as particularly arousing. On the face of it this finding appears hard to reconcile with Schachter's theory, but further research has shown that speeded false heartbeats actually produce arousal and faster heartbeats in the subjects who hear them. So Valins's findings may not contradict Schachter's theory after all.

There have been some attempts to devise clinical treatments based on Schachter's theory of emotions. In one experiment, insomniacs who had chronic difficulty falling asleep were given a placebo sugar pill. Half the subjects were told that the pill produces relaxation and eases tension; the other half were told that it may produce some signs of arousal (tension, increased heart rate). The experimenter then monitored how long it took subjects to fall asleep. The result was not what you might expect. Those given the "relaxing" pill took 40 per cent *longer* than usual to fall asleep while subjects given the "arousing" placebo fell asleep 20 per cent *faster* than usual. It appears that insomniacs given the "arousing" pill attributed their normal bedtime anxieties about falling asleep to the pill. The ability to attribute tension to outside causes reduced their emotionality and helped them fall asleep. Those subjects told that the pill is relaxing, on the other hand, could only attribute their tensions to themselves. (They may even have believed that they were more tense than usual since they felt anxious despite having received a relaxing pill.) These subjects became *more* emotional and had more trouble falling asleep than they usually did.

Schachter's theory, and his classic experiment with Singer, helped psychologists understand how the same physiological state of arousal could produce different emotions. It set the stage for more sophisticated research on the interaction between social context, autonomic arousal and cognitive interpretations — research that continues to this day.

Further Reading

Darwin, C. R., *The Expression of Emotions in Man and Animals*, John Murray, London, 1872.

Schachter, S. and Singer, J. E., "Cognitive, Social and Physiological Determinants of Emotional State", *Psychological Review*, 69, pp. 379–99, 1962.

PART 3

The Social Animal

When we describe a friend who attends many parties and hates to stay home as *sociable* or when we claim that a tax cheat is *greedy* or a soldier is *courageous*, we are implying that the causes of their behaviours lie within these individuals. That is, we attribute their behaviour to certain character traits. While this is a common way to think about behaviour, it cannot be the whole story. For one thing, people tend to be inconsistent. A soldier may act bravely in some situations but not others. Similarly, "greedy" tax cheats have been known to set up philanthropic foundations and donate millions to charity. To a great extent, how people behave depends not only on their character but also on the context — the particular social situation in which they are currently operating. Discovering how social environments influence our thoughts, feelings and actions is the work of social psychologists.

Although it has become something of a cliché to refer to human beings as "social animals", it is true all the same. Almost from the moment of birth we interact with others. These interactions produce social hierarchies, establish behavioural norms, delineate roles for us to play and help us to establish our identities in our culture. Of course the mechanisms by which social interactions exert their influence on our thought and behaviour are not only the province of social psychology. Anthropologists, sociologists, economists, even political scientists are interested in the same questions. But these disciplines differ from social psychology both in their methods and in their level of analysis. Whereas sociologists focus on large groups (conservative voters or Roman Catholics, for example), social psychologists study small groups, often as small as just two people and rarely larger than 10. Social psychologists are also experimentalists. Much of their research takes place not in the *field* (the everyday world), but in the laboratory. Their laboratory experiments are often artificial and contrived, but they are carefully designed to reveal how social influences operate. Two of the three chapters comprising this section are concerned with laboratory experiments; the third chapter describes field research.

Although social psychologists study a bewildering array of problems, there are several recurrent themes. One concerns the common tendency to alter our opinions in line with group pressure. Opinion change takes place every day when juries deliberate on a verdict. Those who dissent in the beginning frequently change their opinions to coincide with those of the majority. Chapter Seven is concerned with how group pressure and social status produce such conformity. Another common social psychology theme concerns altruistic behaviour. Why, and under what circumstances, do people help one another? An experimental study of this subject is described in Chapter Eight. Chapter Nine describes research concerned with another aspect of social behaviour — how social groups determine what behaviours are acceptable and how they enforce these "social norms".

CHAPTER SEVEN

CONFORMITY AND OBEDIENCE

Nonconformist. The very word calls forth an image of a rugged individualist; a person who, with little regard for the stifling mores of contemporary society, controls his own life and makes his own destiny. Conformist, on the other hand, is a word used to describe an inadequate little person, a slave to social custom who dresses and thinks like everyone else and who spends each day worrying about what the neighbours will think. With attitudes like these, no wonder most people describe themselves as nonconformists.

But there is another dimension to nonconformity, one that calls forth rather different images. Criminals, after all, are nonconformists; so are the insane. Such people hardly fit the romantic stereotype of the rugged individualist. In fact there appears to be a point where nonconformity shades into deviance; at this point nonconformity seems no longer an admirable trait. The problem is that the behaviour of extreme nonconformists is unpredictable. Social relations are, to a large extent, based on a shared knowledge of how people will act in familiar situations. If everyone behaved unpredictably, society as we know it would be impossible. Thus despite our favourable view of nonconformists, there are times when conformity is desirable. Team players — not stars — win football games, and nonconformist soldiers can wind up court martialled (or dead). What is required is a balance between individuality and conformity to social norms. Extreme nonconformity results in chaos, while too much conformity is the hallmark of totalitarianism.

In practice such a balance has proved difficult to achieve. The result is that most of us are ambivalent about nonconformity. Sometimes we wish to follow our own ideas; at other times we prefer to conform. Psychologists have tried to discover the social influences determining whether or not we conform. Two classic experiments on conformity are described in this chapter. The first is concerned with group pressure to conform, the second with the importance of authority.

GROUP PRESSURE TO CONFORM

Psychologists define conformity as a change in a person's opinions or behaviour as the result of pressure from a group or another individual. This pressure, by the way, need not be overt; it need not even be real. Imagined pressure can produce conformity if the circumstances are right.

Aristotle wrote about social influences on persuasion as long ago as 350 BC, but experimental studies of conformity did not begin until the twentieth century. One of the earliest was conducted by Floyd Allport in 1924. Allport asked the subjects in his experiment to judge the pleasantness of a series of odours. His subjects did this alone and in small groups. He found that when working together, subjects did not make the same judgements they made when working alone. Instead their judgements tended to approach the mean of their group. Allport concluded that his subjects (who, by the way, did not communicate directly with one another) were making an effort to "belong" with others by adjusting their judgements to coincide with those of the other members of their group.

An even more dramatic illustration of conformity was reported by psychologist Muzafir Sherif in 1936. Sherif based his experiment around what perceptual researchers call the autokinetic effect. When a single point of light is displayed in a completely dark room it will appear to move about erratically even though it is perfectly stationary. This effect was first discovered by astronomers staring at single stars in the black night sky.

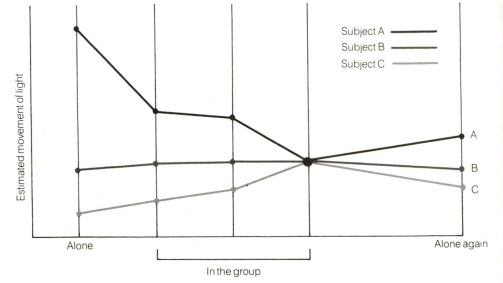

FIG. 55. *When subjects in Sherif's experiment were tested alone, their estimates of the distance the light moved varied widely. When tested in groups, however, their estimates became increasingly similar and remained so when again tested alone*

Each subject in Sherif's experiment was placed alone in a dark room and asked to look at the light for a brief exposure. They were then required to estimate the direction and distance the light moved. The distance estimated varied widely from subject to subject. Some thought the light moved only a few centimetres, others estimated its movement in metres. Sherif then combined individuals with different average estimates into small groups and asked them to repeat the task reporting their judgements aloud. Although their initial judgements differed widely, after a few exposures the judgements of the group members tended to converge, usually somewhere around the mean of their initial judgements. In other words, subjects changed their estimates (some increased, others decreased) in order to produce one estimate they all felt comfortable with. When the subjects were retested again individually, they continued giving the group estimate rather than reverting to their original judgements.

In both Allport's and Sherif's studies the experimenter did not require the subjects to reach a common judgement and there was no punishment for disagreeing with the other group members. Moreover, no group members overtly attempted to persuade others to alter their judgements. In fact in Allport's experiment subjects did not even directly communicate with one another. Yet there was a strong tendency in both experiments for subjects to move toward a similar position.

Although these studies demonstrate a strong tendency to conform to group judgements, there is one aspect of these experiments that deserves closer scrutiny. That is, there were no objectively correct answers. Allport had his subjects make an aesthetic judgement about odours while Sherif's subjects judged the movement of a stationary light. Since the subjects in these experiments had no objective way to verify their judgements, they were forced to rely on "social reality" as a guide to proper behaviour. They conformed not because they feared punishment from the group but because the group's behaviour was their only guide to what was expected of them. This explanation for conformity depends on the actual physical reality being in doubt. It implies that people will not conform when physical reality is clear. This hypothesis was tested in Solomon Asch's classic experiment.

CLASSIC EXPERIMENT 9:

ASCH'S CONFORMITY STUDY

FIG. 56. *Solomon E. Asch (1907–) investigated causes of conformity to group pressure*

Solomon Asch was born in 1907 in Warsaw, Poland. He emigrated to America in 1920 where he attended high school in New York City. He then went on to the City University of New York where he received a bachelor's degree in 1928. He received his Ph.D. from Columbia University in New York in 1932. After receiving his doctorate Asch taught at Columbia, Brooklyn College and the New School for Social Research, all in New York City. In 1947 he took up the Chair of Psychology at Swarthmore College where he stayed until 1966, when he joined the staff of Rutgers University as Distinguished Professor of Psychology. Asch has held visiting appointments at Harvard University, the Massachusetts Institute of Technology, the Centre for Advanced Study in the Behavioural Sciences at Stanford University and the Institute for Advanced Study at Princeton. He has been a Guggenheim Fellow and has won the Distinguished Scientific Contribution Award from the American Psychological Association; he is also a member of the American Academy of Arts and Science. Asch has performed several influential experiments in social psychology and is the author of a popular social psychology textbook. His most famous experiment, however, concerns conformity.

Suppose you are one of the volunteer subjects in Asch's experiment. You could be assigned to either an experimental or control group. If you are in the experimental group, you enter a room along with seven other subjects. The room is arranged with a row of eight chairs facing front. Somehow the other subjects manage to take their seats first, leaving you the one on the extreme left.

The experimenter explains that he is interested in the ability to judge the length of lines. He shows you a straight line (labelled ✕ in Figure 57). This is the standard line. The experimenter also shows you three comparison lines (labelled A, B, and C) and asks you to choose which of the three comparison lines is closest in length to the standard.

Beginning at the right, each subject is asked to make his judgement aloud. The task is extremely easy. It is immediately apparent that the answer is line B. And this is in fact the answer given by every subject. The procedure continues for several trials, each time with different lines, until suddenly something very strange happens. The first subject, the one sitting at the extreme right, appears to make an obvious error. Instead of giving the correct answer the subject chooses a line that is clearly smaller than the standard. Well, perhaps he just made a mistake. But then the second subject also gives the wrong answer — the same wrong response given by the first subject. You begin to think these people are going blind. When the third, fourth and fifth subjects also make the same mistake, you begin to worry that maybe it is you who are going blind. When all seven subjects have made the same incorrect choice, it is now your turn. Do you go along with the evidence of your senses and give the answer you believe correct, or do you go along with the group and give the incorrect answer? Your palm gets sweaty and your heart speeds up while you decide. Finally you give in and go along with the group.

The procedure continues. On several occasions the same peculiar thing happens — everyone makes an obviously incorrect response. On many of these occasions you concur with the group.

Although it certainly looks as if you are conforming to group pressure, it is always possible that you find the line task so difficult that, like Allport's and Sherif's subjects, you are forced to rely on "social reality" as a guide to proper behaviour. In order to assess the difficulty of the line discriminations, half the subjects in the experiment are assigned to a control condition. Subjects in this con-

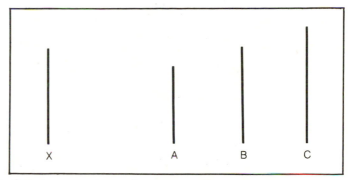

dition were given the same task as those in the experimental condition. They too judged line lengths; the difference was that they did so alone. Subjects in the control group rarely made any errors.

In this experiment Asch set up a conflict between his subjects' knowledge of physical reality and "social reality" as established by the group. He arranged this conflict by rigging the experimental situation: although the person sitting on the extreme left (as you were) is always an experimental subject, all of the other participants are actually confederates of the experimenter. They know their judgements are incorrect; they are making them at the experimenter's request in order to pressure the real subject to conform. And they are successful. Overall, 35 per cent of the real subjects' responses conformed to the group's incorrect judgements — not a majority of responses but still a substantial minority. As in earlier experiments, subjects conformed even though there were no sanctions for not conforming and no rewards for going along.

Since members of the control group rarely made any errors judging line length when working alone, Asch felt confident that his results were not due to the difficulty of the task — the correct answers were just too easy for doubt. Instead, Asch argued that there are two possible explanations for conformity in his experiment. Either group pressure actually convinced subjects that their perceptions were wrong or the subjects knew the

FIG. 57. *Asch's conformity task. Subjects judged which of the three comparison lines (A, B, C) was the same length as the standard line (X)*

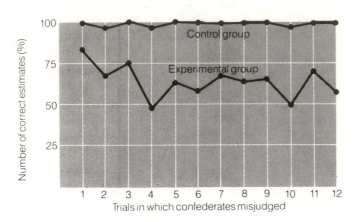

FIG. 58. *Results of Asch's experiment. Control subjects judged line length alone and rarely made any errors. Experimental subjects made their judgements in the presence of group members who were purposely making errors*

group's response was wrong but went along anyway to avoid being disagreeable. The latter explanation implies that for many people being liked and accepted is more important than being correct. After the experiment Asch asked his subjects about their reasons for conforming. Some said they conformed in order to be one of the group, but others claimed that the group's unanimous incorrect response actually changed their perception. That is, the incorrect response came to look correct. Although something like this might happen, Asch was a bit sceptical. He thought that the subjects could just be too embarrassed to admit being persuaded by group pressure. After all, no-one wants to appear weak and easily swayed.

In order to determine whether subjects' perceptions actually change as a result of group pressure, Asch ran another experimental condition. This one was identical to the original experiment in all but one crucial aspect. Subjects heard the reports of the other members of the group but they were asked to make their own judgements in private. In this situation Asch found that subjects *do not* conform to incorrect group judgements. Thus his scepticism was well founded. Group pressure affects only public responses, not private beliefs. In this experiment, at least, group pressure did not change the subjects' perception of physical reality.

Asch's experiment has been repeated with different tasks. Whether subjects have to count the number of beats made by a metronome or the aesthetic value of art works, the results are the same — group pressure leads to a change of public (if not private) beliefs. Asch also repeated his tasks using different-sized groups. He found that conformity increases with group size only up to a majority of three. Beyond this the size of the majority does not increase the tendency to conform. It appears that one or two people can still be treated as individuals whose opinions are theirs alone. However, three or more people giving the same incorrect response constitute a group — a more potent social force.

AFTERMATH

Asch's dramatic demonstration of the power of group influence made a deep impression on social psychologists. Unlike Sherif's and Allport's subjects who had no "correct" judgement to guide them, Asch's subjects were very clear about the nature of physical reality. What Asch showed was that when a conflict was created between our perception of physical reality and the social judgement of a group, we will often publicly go along with a group even if this means contradicting the evidence of our senses.

Although the tendency to conform is an important finding, it is worthwhile keeping in mind that subjects did not conform at every opportunity. What is more, 25 per cent of Asch's subjects never conformed at all. Further research was conducted to try to identify the forces in the experiment and the individual that lead to conformity. One important finding is that a unanimous group is a prerequisite for conforming in Asch's situation. If just one other person produces the correct response, the subject will be unlikely to conform to the majority's incorrect judgement. Researchers have also found that conformers are more likely to have lower self-esteem than nonconformers. Those with poor self-images apparently have stronger needs to be accepted by the group and therefore are more likely to "go along to get along".

The strength of Asch's finding is illustrated by similar experiments in which people have been induced to take public stances very different from those they hold privately about issues more personally important than line length. For example, military officers, who in private all believed they were good leaders, agreed that they were poor leaders when the majority was against them. In another study, 58 per cent of college student subjects were persuaded to agree to the proposition that the right of free speech should be suspended when the government feels threatened. This was a position that none held privately. Even absurd statements such as, "Sixty-five per cent of the population is over 70 years old", have been publicly accepted by subjects placed in Asch-type situations.

Although these experiments demonstrate the importance of group pressure on conformity (at least public conformity), they do not illustrate that such conformity is bad. After all, the subjects knew they were participating in a laboratory experiment. Their conformity, although embarrassing, never really harmed anyone and their private beliefs remained unchanged. If this is all there is to conformity, perhaps it is nothing to worry about. There are worse goals than trying to get along with others. But what happens when conformity does lead to someone getting hurt? The notion that conformity is a benign way to ensure social harmony was challenged by Stanley Milgram in one of the most harrowing social psychological experiments ever conducted.

CLASSIC EXPERIMENT 10:

OBEDIENCE TO AUTHORITY

Obedience to authority is a basic aspect of human social organisation. Virtually every society has developed hierarchies in which some people are given authority over others. Teachers, for example, have authority over their students, headmasters and principals have authority over teachers and government education officials exercise authority over principals. Workers obey managers, soldiers obey their officers and children obey their parents (at least most of the time). It is difficult to see how society could operate any other way.

But there are times when authority and private conscience come into conflict. Indeed, the resolution of such conflicts represents one of the oldest problems in philosophy and religion. Abraham, commanded by God to kill his beloved son Isaac, was placed in a conflict between his love for his son and his obedience to God. The Greek legend of Antigone concerns a similar conflict between the love for a brother and the demands of the state. Over the centuries philosophers have wrestled with the conflict between private conscience and obedience to authority, but the issue remains unresolved. Thus even today we are unclear when to follow our conscience and when to succumb to authority. Take but one example. Should soldiers obey orders? Most of us believe they should. But what happens when such orders require that they kill innocent civilians? Should orders be ignored in such cases? How does a soldier decide when to "do his duty" and follow

orders and when to defy orders that conflict with his conscience? History tells us that few people placed in such a conflict actually defy authority. Perhaps this is why C. P. Snow wrote: "More hideous crimes have been committed in the name of obedience than have ever been committed in the name of rebellion."

Obedience to authority is a form of conformity, and like other types of conformity it has been studied in the psychology laboratory. In Stanley Milgram's classic experiment a conflict is established between a subject's moral beliefs and the demands of authority. The aim of the experiment is to learn how such conflicts are resolved.

Stanley Milgram was born in 1933 in New York City. He grew up during the Second World War and began studying psychology at a time when Nazi atrocities were still fresh in everyone's mind. After attending a public high school he took a bachelor's degree at Queens College. While at Queens College he received a Ford Foundation fellowship to pursue postgraduate study at Harvard University. Milgram received his doctoral degree from Harvard University in 1960 and taught there for several years. In the early 1960s Milgram moved to Yale University, the university where his classic experiment was conducted.

In the years following the Second World War, social psychologists studied the personality traits of Germans. These studies were supposed to have shown that Germans have *authoritarian* personality traits and are therefore more likely to obey the wishes of authority than others. These studies were offered as explanations for German war crimes. Milgram's classic experiment shows that obedience to authority is not nearly so simple a matter, nor is it confined to Germans.

The story of Milgram's experiment should actually begin not in the laboratory but in a lecture theatre. The audience includes psychiatrists, university students and middle-class adults of various occupations. They have come to hear a lecture about obedience to authority. During the course of the lecture the audience is asked to imagine the following experiment.

In response to a newspaper advertisement offering $4.50 (a fair amount in 1963) for one hour's participation in an experiment on "memory and learning", you turn up at the Yale University psychology department. You are shown into an elaborate laboratory and introduced to the experimenter, a 31-year-old man dressed in a grey technician's coat. The experimenter is business-like and rather stern. You are also introduced to another person in the room who, you are told, has also volunteered for the experiment. In contrast to the experimenter the other volunteer is friendly and likable.

Once the introductions are complete the experimenter explains that the purpose of the research is to study the effect of punishment on learning. You are told that the aim is to find out how much punishment is needed for learning and whether it is important who acts as teacher (administers the punishment) and who acts as learner (receives the punishment). You and the other subject are then asked to draw lots from a hat to determine who will be teacher and who learner. You draw the teacher's role. The three of you then proceed to an adjacent room where the other subject is carefully strapped into a chair. The straps, says the experimenter, are merely to prevent excessive movement. But you can see by the way they are tied that the straps make it impossible for him to escape. An electrode is then placed on the learner's wrist and some electrode paste is applied in order "to avoid blisters and burns". Both you and the learner are told that the electrode is attached to a shock generator in the next room. The shocks will serve as punishment in the experiment. When the learner asks if the shocks will hurt, the experimenter replies: "Although the shocks may be extremely painful, they cause no permanent tissue damage."

The experimenter then takes you to the next room where he shows you the shock generator. The apparatus has 30 switches each labelled with a voltage ranging from 15 to 450 volts.

FIG. 59. *Stanley Milgram (1933–   ) examined the role of social factors in obedience to authority*

114

Starting from the left, there is a 15-volt increment from one switch to the next. In addition each group of four switches is given a descriptive label. These range from SLIGHT SHOCK at the low end to MODERATE SHOCK, STRONG SHOCK, VERY STRONG SHOCK, INTENSE SHOCK, EXTREME INTENSITY SHOCK and DANGER: SEVERE SHOCK. The two switches at the extreme right are labelled XXX.

test, you would read blue followed by sky, ink, box, lamp. The learner's job is to indicate that the third response, box, was paired with blue. Since the learner is in a different room, he communicates his answers by pressing one of four switches on his chair. These switches illuminate a set of lights mounted on the shock generator and each light corresponds to one of the four choices.

The experimenter tells you that

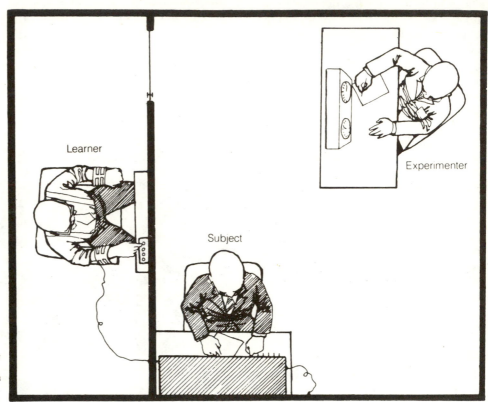

FIG. 60. *Milgram's experimental arrangement. Each time the learner makes an error, the subject–teacher administers an electric shock as the experimenter looks on*

You are told that the experiment involves a "paired-associate" learning task. You as the teacher will read a series of word-pairs to the learner. The learner's task is to remember which words go together. On future presentations you will read aloud only the first member of each pair. You will then give the learner a choice of four words. The learner must indicate which of these four was the word originally paired with the first word. For example, the original word pairs might include blue-box, nice-day, and wild-duck. During the actual

every time the subject makes an incorrect response you are to give him a shock. At the outset the shocks delivered are 15 volts, but you are to move to the next highest voltage level with each error. In order to be sure the equipment is working properly the experimenter gives you a sample shock.

Now the experiment begins. The learner is finding the task difficult and he makes several errors. After each error you administer a shock. At first the shocks are weak but they soon move into the more severe range.

After receiving a 75-volt shock the learner grunts loud enough for you to hear him through the wall. The same thing happens at 90 and 105 volts. At 120 volts the learner says the shocks are getting painful and at 150 he cries: "Get me out of here! I won't be in the experiment any more. I refuse to go on." Protests of this type continue with increasing intensity. If at this or any other time during the experiment you question whether you should continue, the experimenter tells you to keep going. If you press the point he says that the experiment depends on your continuing. He may even say that you have no other choice, you must go on. As the shocks increase even further the learner yells out, "I can't stand the pain", and begins to scream in agony. At 300 volts you can hear the learner pounding on the wall. After this he no longer responds to the task, he just screams in agony when shocked. After 330 volts the learner is not heard from again. At this point the experimenter tells you to treat the learner's failure to respond as an incorrect choice and to continue increasing the shock.

This is the experiment described during the lecture. Each member of the audience was asked to reflect on the experiment and to privately record how he himself would behave. All groups, psychiatrists, university students and middle-class adults, responded similarly. They all saw themselves as disobeying the experimenter somewhere along the line. On average the psychiatrists predicted that they would cease shocking at around 120 volts. Some said they would refuse to shock anyone at all. On average, university students and middle-class adults said they would cease shocking at around 135 volts. Recall, this is the level at which the learner indicates the shocks are painful and well below the level at which the learner first asks for the experiment to terminate. No-one in any group thought he would continue administering shocks beyond 300 volts.

When asked to explain their disobedience, the members of the audience said that they did not wish to hurt anyone. Most agreed that since participation in the experiment is voluntary, the learner should be permitted to quit whenever he asks. In other words, subjects saw their disobedience as motivated by empathy for the subject, compassion for those in pain and a sense of fairness.

It is of course quite common for people to portray themselves in the best possible light. Therefore, the audience members may have been exaggerating when they said they would have defied the experimenter's commands as soon as the learner began to complain. For this reason Milgram also asked them how they thought others would behave in the experiment. It turned out that the members of the audience expected others to be more compliant with the experimenter's demands than themselves (people really do have flattering opinions of themselves). However, obedience was not expected to be very strong. The psychiatrists, for example, estimated that only four per cent of people would reach 300 volts and only one in 1000 would proceed to the highest point on the shock generator. These latter individuals were seen as pathological sadists. That is, psychiatrists believed that only those with psychological disabilities would continue to administer painful shocks after it became clear that the subject had had enough.

Up to this point we have been discussing a hypothetical experiment. But in fact the experiment described to the various audiences was actually conducted. What is more, the results differed markedly from the predictions made by the psychiatrists and other members of the lecture audience. When Milgram actually conducted the experiment he found that with a little prodding the majority of subjects (more than 60 per cent) continued to obey the experimenter, administering shocks right through to

450 volts. These were not psychopaths or sadists either. They were everyday people taken from many walks of life who were willing to go to very extreme lengths to obey someone in authority.

At this point you may be wondering how such an experiment could be conducted. What sort of experimenter would arrange to have painful electric shocks administered to innocent volunteers? The truth is, except for the sample shock given to the subject playing teacher in order to convince him that the equipment was real, no-one actually received any shocks in the experiment. The learner was actually the experimenter's accomplice, a person specially trained to play the role of someone getting shocked. The drawing of lots for who plays teacher and who learner was rigged so that the accomplice always played the part of learner.

Although no-one actually received any shocks in this experiment, Milgram's research was strongly criticised because of the effect it had on the teachers. The experimental situation was extremely realistic. In a post-experimental interview Milgram asked the subjects. "How painful to the learner were the last few shocks that you administered to him?" The teachers were asked to give their answer by choosing a point on a 14-point scale (1 equals "not at all painful" and 14 equals "extremely painful"). The typical response was 14, or "extremely painful". Although most subjects obeyed the experimenter there were obvious signs of their discomfort, especially when administering the most powerful shocks. Subjects were observed to tremble, stammer, bite their lips, groan and dig their fingernails into their skin. Many subjects showed signs of nervous laughter and a few developed uncontrollable "seizures".

One observer described the emotional strain of one of Milgram's "teachers" as follows:

I observed a mature and initially poised businessman enter the laboratory smiling and confident. Within 20 minutes he was reduced to a twitching, stuttering wreck, who was rapidly approaching a point of nervous collapse. He constantly pulled on his ear lobe, and twisted his hands. At one point he pushed his fist into his forehead and muttered: 'Oh God, let's stop it.' And yet he continued to respond to every word of the experimenter, and obeyed to the end.

Milgram placed his subjects in a position where they had to choose between the conflicting demands of the learner who wished to be released and the experimenter who wanted them to continue administering shocks. Both demands cannot be met simultaneously. The subject had to choose between the moral strictures against hurting another person and the tendency to obey those perceived as legitimate authorities. It did not seem to matter that in this situation the authority had no means of enforcing his demands nor did it matter that subjects were obviously distressed by what they were doing — they continued nevertheless.

Contrary to the predictions of both laymen and psychiatrists, and despite their obvious discomfort and distress, Milgram found that most subjects continued to obey the experimenter even if this meant harming another person. Clearly such a finding is at one time both provocative and dismaying. Comparisons were immediately drawn with Nazi concentration camp officers who complied with orders to murder millions of people, and Vietnam massacres of innocent women and children by soldiers following what they believed to be their superiors' orders. The implication is that anyone placed in the right circumstances could behave similarly. That is, rather than inhuman monsters, the Nazi murderers were merely average bureaucrats following orders and trying to do their job as well as they could.

Milgram's interviews with his subjects tended to confirm the view that ordinary people can hurt another person under the proper circumstances. For example, Milgram described the behaviour of a 40-year-old housewife and part-time nurse, a devout Catholic married to a plumber. According to Milgram, she gave the impression of extreme humility. It was as if her every assertion carried the emotional message: I'm just an ordinary person, don't expect a lot from me. At 225 volts she turned to the experimenter and stated in a tentative voice, so as not to offend, "I hesitate to press these". But when the experimenter instructed her to go on, she did. She questioned again, but still continued as ordered, right to the end. During a post-experimental interview she had the following exchange with the interviewer:

INTERVIEWER: *Did you think of stopping at any time?*

SUBJECT [in a lackadaisical tone]: *He said 'Go ahead'. I did. I said to him, 'I don't think I should go any further'. He said, 'Go on with the experiment'.*

INTERVIEWER: *Is there anything Mr Wallace* [the learner] *could have said that would have caused you to stop the experiment?*

SUBJECT: *I don't think so.*

Another subject, a housewife, described her background in obviously proud terms. She had graduated from university 20 years earlier, she was doing volunteer work with juvenile delinquents and was active in the local girl scouts' organisation as well as the PTA. She expressed concern as the shocks moved up the scale but always obeyed the experimenter's instruction to continue. She muttered to herself, "I'm shaking here", but she went right up to 450 volts, which she administered three times. In the interview she said she believed that the shocks she administered were painful. When asked the highest shock she herself would be willing to undergo as a sample, she said 15 volts: "If I were to get any, and I wouldn't want even that. I don't think

it's necessary." Yet she had given the learner 450 volts. Several months after the experiment this subject stated in a follow-up questionnaire that she had not really believed the learner was getting shocks, thereby rationalising her behaviour.

A male subject, a 39-year-old social worker, was described at the outset of the experiment as serious beyond his years and appearing intelligent and concerned. As the experiment proceeded this subject began to giggle and laugh. The laughter got increasingly louder and disruptive. Each outburst was triggered by the learner's screams. Sometimes his laughter appeared totally out of his control. In the post-experimental interview this subject described his reaction as "awfully peculiar". "This isn't the way I usually am." He felt ". . . caught up in a set of circumstances where I just couldn't deviate and I just couldn't help". Another subject, a 43-year-old water inspector, was so convinced by the experiment he believed the learner's silence meant he was dead. He was relieved to find that it was all a hoax; nevertheless, when his wife asked him how he would feel if the man really was dead, he replied: "So he's dead. I did my job."

These apparently ordinary people all administered severe shocks to an innocent victim. Although they appeared uncomfortable doing so, they did not disobey. But other subjects did refuse to obey the experimenter. These subjects were also interviewed. One, a Professor of Divinity, baulked at going further than 150 volts. When he was told that it was essential to the experiment that he continue, he responded: "I don't understand why the experiment is placed above this person's life." No argument could convince him to continue. Another subject, a 32-year-old engineer, stopped at the 225 volt level. The experimenter tried to bully him into continuing, finally saying that he *must* continue: "You have no other choice." To this the engineer replied: "I *do* have a choice. Why don't I have a choice? I came here on my own free will." Upon further questioning it became clear that this subject believed he was "responsible" for his actions and that he did not wish to harm another. A 31-year-old female medical technician, who refused to continue beyond 210 volts, also emphasised the voluntary nature of her participation and her sense of personal responsibility. "I don't want to be responsible if . . . anything happens to him."

In Milgram's experiment, those who took responsibility for their own actions were more likely to terminate the shocks than those who viewed the experimenter as responsible for anything that happened in the experiment. These subjects saw themselves as merely "following orders". It seems that there were more of the latter than the former. In our society there are strong pressures to conform in the interest of efficiency. In fact those who conform usually move up the hierarchy to positions of increased authority. The reward system favours obedience to authority and it takes a strong person to resist.

AFTERMATH

The idea that a psychological experiment could reduce subjects to the "point of nervous collapse" brought forth a storm of criticism. Critics worried that subjects in the experiment might have suffered permanent emotional damage as a result of their participation. For instance, knowing how they behaved could have damaged their self-image. Some critics saw Milgram's experiment as an abuse of trust because subjects were deceived about the true nature of what was going on.

Milgram countered these criticisms by arguing that all subjects were "debriefed" at the end of the experiment. During this debriefing the true nature of the experiment was explained to each subject and they were all told that no shocks were actually delivered. They even met the learner-victim and saw that he was unharmed. Milgram reported that when questioned about the experiment, 84 per cent of the subjects were happy to have participated, 15 per cent were neutral and only one in 100 was sorry to have been involved. Some subjects claimed to have learned something about themselves and thought they would be less certain in the future that authority figures should always be obeyed. One even said he became a conscientious objector partly as a result of participating. Milgram felt that what really troubled his critics was not so much the deception of volunteers or the blows to their self-esteem, but rather the implications of the experiment for our view of human nature. Remember, more than half the volunteers were willing to administer harmful shocks. And this behaviour is not confined to Americans either. Milgram's experiment has been repeated in Australia, South Africa and in several European countries with similar or even more dramatic results. In one German study, 85 per cent of subjects were found to be obedient to the experimenter!

Milgram conducted additional studies to isolate the variables that influence obedience in his study. There were several factors that may have encouraged subjects to obey the experimenter's orders. First, the experiment was conducted at Yale University, a prestigious institution with a good reputation. Subjects may have been influenced by Yale's sponsorship to continue to obey. Second, the purpose of the experiment appears — at least superficially — to be worthwhile. Subjects may have been swayed to obey because they wanted to help contribute to knowledge. Third, subjects realised that both they and the learners were volunteers. In the beginning, at least, no-one forced them to participate. The subjects were told that the shocks are painful but not dangerous, and for a while the learner appeared to be cooperating in the game. Fourth, the learners were out of sight where their suffering could be heard but where the teacher and learner could not see one another. The first two factors may have affected the experimenter's perceived authority while the second two concern how aware the subjects were of the learner's suffering.

Awareness of the learner's plight was investigated in a series of follow-up experiments. Four conditions were employed, each involving a different relationship between the teacher and the learner. In the "remote feedback" condition the teacher and learner were in separate rooms. The learner could not be heard and the only signal the teacher had of the learner's distress was some pounding on the wall when the shock level reached 300 volts. The "voice feedback" condition was the one used in the classic experiment. The learner could be heard but not seen. In the third condition, "proximity", the learner was seated near the subject and could be seen as well as heard. In the fourth condition, called "touch proximity", the teacher was actually required to hold the struggling victim's hand on a "shock plate" in order to give him shocks above 150 volts.

As you may imagine, Milgram found that subjects were less likely to obey the experimenter in the "touch proximity" condition than in the "remote" situation. The percentage of obedient subjects went from 65 per cent in the "remote" condition to 62 per cent in the "voice feedback" condition to 40 per cent in the "proximity" and only 30 per cent in the "touch proximity" condition. It appears to be easier to perform harm when one cannot see the victim — a fact known by most soldiers. While the percentage who obey was reduced by increasing exposure to the victim, it is still sobering to note that 30 per cent of subjects were willing to hold down the hand of a man screaming in pain while giving him severe electric shocks.

In addition to changing the relationship between subjects and their victims, Milgram also conducted experiments designed to alter the relationship between the experimenter and subjects. For example, in one version Milgram had the experimenter leave the room after explaining what was to be done. For the rest of the experiment all communication between the subject-teacher and the

FIG. 61. *Thirty per cent of subjects were willing to hold down the hand of a man screaming in pain so as to administer even stronger shocks*

experimenter was conducted by telephone. Only about 23 per cent of subjects were obedient in this situation as opposed to over 60 per cent when the experimenter was present. A few subjects resolved the conflict between obedience and humanity in this situation by telling the experimenter (who was listening on the telephone) that they were increasing the shock when, in fact, they were continuing to administer the lowest level.

These experiments indicate that the tendency to obey can be manipulated by changing the experimental situation but they do not directly address the role of the experimenter's authority. It is still possible that the experiment's location, Yale University, conferred a certain legitimacy on the proceedings. The subjects could have assumed that no-one associated with such a prestigious institution would ever allow an unethical or harmful experiment to take place. In order to examine the importance of the setting, Milgram moved his apparatus to a rather rundown office building in nearby Bridgeport, Connecticut. Instead of Yale University, subjects were told that the experiment was being conducted by a fictitious firm called Research Associates. Moving the experiment had an effect. Only 48 per cent of subjects were fully obedient as compared with over 60 per cent who participated at Yale. Still nearly half the subjects remained totally obedient.

Milgram also looked for differences between people that might predict who would and who would not obey. Males and females were equally obedient (although females were more nervous) and although those who took responsibility for their actions were less likely to obey than those who assigned responsibility to the experimenter, it was not easy to tell who these people were prior to their participation in the experiment. There was also a tendency for educated subjects to be less obedient, and those who had spent time in the military to be more obedient. Overall, however, the relationships between subject characteristics and obedience were very weak. Most of the time it was impossible to predict who would obey and who would not.

Milgram felt that his results held relevance for understanding such behaviours as the Nazi war crimes and Vietnam massacres already mentioned. He notes that Nazis frequently described themselves as helpless parts in a big machine. He also cites their tendency to devalue their victims. European Jews were the subject of a propaganda campaign designed to make them appear to deserve punishment. Milgram found a tendency to devalue the learner among his subjects as well. Many described the learner as stupid and slow and one even said the learner was so dumb he "deserved to get shocked".

There is clearly food for thought in Milgram's findings, but it is a long way from the psychology laboratory to Nazi Germany or Vietnam. Subjects in Milgram's experiment were being asked to increase human knowledge, a culturally positive goal, whereas the goal of Nazi Germany, mass murder, was morally appalling. Also Milgram's subjects stopped obeying when the experimenter was out of sight, whereas many war crimes did not require a supervisor standing over the perpetrator. Another difference between the two situations is that while some war criminals took sadistic pleasure in their crimes, Milgram's subjects were quite distressed by what they were doing. Finally, Milgram's subjects operated alone. Citizens of Germany had other people working along with them supporting their actions. Social support can exert a strong effect on conformity. Milgram himself demonstrates the importance of social support in another follow-up experiment in which two accomplices were assigned to the teaching role along with the subject. If these accomplices refuse to obey the experimenter, 90 per cent of the time the subjects refuse as well.

Although Milgram's research has been criticised as being "artificial", further experiments conducted by other psychologists suggest that his findings would be obtained even under more natural conditions. In one experiment, nurses on duty in several different hospitals received a telephone call from a doctor whom they had never met. The doctor gave his name and said that he had been in to see one of the patients on the nurse's ward earlier that day. The doctor said he would be back later but would like the patient to receive medication before he visits. The doctor asked the nurse to check the medicine cabinet to see if it contained the drug Astroten. The nurse checked the cabinet and found a box labelled:

ASTROTEN
5 mg capsules
Usual dose: 5 mg
Maximum daily dose: 10 mg

When she returned to the phone the doctor instructed the nurse to give the patient 20 milligrams of Astroten. He said he would be there in 10 minutes to sign the order but he would like the drug administered immediately. An observing staff doctor terminated the experiment after noting the nurse's behaviour.

The doctor's request violated several hospital rules. Not only was the amount prescribed twice the maximum daily dose, medical orders are not permitted by telephone. Furthermore, the medicine was not on the hospital's list of approved drugs and it was ordered by someone the nurse did not know. Nevertheless, 95 per cent of the nurses contacted started to administer the medicine.

Milgram's work has been repeated many times with many modifications. It has also been the subject of a television play called "The Tenth Level". Not only does his classic experiment reveal an important facet of human nature — behaviour that was not predictable even by a panel of psychiatrists — it also highlights the ethical issues involved in social psychological research. Milgram has received many awards for his work including a Guggenheim Fellowship and his obedience experiment won the Sociopsychological Prize of the American Association for the Advancement of Science in 1964. In 1983 he was elected to the American Academy of Arts and Sciences.

Further Reading

Asch, S. E., "Opinions and Social Pressures", *Scientific American, 193*, pp. 31–5, 1955.

Milgram, S., *Obedience to Authority*, Tavistock, London, Harper & Row, New York, 1974.

CHAPTER EIGHT

THY BROTHER'S KEEPER

In the early evening of January 13, 1982, a jet plane took off from Washington, D.C.'s National Airport on its way to Florida. The passengers were looking forward to their holiday in the sun; the winter in Washington had been particularly severe. Even as the vacationers boarded the flight, an icy rain fell on the city. Due to the bad weather, takeoff was delayed but eventually the Boeing 737 was hurtling down the runway. National Airport is located close to the city and planes must ascend quickly to avoid hitting nearby obstructions. Unfortunately, ice on the wings prevented the Florida-bound plane from gaining altitude quickly enough and it crashed into the nearby 14th Street Bridge. The plane plummeted through the ice of the frozen Potomac River coming to rest upside down at the bottom. Lenny Skutnick, an office worker and father of two, was on his way home from work when he saw the crash. By the time he reached the scene, rescue workers were already attempting to save the survivors. He saw that some victims were being flown to safety by rescue helicopters. But he noticed that one woman appeared to lack the strength to hold on to the rope lowered from the helicopter. Skutnick realised that the woman would surely drown if no one helped her. So, ignoring the jet fuel (which could easily ignite) and the floating chunks of ice, he jumped into the freezing river and held the woman afloat until she was rescued. Lenny later told newsmen that he knew "she was going to drown if I didn't go get her, because nobody else was going to".

Late one night in 1964 in the New York borough of Queens a woman named Kitty Genovese was attacked by a madman with a knife. She screamed and struggled as he stabbed her. Her screams were so loud she awakened many of the people living in the area. Lights were switched on in nearby windows as the residents peered out to see what was going on. Thirty-eight people were alerted by Kitty Genovese's cries and their lighted windows scared off her attacker. Kitty lay in the street, bleeding but not yet dead. Not one of the 38 witnesses offered her any help. Not one called the police. Instead, they all watched as the attacker fled and later returned to finish off his victim. All told, it took 30 minutes for Kitty Genovese to die and throughout this period not one of the 38 witnesses called the police or an ambulance. After she died, one witness finally called the police. But not before he called a friend living in another part of the city to seek advice.

These two news stories, one of heroism the other of shameful disregard, can be repeated many times over. In 1983 a teenage girl living in northern Australia jumped into a river in which a man she had never seen before was being devoured by a crocodile. The girl struggled with the animal and managed to pull the man free. In contrast, a boy was stabbed on a New York commuter train while 11 people watched. Although the assailant left the compartment immediately, none of the witnesses came to the boy's aid until after he had bled to death.

Why do some people risk their own safety to come to the aid of a victim in distress while others refuse to get involved? Can we characterise the variables that determine who will be helped and under what circumstances? These are the questions addressed in the classic experiment on "bystander intervention" to be described in this chapter.

ALTRUISM AND APATHY

The idea that people have been allowed to die by onlookers who fail to offer any aid is justifiably horrifying. For this reason such instances receive widespread publicity. The story of the boy stabbed on the train, for example, served as the basis for a feature film called *The Incident*. The Kitty Genovese story has been told in television shows, magazines, newspapers, a play and in a book written by the editor of the *New York Times*. Obviously the public is shocked and surprised when witnesses fail to help the victim of a crime. However, from a psychological viewpoint, altruistic behaviour — self-sacrifice for the benefit of others — is even more surprising.

Traditional psychological theories have a hard time explaining why anyone would risk death to save another. This is because most psychological theories assume that we are motivated solely by considerations of personal reward and punishment. Nevertheless, altruistic behaviour does seem to occur and psychologists have had to modify their theories to contend with such behaviour. Social psychologists have come up with two rather different explanations for altruism; sociobiologists have added a third.

Empathic sympathy

Psychologists have attempted to account for altruism within the traditional framework of rewards and punishments. They do this by postulating that altruism really is rewarding — but not directly. One psychological theory of altruism, for example, claims that the sight of someone in distress produces "empathic sympathy" in the observer; the observer actually suffers along with the victim. For this reason coming to the aid of another alleviates not just the victim's distress but also the observer's empathic suffering. According to this theory by helping victims we also help (reward) ourselves.

Adherence to a social norm

Another theory put forth by psychologists is that altruism results from a desire to "look good" in front of others. This theory holds that there is a "social norm" demanding that we help those in need. If we observe someone in distress and fail to help, we think less of ourselves and we fail to receive the social rewards granted to heroes. According to this explanation altruism results from a desire to avoid censure and gain social respect.

A genetic trait

A third possibility — the one favoured by sociobiologists — is that altruism is a basic human instinct. That is, like thirst, hunger and sex, altruism may be a biological drive. Certainly this appears to be the case in other species. For example, lookouts in marmot colonies (a marmot is a type of wild prairie dog) warn other colony members of the approach of a coyote by barking. In doing this, lookouts call attention to themselves; they put their own lives in danger to save others. Similarly some birds pretend to act injured when a predator is around in order to draw attackers to them and away from the young in the nest.

Although it is possible that altruism is a biological drive, it is strange that such a trait should survive through the generations. After all, self-sacrifice is clearly not adaptive for the individual involved.

From an evolutionary viewpoint altruism should eventually disappear because those who possess the trait die before they can pass it on. How, then, can altruism become part of a species' heredity if those who behave altruistically die while the others survive? The answer, according to sociobiologists, is that altruistic individuals share "altruistic" genes with their kin. Since relatives tend to live near one another, the performance of an altruistic act will save the lives of many kin who also possess altruistic genes. By sacrificing itself, the altruistic individual ensures that others who have genes for altruism are saved. In fact more altruistic genes may be saved than lost by the sacrifice of a single individual.

Since *species* with altruistic genes are better adapted to survive, the trait becomes established.

Are Current Theories Sufficient?

As you can see, the sociobiology argument is rather different from the two psychological explanations for altruism; it is based on what is good for the group (or species) rather than the individual. It also sees altruism as a positive behaviour — something done for its own sake, rather than as a behaviour designed to avoid empathic suffering or social censure. Nevertheless, it is difficult to say just how far the sociobiological explanation for altruism applies to human beings. We are all aware that human behaviour is strongly shaped by the environment and in practice it is often impossible to disengage environmental factors from biological ones. For example, are rescue workers who put their own lives at risk to save a child who falls down a disused water well demonstrating the influence of a biological trait, or are they adhering to a "social norm" that says we must help others in distress? Perhaps they empathise with the child and reduce their own suffering by rescuing him or maybe their behaviour results from all three factors. No-one knows. And no-one is likely to know until we develop much more complicated theories of altruism than any advanced so far.

The main problem with all three explanations for altruism is that they are designed to explain why altruism occurs. Not one offers any explanation for why it sometimes does not. Why, for instance, did no-one help Kitty Genovese? Did the witnesses fail to empathise with her plight? Was there no social norm operating? Were all of the onlookers short on altruistic genes?

A. M. Rosenthal, author of *Thirty-eight Witnesses*, a book about the Kitty Genovese incident, asked various experts to explain why no-one came to the woman's aid. Each expert gave a different explanation. One sociologist said the bystanders' behaviour was the result of a "disaster syndrome". Witnessing the killing "shook the safety and sureness of the individuals involved and caused psychological withdrawal from the event by ignoring it". A psychoanalyst assigned the witnesses' behaviour to "the megalopolis in which we live, which makes closeness very difficult and leads to the alienation of the individual from the group". A psychiatrist blamed television violence: "We underestimate the damage these accumulated images do to the brain ... they were deaf, paralysed, hypnotised with excitation." About the only recurring theme Rosenthal was able to identify was *alienation*. Everyone described the witnesses as "detached" and "apathetic".

Yet "apathetic" does not seem a very good word to describe the witnesses' behaviour. They did not simply look outside, observe the carnage, give a yawn and return to bed. They stared out their windows for 30 minutes, horrified yet unable to turn away. Moreover, the witnesses were quite distressed and frightened by what they saw. They may not have tried to help, but they were certainly not apathetic. The truth is the various experts quoted in *Thirty-eight Witnesses* had no idea why the onlookers failed to help. All they could offer were comforting bits of professional jargon and a few facile jabs at metropolitan life and television violence. If they were asked, these experts would have an equally difficult job explaining why Lenny Skutnick jumped in the Potomac to save a total stranger.

The problem is that most theories of altruism are too abstract to be of much use in understanding behaviour in particular situations. They identify some general factors determining whether one will act altruistically, but they ignore the specific circumstances that make each incident different. The identification of one of these specific situational influences was the aim of the classic experiment described next.

CLASSIC EXPERIMENT 11:

DIFFUSION OF RESPONSIBILITY

John Darley and Bibb Latané were both living in New York when Kitty Genovese was murdered. Darley, who had recently received his doctorate from Harvard University, was teaching at New York University and Latané had recently come to Columbia University after receiving his doctorate at the University of Minnesota. Both psychologists were still in their twenties at the time. They, like everyone else, were shocked by the behaviour of the witnesses but neither believed that the simple explanations offered (alienation, television violence, disaster syndromes and so on) really accounted for the witnesses' inaction. As experimental psychologists they attempted to find an answer in the psychology laboratory. They believed that the circumstances surrounding an incident are more important determinants of whether people will help than abstract factors such as "empathic sympathy", "social norms" or even "altruistic genes". In their classic experiment they were concerned with one aspect of emergency situations — the number of witnesses.

A great deal had been made of the number of people who watched Kitty Genovese's attack. Many experts argued that since 38 people witnessed the crime, at least one should have been expected to help. The unstated rule seems to be that there is "safety in numbers". The more people who observe an incident, the more likely the victim is to be helped. Darley and Latané challenged this view, arguing that a victim observed by just one bystander might actually be in a better position than one observed by many. Their reasoning went like this: when there is only one witness the responsibility to help clearly falls upon a single person (there is no-one else). On the other hand, when there are many witnesses no single individual may feel responsible. Darley and Latané called this phenomenon *diffusion of responsibility*. They claimed that diffusion of responsibility is the reason why motorists are actually more likely to get help if they break down on a deserted highway than on a busy street. In the first instance anyone who passes realises that if he does not help, no-one else will. On a crowded street, however, no single driver feels responsible. Instead responsibility is diffused among all passing motorists. Put simply, Darley and Latané hypothesised that one factor determining whether someone will help another is the extent of personal responsibility the witness feels.

FIG. 62. *Bibb Latané (1937–   )*

By-standers are more likely to help when they are alone than when they are among many witnesses.

Darley and Latané tested this hypothesis in a classic laboratory experiment. The subjects in the experiment were student volunteers, who found, upon their arrival in the laboratory, a long corridor with doors opening into several rooms. The experimenter escorted the volunteer into one of the rooms and seated him at a table. Each volunteer was asked to put on a set of headphones; no other equipment was used in the experiment. The experimenter left the room, carefully shutting the door.

Over the headphones the subject heard the experimenter explain that he was interested in the personal problems facing university students, especially those in a high-pressure urban environment. The headphones and microphone were described as a way to avoid embarrassment and maintain anonymity while still allowing subjects to talk about their personal problems. Instead of face-to-face conversations, subjects would communicate with one another over the headphones. The experimenter said that he would not listen to the discussion as this could prove inhibiting. Instead he would get their reactions later, by questionnaire. Since the experimenter was not going to listen, the subjects were told that some organisation would be required. Each person would speak in turn, followed by comments and a free discussion. Microphones were controlled by a switching device that gave each subject two minutes to talk. While one subject's microphone was on, all others would be off — only one subject could be "on the air" at any one time. Depending on the experimental condition, subjects were led to believe there were either two, three or six subjects taking part in the experiment. In reality there was only one real subject; all of the other student voices were merely tape-recordings. The real subject was the last to speak.

The first "person" to speak in the discussion admitted to finding New York City and his academic work hard to get used to. In an embarrassed voice this person described having epileptic seizures especially when working hard and around exams. All of the other "subjects" (including the real one) then contributed their two minutes each in turn. None of the others mentioned seizures. When it was the first person's turn to speak again, he made a few comments and then began to sputter incoherently:

I-er-um-I think I-I need-er-if-if could-er-er-somebody er-er . . . give me a little-er-give me a little help here because-er-I-er-I'm-er-er-h-h-having a-a-a real problem-er-right now and I-er-if somebody could help me out it would-it would-er-er s-s-sure be-sure be good . . . because-er-there-er-er-a cause I-er-I-uh-I've got a-a one of the-er-seiz-----er-er-things coming on and-and-and I could really-er-use some help so if somebody would-er-give me a little h-help-uh-er-er-er-er c-could somebody would-er-give me a little . . . [choking sounds] . . . I'm gonna die-er-er-I'm . . . gonna die-er-help-er-er-seizure-er [chokes then quiet].

The experimenters' interest was in observing whether the real subjects would leave their rooms in order to help the student they believed to be in distress. They also measured how long, from the start of the "seizure", it took for each subject to seek help. Those subjects who did leave their rooms encountered the experimenter seated at the end of the corridor and invariably went to him for help. If the subject reported nothing for six minutes the experiment was terminated.

All but two subjects were taken in by the deception. Most were nervous and agitated when they reported the seizure to the experimenter and surprised when they learned that it was really simulated. Many subjects also made comments out loud (when they thought their microphones were off) that indicated they believed the seizure was real. Even subjects who failed to help the victim later admitted to believing his seizure was real. Their trembling hands and sweaty palms suggested that many of these non-interveners were even more emotionally aroused than those who did seek help.

The main experimental manipulation was the number of "students" in each group. Recall that some subjects heard only one other person speak in the first round — the person who later had the seizure. Some subjects heard two other students speak and still others believed that they were one of six students having a conversation. The number of bystanders the subjects believed to be present exerted a strong effect on whether they sought help. Of those who thought they were the only witnesses to the seizure, every single subject reported the emergency. In fact most subjects in this condition sought help while the seizure was still being broadcasted. Their average time to respond was 52 seconds. Eighty-five per cent of the subjects who believed they were members of a three-person group reported the emergency in an average time of 93 seconds. Those in the "six-person" condition were much less likely to seek help. Only 62 per cent of these subjects sought assistance and their

average time to react was 166 seconds. Since all subjects were exposed to exactly the same emergency (they all heard the same tape), it seems clear that diffusion of responsibility occurred.

An interesting aspect of these findings is the relationship between the likelihood of offering aid and the speed with which it is offered. Not only were those who thought themselves members of a large group less likely to offer aid, they were also slower to respond. From the viewpoint of the subject, the probability of getting speedy help (within 45 seconds) was about 50 per cent in the single bystander condition and nil when there were five bystanders.

Darley and Latané's study was a dramatic illustration that behaviours like altruism are strongly affected by situational factors — in this case, the number of witnesses present. Victims received more help more rapidly when there was only a single bystander than when many were present. There was no evidence for apathy or alienation among the subjects in this study; those who failed to help the victim appeared as upset as those who did. Instead the presence of others diffused the responsibility to act among many people. Darley and Latané's results imply that one reason no-one helped Kitty Genovese is that the witnesses could see one another in their lighted windows. With 38 witnesses considerable diffusion of responsibility would have occurred.

Darley and Latané demonstrated that the common explanations for altruism are too abstract to account for behaviour in specific situations. Rather they showed that carefully controlled experiments can isolate those factors that determine whether someone will help in an emergency. Their original experiment was followed by many additional studies designed to identify other factors affecting altruistic behaviour. Some of these experiments are discussed in the next section.

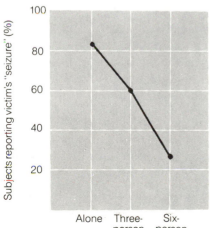

FIG. 63. *The probability that a subject will seek help in Darley and Latané's experiment decreased as the number of supposed group members increased. These results indicate that diffusion of responsibility occurred*

AFTERMATH

Darley and Latané eventually developed their own theory of the bystander intervention process. According to this theory there are five steps leading up to intervention:

1. A potential emergency must be observed.
2. The situation must be defined as an emergency.
3. The witness must accept responsibility for helping.
4. The witness must know how to help.
5. Help is offered.

The classic experiment provides information only about step 3. However, research has been conducted on several of the other steps as well. Most of this research has been concerned with steps 1 and 2.

Defining the Situation

Most emergencies begin ambiguously. The man you observe staggering in the street may be sick or he may be drunk. The white clouds you see coming from the window across the street could be smoke or simply steam from a hot shower. In both cases you have noticed a potential emergency (step 1) but you are not sure whether the emergency is real or imagined. Before you act — before you run to the man's aid or call the fire brigade — you must first define the situation as a true emergency (step 2). But how do you go about making such an interpretation? After all, emergencies occur very rarely and most of us have little experience in dealing with them. So where do you get the information to decide whether an emergency is in progress? According to Darley and Latané you get it from other people. That is, you look around to see what others are doing. If they remain untroubled, you assume that nothing is wrong.

A potential difficulty with relying on the reactions of others to help interpret whether an event is an emergency is that they may have no better idea than you. In fact they may be standing around waiting for *you* to do something. In such a situation a state of what has been called *pluralistic ignorance* can arise. Everyone misleads everyone else into doing nothing even when an emergency is occurring.

In one experiment dealing with interpreting emergencies, Latané and Darley had subjects sit in a small waiting room and fill out a questionnaire. Before long, smoke started to come out of a wall vent. Some subjects were alone in the room; others were in groups of three. The experimenters observed subjects' reactions through a one-way mirror. They found that 75 per cent of subjects tested alone reported the smoke within two minutes. Only 13 per cent of subjects tested in groups of three reported the smoke this rapidly. Even when the room was literally filled with smoke, few people in groups of three bothered to tell the experimenter what was going on. In a third experimental condition, subjects were placed in the waiting room with two confederates of the experimenter. These confederates were instructed to ignore the smoke and continue completing the questionnaire. Only 10 per cent of the subjects in this condition reported the smoke even after six minutes. When asked about their behaviour after the experiment, those who did not report the smoke explained that they had decided it was faulty air-conditioning, or steam or some other non-threatening phenomenon. It seemed that no-one wanted to appear foolish by complaining about a situation that may not have actually constituted an emergency. In this experiment subjects permitted bystanders to define whether or not the smoke constituted an emergency. The result was a state of pluralistic ignorance.

In another experiment conducted by Latané and Judith Rodin, subjects in a testing room heard a female experimenter (who was behind a curtain) climb on a chair to retrieve a book from a high shelf. They then heard the experimenter fall to the floor and groan: "Oh, my God — my foot ... I ... can't move it. Oh ... my ankle ... I can't get this thing off me." Her groans continued for another minute. The entire episode lasted about two minutes. This time there was no potential danger to the subjects themselves and there was no chance that they would appear cowardly if they went to the experimenter's aid. Despite these differences the results were similar to those of the "smoke-filled room" experiment. Nearly twice as many subjects helped when they were alone as when there were two witnesses to the "accident". Once again, when questioned after the experiment, those who did not offer help said they were not sure that a real emergency had taken place. As in the "smoke" experiment subjects were lulled into a sense of security by the calmness of others.

These studies, along with the classic experiment, seem to support at least the first three steps in Darley and Latané's theory. Before bystander intervention is possible the witness must first notice a potential emergency then interpret the situation as dangerous and take responsibility for acting. It follows, then, that if pluralistic ignorance and diffusion of responsibility can somehow be overcome, people will be more likely to help one another. An experiment conducted on the New York subway by psychologist Ira Piliavin and his associates 'was designed to assess the accuracy of this prediction.

Two male and two female experimenters boarded the subway separately. The two females took seats and recorded the results. The two men remained standing. As the train began to move one of the men lurched forward and collapsed. He lay on the floor, face upward, staring at the ceiling until someone came to his aid. If no-one helped, the other male experimenter

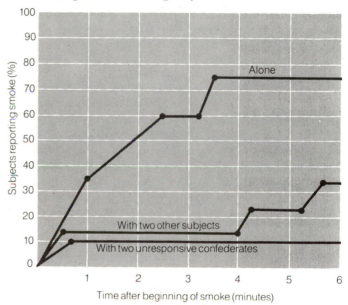

eventually helped the "victim" to his feet. Several variations of this incident were staged by the experimenters. Sometimes the victim carried a black cane and looked ill, sometimes he smelled of alcohol and carried a bottle of liquor in a brown paper bag. Sometimes the victim was white, other times black. The experimenters reasoned that: 1. every passenger in the car would observe the potential emergency (they would see the man fall down); 2. the situation would be interpreted as an emergency and 3. diffusion of responsibility would be minimal because the passengers would observe whether or not someone else intervened. In short, the experimenters predicted that people should help in this situation.

FIG. 64. *Percentage of subjects who reported smoke in Darley and Latané's experiment. Subjects were more likely to report the emergency when they were alone than when accompanied by two seemingly untroubled people*

The results supported their prediction. The victim carrying the cane received help 95 per cent of the time, usually within five seconds of falling. The "drunk" victim received help 50 per cent of the time in an average of 109 seconds. A possible reason for the different response rates was that witnesses may have considered the drunk victim "responsible" for his own plight whereas what was happening to the other person was clearly not his own fault. Bystanders may have also believed that helping the drunk involved greater cost (he could vomit on them or even turn aggressive) than helping the other victim. Both black and white victims were helped by black and white witnesses and there was no relationship between the number of bystanders and the speed with which help was offered. People helped just as often and just as fast on crowded as on nearly empty trains. Diffusion of responsibility had, it appeared, been minimised in this experiment probably because bystanders on the train could not simply walk away. They could not assume that "someone else will help" when they, in fact, could see that no-one had. (Even the witnesses to the train stabbing mentioned earlier eventually tried to help the victim.) This study offers considerable support to Darley and Latané's model of bystander intervention. The findings also suggested another factor that may influence altruistic behaviour — modelling someone else.

The experimenters noted that as soon as one person came to the victim's aid several others jumped up to help as well. This happened whether the victim was sick or drunk. This observation suggests that we not only rely on others to tell us when a situation is *not* an emergency (as in the "smoke-filled room" experiment) but also to show us when helping is required. The importance of a helping model was highlighted by an experiment in which the number of drivers who stopped to help a woman with a flat tyre served as the dependent variable. There were two conditions in the experiment. In the control condition only the woman and her car were on the road. In the experimental condition another car with a flat tyre was parked along the highway about half a kilometre before the woman's car. This first car was raised on a jack. A man was changing the flat tyre while a woman watched. Four thousand cars passed the second car during the course of the experiment. Ninety-three of these stopped to help the woman change her tyre. Of these, 35 stopped in the control condition and 58 stopped in the experimental condition. In other words, observing an appropriate "model" (in this case someone helping a woman change a tyre) almost doubled the number of people who stopped to help. These results confirm that we rely on others not only to tell us when not to act in an emergency but also when to stop and help.

The subway train experiment showed that a victim's appearance affects whether help is offered. The drunk is not helped as often or as quickly as the sick man carrying the cane. Researchers have also looked at other victim characteristics in order to determine whether these too determine who will be helped. One such characteristic is race. Although no difference was noted in the subway experiment between aid offered to black or white victims, other studies have found that race does exert an effect. In certain situations whites have been found to be more likely to come to the aid of whites than blacks. Another finding is that attractive victims are more likely to be helped than unattractive ones. Thus in addition to whether the victim is viewed as responsible for his or her plight, the victim's race and attractiveness also determine whether they will be helped. It is as if the observer calculates a complex cost and benefit equation before deciding to help. The costs of helping (self-blame, possible physical harm) are balanced against the benefits (praise, self-esteem) and even small things such as the victim's appearance can tip the balance one way or another.

The evidence presented so far applies to the first three steps of Darley and Latané's bystander intervention theory. But what about step 4? Are those who know *how* to help more likely to give help? The answer is yes. Training in what to do in an emergency prepares people to take action. People who take courses in cardiopulmonary resuscitation, for example, are more likely to help heart-attack victims than bystanders without this specialised knowledge. Even studying the experiments described in this chapter can make a difference. In one experiment students who had studied the research on bystander intervention and those who had never been exposed to these experiments were confronted with a simulated emergency while walking with an assistant of the experimenter. They encountered a male student unconscious on a hallway floor. The assistant did not react as if the situation was an emergency. Nevertheless, of those who had studied the research, 43 per cent offered help compared with only 25 per cent of those who had not studied the literature. Perhaps studying social psychology is one way to create good Samaritans.

One point that seems clear from all of these studies is that the stereotype of the alienated bystander, too apathetic to come to the aid of someone in danger, is not really accurate. Bystanders often will help, but whether they do depends on a combination of factors. They must observe a potential emergency, define the situation as an emergency requiring help, take responsibility for helping, know what to do and finally take action. At each of these steps bystanders are influenced by the number and actions of those around them as well as the characteristics of the victim.

These studies illustrate the social nature of much of our behaviour. Other people serve as an audience for what we do and we do not wish to appear foolish in front of them. Others also serve as guides for our behaviour. In ambiguous situations, when we do not know what is going on, we depend on the reactions of others to guide us. In addition, when many people are looking on, no single person takes full responsibility for acting. Darley and Latané's classic experiment was a major attempt to analyse an important behaviour — altruism — in a controlled laboratory experiment. Their research won the Sociopsychological Prize of the American Association for the Advancement of Science. However, an even more important indicator of its importance is the great number of additional experiments it has spawned. Even today it serves as a model of how important variables operating in social situations can be studied experimentally.

Further Reading

Latané, B. and Darley, J. M., *The Unresponsive Bystander: Why Doesn't He Help?*, Appleton-Century-Crofts, New York, 1970.
Rosenthal, A. M., *Thirty-eight Witnesses*, McGraw-Hill, New York, 1964.
Piliavin, I. M., Rodin, J. and Piliavin, J. A., "Good Samaritanism: An Underground Phenomenon?", *Journal of Personality and Social Psychology*, 13, pp. 289–99, 1969.

CHAPTER NINE

THE HAWTHORNE EFFECT

In 1898 a psychologist named Norman Triplett performed the very first social psychological experiment. Triplett had noted that bicycle racers made faster speeds when they raced against one another than when they raced individually against the clock. From this observation he developed the hypothesis that performance improves in competition with others. He tested this hypothesis in his laboratory by having children turn fishing reels. The children were asked to turn the reels as quickly as they could and he measured their speed. He found that when two children worked together (each with his own reel), their respective speeds exceeded either child's pace when working alone. Triplett's observation has been repeated many times since. The effect — enhanced performance when working competitively — has come to be called *social facilitation*.

More recent experiments have shown that competition is not the essential factor underlying social facilitation. Just having an audience can improve performance. The best example of this was an experiment conducted in primary-school classrooms by psychologist Robert Rosenthal. Randomly chosen children were singled out for observation by experimenters who periodically visited the class. Just being observed was found to improve the children's school performance.

The exact mechanism by which social facilitation operates is unknown. However, one thing is quite clear — its very existence presents a problem for social psychologists. If people change their behaviour simply because they are being observed, then the possibility exists that subjects in psychological experiments (who know they are being observed) may not be reacting in their normal manner. Social facilitation rather than the experimenter's manipulations may be responsible for any changes in behaviour. This means that social psychologists who design experiments to measure one variable may find that they are studying something quite different. This is exactly what happened in the classic experiments at Hawthorne.

THE EXPERIMENT THAT TRIGGERED
THE HAWTHORNE RESEARCH

Employee Relations

In the years preceding the Great Depression of the 1930s manufacturing industries grew at incredible rates throughout the industrialised world. Economies boomed throughout the 1920s and unemployment was relatively rare (but not unheard of). Although profits were healthy, little of this money actually filtered down to the workers. Wages were often barely above subsistence level.

What is more, working hours were long (50 hours per week was not uncommon) and conditions were harsh. Coffee breaks were unknown and worker exploitation was common. Workers were often forced to kick back part of their wages to their supervisors, they could be fired without notice (and without cause) and sexual exploitation of female employees was routine. There were few strong unions to protect workers in those days; the power was almost entirely with management.

Against this background the Western Electric Company's plant at Hawthorne, Chicago (known as the Hawthorne Works), was something of a model of industrial enlightenment. The plant was owned by the giant American Telephone and Telegraph Company and manufactured telephone equipment. Even in the 1920s the Hawthorne Works included an industrial relations branch which looked after all aspects of employee relations. The branch saw to it that workers were placed in jobs best suited to them. It arranged for extra training for those workers keen for advancement and it even undertook to advise employees about personal problems, education, health, advancement and savings. The company ran a stock participation plan in which employees could buy shares in the company; an insurance office was set up in the plant to advise workers on their insurance needs; a building society association was established to help employees buy homes; sickness, accident and death benefit plans were operated by the company; the company even ran a recreational and social programme.

While the Hawthorne Works could hardly be compared to some of the sweatshops operating early in this century, it should be made clear that its industrial relations policies were not entirely benevolent. Workers still could be dismissed without notice and any attempt to form a union was quashed rapidly. In fact many of the employee benefits were designed to keep workers happy and non-unionised.

Perhaps because of their appreciation of the "human element" in the workplace, Western Electric managers were anxious to involve the newly developing field of *industrial psychology* in their manufacturing plants. In 1924 the Hawthorne Works, in collaboration with the National Research Council, began a series of experiments on the factors influencing industrial output in their Chicago plant. These experiments were the beginning of a research programme that lasted until 1932.

The Illumination Experiments

Although psychologists began doing research in industry before the turn of the century, industrial psychology was hardly a burgeoning field even in the 1920s. Practically all of industrial psychology was concerned with the influence on worker output of the "physical" conditions prevailing at a factory. Indeed, most industrial psychologists were behaviourists who eschewed all motivational and social influences on the individual. They acted as if changes in the physical environment (number of rest pauses, amount of light, temperature, and so on) directly affected output. Workers were viewed as extensions of the machines they operated, mere cogs in a giant assembly line whose feelings, desires, needs and motives could be safely ignored.

It should not be surprising, therefore, that the National Research Council's industrial psychologists decided to investigate the effects of a physical variable — level of illumination — on productivity at the Hawthorne Works. The research began in 1924 with observations of workers in three departments, each engaged in different work. Without warning the workers, illumination in each of the three departments was progressively increased. The researchers expected all three groups of workers to increase their output with increased illumination. But things did not quite work out this way. Despite identical treatment, the three groups responded differently. In one department, illumination and productivity were totally unrelated. In the others, output sometimes increased and at other times did not. There seemed to be no consistent relationship between illumination changes and productivity.

The researchers worried that their results could be due to the different work being done in the three departments. They reasoned that some jobs might be more sensitive to light levels than others. So they decided to conduct a controlled experiment using workers from just one department. Two groups of workers were chosen so as to be about equal in experience. The first group was designated the control group. Control group workers continued to work in the conditions to which they were accustomed. The experimental group, however, worked under light intensities that were systematically varied. Sometimes the illumination was increased; at other times it was decreased. The results, however, were not quite what the experimenters expected. They did find that illumination increases led to increased productivity in the experimental group, but productivity also increased in the control group whose illumination level remained unchanged. Even more surprising was what happened when light levels were *decreased* in the experimental group. Their productivity continued to rise! Further manipulation of light levels only served to confirm these observations. Productivity continued to rise in both the experimental and control groups irrespective of whether illumination was increased, decreased or remained the same. The only way the researchers could actually produce a decrease in productivity was by reducing the level of illumination in the experimental group to the equivalent of moonlight!

The researchers were naturally perplexed by their results and undertook to repeat the experiment again with tighter controls over illumination levels. The results, however, were the same. Experimental groups working under increasing illumination increased their productivity, but so did the control group whose physical environment was unchanged. Even those workers who had their light levels decreased produced more. In short, no matter what the experimenters did to the light levels, productivity increased by the same amount in all groups.

From today's perspective, these findings can be viewed as constituting another demonstration of the influence of social facilitation. Somehow subjects chosen to participate in an experiment — who knew they were being observed — altered their behaviour. Even those in the control condition, who were working under the same physical conditions that they always worked under, improved their performance when they were being watched. However, there is a big difference between labelling a phenomenon "social facilitation" and explaining how it works. The researchers realised that their apparently contradictory results had to be caused by uncontrolled variables operating in the experiment. But they made no attempt to identify these variables or explain their findings. Instead, they recommended that more research be conducted. This recommendation was followed by psychologists from Harvard University who, along with their colleagues at Hawthorne, were responsible for the classic experiments described next.

CLASSIC EXPERIMENT 12:

SOCIAL RELATIONS AT WORK

The Hawthorne experiments were actually a collaborative effort, but their results were popularised by the leader of the research team, Elton Mayo. Mayo was born in 1881 in Adelaide, South Australia. He received his initial education in South Australia, graduating from the University of Adelaide in 1899. Mayo's academic career began at the University of Queensland in Brisbane where he lectured in philosophy and logic, eventually becoming a professor in 1919. Mayo emigrated to America in the 1920s. He first took up an academic post at the University of Pennsylvania and then moved to Harvard University in 1926. Mayo's appointment at Harvard was not in psychology but in industrial relations. He was appointed head of the newly formed department of industrial research in the Harvard Graduate School of Business Administration. The new department was largely funded by John D. Rockefeller Jr, a person Mayo came to know quite well.

Mayo's appointment to this new department indicated a shift in thinking in the field of industrial psychology. Unlike the typical industrial psychologist, Mayo was not nearly so interested in the physical conditions governing output as he was in the social relationships among workers, and between workers and their supervisors. Mayo had some research experience in industry but he was mainly known as an integrator of various social science areas. He had written on psychiatry, social psychology, anthropology and politics. Mayo viewed his new job as a way to apply social and clinical psychology in the workplace. His interest was in determining how the social and emotional needs of workers operate to affect productivity. He also believed that enlightened human relations in industry would increase industrial harmony and decrease worker–management conflict.

Mayo joined Harvard at the time the illumination experiments were being conducted at Hawthorne. These experiments ended the research collaboration between the National Research Council and Western Electric. In 1927 a new collaborative research programme began, this time between the Harvard industrial research group led by Mayo and the Hawthorne researchers. This

FIG. 65. *Elton Mayo (1881–1949) organised and directed the Hawthorne research*

research programme lasted six years; the outcome was what later became known as the "human relations" movement in industry.

Although the Hawthorne research programme actually consisted of several experiments as well as an attitude survey, most historical attention has been given to the first experiment which was concerned with worker fatigue. The experiment began as another attempt to investigate the effects of changes in the physical conditions of work on productivity. The main focus was on the effect of rest pauses and shorter working hours on worker output. The experiment was designed to eliminate (or control) those variables that the researchers believed may have confounded the results of the earlier illumination studies. To give but one example, the researchers chose employees whose rate of productivity was determined entirely by themselves rather than workers whose job involved interacting with a machine. The authors argued that in the illumination experiments, workers could have adjusted their pace to the machine's speed, thereby rendering themselves relatively insensitive to changes in illumination.

The experiment was named after the area of the plant in which it was conducted, the Relay Assembly Test Room. Six highly experienced female employees were recruited by asking two who were known to be friends to choose four others. Before the experiment began the workers received an explanation of the purpose of the research. They were asked not to strain to overproduce but to work as they normally would. Each change in the research project was similarly explained before it was introduced. The workers had the opportunity to make suggestions about proposed modifications and their ideas were often incorporated into the experimental procedures.

When the experiment began the workers were taken out of their nor-

mal departments and put in a special area separated from the rest of the department by a three-metre partition. This area was designated the Relay Assembly Test Room. The room was well lit and its temperature and humidity were carefully regulated. In addition the six employees were given regular medical check-ups.

The room contained an assembly bench at which five of the women sat assembling telephone relays. The sixth worker provided the others with a constant supply of parts. Constructing the relays required a fair degree of skill. Each relay consisted of a coil armature, contact springs, an insulator and many fasteners (35 parts in all) secured into a fixture with four screws. The workers chosen for the experiment produced about 500 relays each in an average day.

The experiment began in April 1927 and lasted for more than two years; it consisted of 13 periods. Period 1 actually occurred before the beginning of the experiment. For two weeks prior to the move to a separate room, and unknown to the women, a record had been kept of their productivity. This record was used as a baseline upon which to evaluate later changes in their output. During the experiment productivity was measured in two ways. First, an observer and several assistants were placed in the room and told to record "everything that happens". In addition, as each completed relay was dropped in a slot in the bench, a specially constructed mechanical device automatically kept a tally of each worker's productivity. During their first five weeks in the test room no changes in hours or rests were introduced. This provided the authors with another five weeks of baseline data and also told them whether just moving to a new room affected productivity. These five weeks constituted period 2.

At the end of period 2 a new method of incentive payment was in-

FIG. 66. *Operators working in the Relay Assembly Test Room*

troduced. Before moving to the test room the workers were paid according to the production level of their entire department. The six workers in the experiment, however, were taken off this pay system and were formed into a special group for pay purposes. This meant that their earnings would be more closely tied to their own, rather than the whole department's, productivity. This change in pay was period 3 of the experiment.

Following the introduction of the incentive payment scheme, rest pauses were introduced into the working day. Several different varieties of rest pauses were instituted. Each type was evaluated for a fixed period before the next type was tried. In sequence, the workers received:

Period 4. Two five-minute rest pauses (one in the morning and one in the afternoon).

Period 5. Two 10-minute rest pauses.

Period 6. Six five-minute rest pauses distributed throughout the day.

Period 7. The company provided snacks during a 15-minute morning break; a second 10-minute pause occurred in the afternoon.

Following these manipulations the investigators began to introduce variations in the length of the working day. Again, in sequence, the working day was changed so that:

Period 8. Work ended at 4.30 p.m. instead of 5 p.m.

Period 9. Work ended at 4 p.m.

Period 10. Work conditions reverted back to those of period 7.

Period 11. Saturday work was eliminated.

Period 12. Work conditions reverted back to those of period 3.

Period 13. Work conditions reverted back to those of period 7.

Although the various periods were not of equal length, no period, except for the original two-week base-line, lasted less than four weeks and many lasted for two or three months. Productivity data were examined for each of these 13 periods. In addition the workers were interviewed and their interpersonal behaviour at work was also recorded. As might be imagined, after more than two years of recording, the experimenters had collected a mountain of data. The experimenters chose to emphasise one aspect of their data — the one they found most surprising. This was that, with only small variations, productivity showed an almost unbroken rise from period 1 to period 13. The experimenters contended that no matter what the conditions prevailing in a period and despite the reversion to a longer working day in period 12, the women continued to increase the number of relays they produced. At the beginning of the experiment the women produced about 2400 relays in an average week. Two years later the average was 3000. Although periods 7, 10 and 13 had very similar working conditions (morning and afternoon breaks with a morning snack), the average output climbed from 2500 relays per week in period 7 to 2800 relays in period 10 and 3000 relays per week in period 13.

These results are quite similar to those obtained in the illumination experiments. Although the researchers hoped to demonstrate that productivity varies with changes in rest pauses and working hours, they found instead that productivity increased regardless of the manipulations they made. Once again, social facilitation appears to have occurred. But why? The workers themselves were asked why they produced more in the experimental context but they could not say. A partial answer came from the reports of the observers who monitored the experiment throughout the two years. They noted differences between the six workers in the experiment and other workers in the plant. For example, the six workers

rarely missed any days. Their absences from work were only one-third of the average for the plant as a whole. In addition their morale seemed higher. They also grew more friendly toward one another and saw each other socially after work. Not only did they begin meeting together for parties, they also pitched in to help anyone who became sick. Their socialising, their separation from other workers, the envy of the other workers and the experimenters' interest in them, created in the six women a feeling of being different and special. The researchers believed that it was this feeling of being part of a special group that led to increased productivity among the women rather than any changes in working conditions made by the experimenters. In Mayo's own words:

Undoubtedly, there had been a remarkable change in attitude in the group. This showed in their recurrent conferences with high executive authorities. At first shy and uneasy, silent and perhaps somewhat suspicious of the company's intention, later their attitude is marked by confidence and candor ... The group unquestionably develops a sense of participation in the critical determinations and becomes something of a social unit. The developing social unity is illustrated by the entertainment of each other in their respective homes ...

Mayo took the results of this experiment to support the notion that human relations are more important than physical conditions in determining productivity. He believed that the workers began to see themselves as a social unit. He interpreted the improvements in their productivity as the result of group cohesion and morale rather than as the result of changes in incentive payments, rest pauses or working hours. According to Mayo subgroups are formed because "the industrial worker wants ... first, a method of living in social relationship with other people" and "happiness and such sense of personal security as may be found in subordination of an individual to a common purpose".

Of course there is another possible explanation for the findings — one that does not depend on changes in morale but purely on the changed method of payment. Recall that workers in the experiment were taken off the usual pay system. Instead their pay was more closely tied to their own productivity. Thus it is possible that they produced more in the experiment simply because they realised that increased production led more or less directly to higher pay.

In order to determine just how important the wage system was in determining the experiment's results, the Hawthorne experimenters conducted a second study. Called the Second Relay Assembly Group study, this experiment was meant to serve as a control for some aspects of the first. Workers selected for this second experiment were seated next to one another in the regular relay assembly department. They were put on the same incentive payment system used in the first experiment, but except for this change they worked as they normally did. Not only were they not segregated into a separate room, they also received no special rest pauses nor any change in working hours. After nine weeks it seemed clear that productivity had risen among the workers placed on the new incentive pay system. Thus even without the development of group identities and even without changes in their physical environment, these workers increased their output. This productivity increase, which could only be due to the new pay scheme, amounted to about 13 per cent. This was substantial, but only half the gain in productivity observed in the original experiment. Thus the experimenters concluded that changes in the pay system alone could not account for the entire productivity improvement obtained in the first Relay Assembly Room experiment.

AFTERMATH

The results of the Hawthorne experiments or, more specifically, Mayo's interpretation of them, led to the development of human relations as an important research area not only for psychologists but also for industry. After Hawthorne, industrial psychologists could not continue to look upon workers as just a bundle of skills hooked onto the end of a machine. No longer was it possible to view workers as responding automatically to changes in physical conditions such as light, heat or rest. Instead the human relations movement forced managers and researchers to look upon workers as flesh-and-blood organisms with feelings and instincts, whose relationships with those around them influence how they behave.

The Hawthorne research programme did not end with the two experiments already described. There were further studies as well as a large-scale attitude survey designed to uncover employee attitudes toward management and their feelings about one another. Of this additional research the experiment that received the most attention is known today as the Bank Wiring Observation Room experiment. Actually this was not an experiment at all. There were no control groups and no true experimental manipulations. Instead the research consisted of the close monitoring of the performance of nine male workers. Like the workers in the Relay Assembly Test Room, the nine male workers were isolated from the others. Their task was wiring and soldering banks of terminals. Once again a baseline measure of productivity was taken. After this period the men were placed on a sophisticated wage-incentive system modelled on the one introduced in the Relay Assembly Room experiment. The system ensured that those who produced more would receive greater rewards.

Although the incentive pay system rewarded maximum individual productivity, the researchers found that workers failed to maximise their output. Instead productivity changed very little from week to week and from person to person. When questioned about their performance, the workers in the Bank Wiring Observation Room made it clear that they believed that wiring two banks (6000 terminals) constituted a "fair day's work". This view was so widely held that instead of maximising their output, the workers adjusted their reported productivity to conform with this group "norm". Thus when reporting their productivity some workers overestimated what they had done, others underestimated. The effect was to keep the average output at two banks per day. When the experimenters analysed the actual production data — rather than the output reported by the workers — they found that only three of the nine men consistently produced as much as they claimed. The others misrepresented their productivity.

The experimenters concluded on the basis of their observations and interviews with the workers that the group was operating well below its capability in order to protect itself. The workers feared that increasing their output could lead to a cut in the incentive rate (the pay per bank) or an increase in their expected daily output. Some believed that greater productivity could lead to layoffs, especially of the slower workers. To avoid these consequences the group established a productivity norm — not too low or too high — and then made sure that their reports reflected this norm. The group developed rules of conduct: do not be a rate buster (turn out too much work); do not be a chiseler (produce too little); and do not turn in any of your fellow workers. Those who did not adhere to these norms were ostracised, ridiculed or even, on occasion, physically assaulted.

Partly because of the Hawthorne experiments the development of group norms has become an important area of research in social psychology. We now know that social interactions almost always take place in the light of group norms. These norms are consensual agreements about how to act in particular situations and may be explicit (No Parking, No Smoking, No Talking) or they can be unspoken (wait for everyone to be served before eating). The influence of social norms is particularly noticeable when you visit another culture in which norms are different. For example, in some societies it is considered a sign of politeness to burp loudly after a good meal; this shows the host that you appreciate the cooking.

Of course we do not and we cannot follow all of the norms established in a society. Instead we tend to have reference groups with whom we identify. Sailors who identify with their reference group get themselves tattooed; executives following their reference group's norm wear pinstriped suits. Social reference groups serve to guide their members' behaviour while at the same time providing them with a social identity. This sort of reference group identification is what Mayo and his colleagues believed was going on at Hawthorne. Productivity, they believed, was governed not solely by economic interests or by physical working conditions but by the social relationships among workers and between workers and supervisors. Mayo believed that when human relationships were taken into account, management and workers could cooperate in their common interest.

The Hawthorne research made Elton Mayo famous. He used the Hawthorne data as the basis for three books on the problems of industrial civilisation: *The Human Problems of an Industrial Civilization, The Social Problems of an Industrial Civilization*, and *The Political Problems of an Industrial Civilization*. He received honorary degrees including one from Harvard and was elected a Fellow of the American Academy of Arts and Sciences. He retired from Harvard in 1947 and moved with his family to England where he died in 1949.

Although Mayo's fame was great, the Hawthorne experiments were not without their critics. Almost from the beginning the research was the focus of intense controversy. Most of this criticism was aimed at Mayo's interpretations. A common theme among his critics was that Mayo underestimated the extent of the conflict between workers and management. Mayo's belief that with the right sort of human relations policy workers and management would work together toward common goals was portrayed as naive. Critics, particularly those with Marxist views, saw the conflict between workers and management as inextricably built into the capitalist system. This conflict, they argued, cannot be eliminated simply by cosmetic changes in supervisory style. Mayo was also accused of being anti-union and pro-management and of treating workers as simple-minded people who could be easily "taken in" by trivial changes in management techniques.

These criticisms are not entirely unfounded. There were no unions at Hawthorne when the experiments were conducted and Mayo did not believe any were necessary. He did seem to identify with management and sometimes described worker behaviour as "irrational". Perhaps even more important than criticisms of Mayo's interpretations were attacks on the Hawthorne experiments' methodology. It is true that none of the experiments was tightly controlled. It is also true that changes outside the plant (the Depression began and deepened while the studies were in progress) could have affected the experiments' results.

Even more troubling was Mayo's habit of playing down the weak points in his data. For example, in the first Relay Assembly Test Room experiment Mayo reports that two of the workers "dropped out" and had to be replaced. More extensive reports of the experiment by Mayo's colleagues suggest that the two dropped workers were not cooperating. If these workers were replaced by two more cooperative ones, then it could be argued that the results of the experiment (continued productivity increases) were rigged by choosing workers whom the experimenters knew would respond in the desired fashion. There is even some doubt about Mayo's presentation of the results themselves. For example, in period 12 when workers in the Relay Assembly Test Room had their working day revert from the shorter hours back to the longer work week — hourly productivity actually fell. Instead of interpreting this fall as a reaction to the lengthened work week, Mayo chose to emphasise that weekly productivity continued to increase. What he neglected to point out was that this increase was the result of working longer days rather than a rise in hourly productivity.

Another example of Mayo's tendency to ignore data pointing toward alternative explanations for his findings is his treatment of the Bank Wiring Observation Room experiment. The nine men working in the Bank Wiring Room were observed during a period of great economic uncertainty. During the course of the experiment the men were put on progressively shorter hours. After a few weeks their work week was actually reduced to four days. Before they could adjust to this the hours were reduced further and the men were working only alternating weeks. Finally, the whole study had to be terminated because there was no work for the men to do. Surely such cutbacks in work (not to mention wages) could have motivated the men to try saving their jobs by restricting their output. Yet this possibility was never seriously considered by Mayo.

The Hawthorne experiments remain controversial; critiques and defences still appear in the psychology literature more than 50 years after the experiments were conducted. Although many textbooks describe the Hawthorne experiments as unqualified proof that human relations are more potent influences on productivity than economic incentives or physical working conditions, most careful readers agree that Mayo and his colleagues exaggerated their findings and ignored contradictory data. Although their precise interpretation will probably always remain in doubt, the original illumination experiments and the subsequent Hawthorne experiments do make one very important point. Observing people in social psychology experiments can change the way they behave. This phenomenon is so closely associated with the Hawthorne experiments that it is today universally known as the *Hawthorne Effect*.

Further Reading

Landsberger, H. A., *Hawthorne Revisited*, Cornell University Press, Ithaca, New York, 1958.

Mayo, E., *The Human Problems of an Industrial Civilization* (second edition), Macmillan, New York, 1946.

Roethlisberger, F. J., Dickson, W. J. and Wright, H. A., *Management and the Worker*, Harvard University Press, Cambridge, Massachusetts, 1950.

PART 4

Critical Periods in Development

The old saying "The child is father to the man", expresses exactly why psychologists study child development. Of course our behaviours and thought processes do not stop changing when we leave childhood; development continues throughout the lifespan. But most psychological research efforts have been directed at the changes occurring in early childhood. This is understandable when we consider just how important the childhood years are for human beings. Of all mammals, humans are the most immature at birth. While some are able to move around almost immediately (horses, for example), human infants are incapable of any locomotion. Humans are slow developers even when compared with their close relatives the primates. Some species of newborn monkeys are on their own only a few weeks after birth, others fend for themselves after a few months. Human infants, on the other hand, are dependent on care-givers for many years before they become self-sufficient.

Developmental psychologists look for age-related changes in behaviour. They are concerned with when specific psychological skills and personality characteristics, such as talking, walking and trusting others, appear. Although interesting in itself, this information also has practical value. Educators who wish to know the best time to introduce certain topics to children, and parents looking for child-rearing advice often rely on data provided by developmental psychologists. In addition clinical psychologists who work with children depend on the results of developmental research to decide whether a child's behaviour is abnormal. This is necessary because many behaviours that are perfectly normal at one developmental stage indicate an emotional problem if present in children at another stage of development.

At first glance it may appear that the work of developmental psychologists is rather easy. As children grow older they gradually get bigger, heavier, better coordinated and perhaps more intelligent. All the psychologist must do is observe these changes and record them. A closer look, however, reveals that the process is not nearly so simple. For example, some of the changes that occur over time are mainly the result of biological factors while others depend on certain environmental experiences. A third group of developmental changes does not fit into either category; these result from biology and experience working together.

Biologically governed development is usually called *maturation*, a term that refers to the biological "unfolding" of the organism under genetic guidance. Sitting up, holding the head upright and walking are examples of maturational development. Although no-one denies that development contains a maturational element, psychologists have been more concerned with the role of experience. They argue that most human abilities (the ability to do long division, swim, read, write poetry) and most psychological problems result not from maturation but from certain critical learning experiences.

Although the distinction between maturation and experience is often made in theoretical discussions, it is not always easy to apply in practice. For example, all around the world children learn to speak their first words at about the same age. Some psychologists have taken this as evidence that language acquisition is a maturational process. However, children in various parts of the world do not learn to speak the same words. Our biological inheritance may give us the capacity to learn a language, but the particular language we learn depends on our experience. Most psychological traits are like language; they represent the interaction of maturation and experience.

Determining the relative contributions of maturation and experience to behaviour is one of the primary tasks of developmental psychology. It is also a matter of considerable controversy. Some psychologists emphasise maturation, others focus on experience. Another related controversy concerns whether development proceeds continuously or whether children move through discrete developmental stages. We are all aware that children grow gradually taller and heavier. Some psychologists have assumed that behavioural development, like physical development, is also continuous. There are other psychologists, however, who do not see development this way. Instead they view it as a series of leaps from one discontinuous stage to another. The stages they have in mind differ from the informal "stages" referred to by parents (the "terrible twos", "teenage rebellion" and so on). Psychological stages revolve around a single theme and each stage differs qualitatively, not just quantitatively, from previous stages. What is more, all children are thought to pass through these stages in the same order. This last point is particularly important. Stage theorists believe that sequence is crucial. A child cannot achieve a later stage without first passing through an earlier one.

The chapters in Part 4 are each concerned with a different developmental issue. Chapter Ten shows how research on animal behaviour illuminates the interaction between maturation and experience. The importance of discontinuous developmental stages is illustrated in Chapter Eleven. Chapter Twelve deals with the influence of one psychological trait — intelligence — across the entire lifespan.

IMPRINTING

Psychologists have always used animals in their investigations. For most of this century dogs, cats, monkeys and that old standby, the laboratory rat, have been the subjects of endless experiments designed to reveal the connections between stimuli (lights, sounds, tastes) and responses (pressing a bar, jumping across a wall). In fact for many years a rat negotiating its way through a maze was most people's idea of psychological research. The aim of these animal experiments was to reveal the "units" of behaviour — the smallest elements from which all complex behaviours are supposed to arise. What all these experiments had in common was a complete disregard for how animals behave in their natural habitats. It was assumed that the essentials of behaviour were the same in the laboratory and in the field. Thanks to the work of ethologists we now know that this assumption is completely false. In this chapter, research by the father of ethology, Konrad Lorenz, is described. Although the subjects of his investigations were animals, his results had a profound effect on virtually all branches of human psychology.

BEHAVIOUR AND EVOLUTION

Prior to the eighteenth century, studying animals in their natural environment was a matter for amateurs, mainly British, with an interest in nature. These students of animal behaviour were called "natural historians". Their ranks included country squires who liked to watch birds while taking their morning stroll, clergymen with an eye for nature, doctors, and Victorian gentlemen with time on their hands. Although they were amateurs much of the work published by the natural historians was of a high standard. Indeed, by the 1850s sufficient observations had been made to permit two men to propose the theory of evolution. After that the experts moved in and nothing was ever the same.

Darwin and Wallace

Evolution by natural selection is a theory that was independently formulated by two men, Charles Darwin and Alfred Russel Wallace. Both had little scientific training (Darwin spent two years at medical school; Wallace was trained as a surveyor). When he was in his twenties Darwin accepted the unpaid post of naturalist aboard a ship called the *Beagle*, which was commissioned by the British Admiralty to survey the South American coastline. During the course of this trip Darwin's interest in botany and zoology grew from scholarly curiosity into an obsession. As a result of his observations on the *Beagle* Darwin concluded that, contrary to most thinking, the various species are not unchangeable. He came to believe that the species change over time, particularly when isolated from others. Unfortunately Darwin had no idea how and why such changes occur. After mulling it over for several years, he hit on an explanation. But he realised that his ideas would shock Victorian society and he was therefore reluctant to publish. So although he wrote a description of his theory, he put it aside where no-one could read it. He left instructions with his wife to have the manuscript describing his ideas published after his death and even left a sum of money for that purpose. And that is how history might have been if it were not for Alfred Wallace.

FIG. 67. *Charles Darwin (1809–82)*

FIG. 68. *Alfred R. Wallace (1823–1913)*

Wallace's work as a surveyor kept him outdoors where he could indulge his interest in plants, animals and insects. While surveying the Welsh countryside for the expanding railroads, Wallace collected all types of specimens. Eventually he gave up surveying to become a full-time "naturalist", supporting himself by selling his findings to museums and collectors. Like Darwin, Wallace also visited South America and, again like Darwin, he was struck by the wide diversity of nature. He also visited other parts of the world and by 1855 had published an essay arguing that the species were not immutable. Wallace sought an explanation for nature's diversity and eventually came up with one — natural selection. He argued that organisms best adapted to their environment survived to pass on their abilities to their offspring. The variability in nature ensured that those not adapted to their conditions were weeded out while the most fit survived to continue their species. This principle he called "survival of the fittest". He sent a paper describing his ideas to Darwin who he knew was interested in such matters. Darwin was stunned. Wallace's theory was the same as his. Darwin could no longer delay publication if he wanted any credit, so he went public. The result was the most important scientific book of the nineteenth century, *The Origin of Species*.

Evolution and Psychology

With the powerful explanatory tool provided by Darwin and Wallace, evolutionary biologists started the work of explaining why animals are built the way they are. For humans the questions addressed included why we walk on two legs rather than four, why our eyes point forward rather than sideways and why we can touch our thumbs to our forefingers while no other animal can. As can be seen, the emphasis was on anatomical structure — how our bodies are shaped by evolutionary pressure. Relatively little attention was given to behaviour. Yet Darwin himself argued that behavioural routines are as important as anatomical structure in determining who will survive. Examples of adaptive behavioural routines can be multiplied indefinitely. Birds who build nests, squirrels who bury nuts, salmon who return to the streams from which they were spawned, all have an edge on those who do not possess these behaviours. Darwin believed that adaptive behaviour patterns like adaptive anatomical traits are naturally selected and passed on from one generation to the next.

Although animals were common subjects in psychological experiments, few psychologists actively attempted to verify Darwin's theory. Most psychological experiments focused on reflexes — simple stimulus–response relationships, usually involving only a single muscle group. For example, a puff of air directed at the eye will cause a blink reflex, a hammer tap below the knee causes a knee-jerk. Even those psychologists interested in the genetics of behaviour failed to take an evolutionary perspective. For example, in one now legendary experiment, rats were tested in laboratory mazes in order to discover which ones were clever maze-runners and which made many errors. The bright rats were mated with one another and the dull ones likewise. Their offspring were also tested in the maze and selectively bred. This went on for seven generations until two quite distinctive strains were created — maze-bright and maze-dull rats. The experimenters had shown that at least part of the ability to run through a maze is genetic. But mating in this experiment was controlled by the experimenter. Thus it shed little light on how intelligence is inherited in the natural environment where there are no mazes and mating partners are chosen by the rats themselves.

Studying animals in their natural habitats was left to the new science of ethology which began to develop in Europe during the latter part of the nineteenth century. The ethologists were interested in animal behaviour but they rejected the artificial laboratory methods of experimental psychologists. They believed that the best way to study animals was to observe them in the wild, but they differed from the natural historians who preceded them by insisting that observations not be haphazard. The ethologists applied rigorous standards to their work and were also not averse to interfering with nature if it meant clarifying how a particular process worked. Where the ethologists differed from the psychologists was in the type of interference they engaged in. Instead of removing animals from their natural worlds into the caged artificiality of the laboratory, the ethologists performed their experiments in the wild.

The major discovery of the early ethologists has come to be known as the *fixed-action pattern*. These are complex behavioural sequences that seem to be triggered by specific environmental stimuli. Fixed-action patterns are obviously related to the reflexes studied by the early experimental psychologists. For one thing, both reflexes and fixed-action patterns are innate; the organism need not learn them. Also members of a species who are separated from others at birth exhibit the same reflexes and fixed-action patterns as normally reared animals when put into appropriate situations. Finally, both reflexes and fixed-action patterns are inflexible. Faced with the appropriate triggering stimuli, an animal cannot prevent either a reflex or a fixed-action pattern from occurring. While reflexes and fixed-action patterns share some similarities, there are some important differences between the two concepts. For instance, fixed-action patterns are more complicated than reflexes. Instead of a single muscle group, they involve many muscles and body parts. An even more important difference is that fixed-action patterns almost always play a role in social behaviour and the survival of the species.

An example of a fixed-action pattern is the threat one bird makes against another who enters its territory. These threats take the form of special noises, a display of feathers and sometimes even a pecking attack. The English male robin, for example, will engage in such threatening behaviour when confronted with another male. These threats usually drive away the intruder, thereby limiting mating and reducing the number of young in the territory. The result is more food for the babies in the nest and a greater chance they will survive. The adaptive value of the robin's threatening behaviour is clear, but what causes it? The easy answer is the sight of another male. But this is not really adequate as it does not say how other males are recognised. Ethologists have found the answer to this question by conducting experiments in which robins are presented with various dummy birds each differing from real male robins in one crucial feature. The idea is to see which characteristics of the male are most important in giving rise to threatening behaviour. The crucial feature actually is the bird's red breast. Even a bundle of red feathers elicits threatening behaviour from male robins, while a full model of a male robin accurate in every detail except the red breast produces no threats at all.

Ethologists call the stimulus that sets off a fixed-action pattern a *releaser* or *sign stimulus*. In the case of a robin defending its nest, the sign stimulus is the red feathers on the invader's breast. Many examples of natural sign stimuli have been recorded over the years. Nikolaas Tinbergen, a famous ethologist who won the Nobel Prize for his work, studied a fish called the three-spined stickleback. This fish, like the robin, has a territory that it defends from other males especially during mating season. It savagely attacks any encroaching males. The invading stickleback begins its attack by turning upside down and showing its red belly to the male defender. Tinbergen constructed various stickleback models in order to demonstrate that the red belly is the sign stimulus triggering the defending stickleback's attack.

Sign stimuli are not always colours of course. Odours and sounds can also be releasers. Sexual activity may be elicited by odours produced by females in heat and hens come to the aid of their young in response to their calls of distress. Sign stimuli need not even be discrete; they can be relational. For example, young thrush birds respond to the return of their parents to the nest by widely opening their mouths. The sign stimulus for this behaviour appears to be the parent's head, but how is the head recognised? In fact the baby birds will perform the same fixed-action pattern when a wooden knob appears overhead, provided it is attached to another larger knob. Any size knobs will work so long as one is bigger than the other. The relationship between the two knobs rather than the absolute size of one knob alone appears to be the releaser of the behaviour. To take another example, plovers recognise their eggs because of the contrast between the dark-brown spots and lighter background on the egg's surface. This was demonstrated by confronting the birds with eggs on which black spots had been painted. The plover preferred these eggs to the real thing. It appears the contrast between the spots and the background releases nesting behaviours in plovers. Heightening this contrast makes the plover prefer artificial to real eggs.

Sometimes the relationship between sign stimuli and fixed-action patterns can get quite complicated. For example, when birds reach puberty they tend to migrate to a breeding area. Although such birds are able to reproduce, they will not do so unless their hormonal systems are exposed to certain environmental releasers. First the male bird must establish a territory, but he will not do this unless he has an exceptionally high blood level of the sex hormone testosterone. And social sign signals cause testosterone to increase in male birds in the first place — the presence of a female raises male testosterone levels as, does the presence of a rival male. In a reciprocal fashion the presence of a male is the sign stimulus for sexual development in the female. Just playing a recording of male songs to a female canary accelerates ovarian development, increases blood levels of sex hormones and elicits nesting activity. Similarly the presence of a sexually active female increases testicular development in males. Even the weather exerts an effect. Fine weather and longer days serve as a signal for mating to occur. An unusually cold or rainy spring reduces hormone levels and, as a consequence, reproduction. The combination of signs and fixed-action patterns is finely balanced to ensure that breeding takes place and the species survives.

The discovery of fixed-action patterns and their releasers was the main activity of the early ethologists and to a large extent this remains true today. The idea that such patterns exist and that they are passed on from generation to generation propelled by evolutionary forces particularly fascinated Konrad Lorenz, whose classic experiments are the main focus of this chapter.

KONRAD LORENZ AND THE BIRTH OF ETHOLOGY

Konrad Lorenz was born in 1903 and spent his childhood in a small village not far from Vienna, Austria. Lorenz's father was a well-known, wealthy orthopaedic surgeon who hoped that his son would follow him in a medical career. The young Lorenz was very fond of animals and, encouraged by his parents, kept many pets. In addition to dogs Lorenz kept ducks, fish and a whole colony of jackdaw birds in the attic of the family home. The Danube River was close to the Lorenz residence; it provided another habitat for the youngster to observe wildlife in a natural environment.

In 1922, because of the encouragement of his father, Lorenz left Austria for New York to study at Columbia University. However, Konrad Lorenz did not care for New York and his stay was very short. Upon returning home he entered the medical course at the University of Vienna. Although he received a medical degree in 1927 Lorenz was more interested in science than in being a doctor. While a student at the University of Vienna Lorenz published his first scientific paper; it contained his observations of the jackdaws he had kept in the attic of his father's house.

After completing his medical course Lorenz took a position as assistant in the department of anatomy at the university. It was while holding this position that Lorenz came under the influence of one of the first ethologists, Oscar Heinroth. Not only did Heinroth teach Lorenz a great deal about animal behaviour and scientific method, he also showed him that it was possible to make a career out of doing what he most liked — observing animals. During the next few years Lorenz became increasingly interested in applying rigorous methods to the study of animal behaviour. He received a doctorate in zoology in 1933 and took a position as lecturer in comparative anatomy and animal psychology. During the 1930s Lorenz and his wife, Margarethe Gebhardt, bought a boat which they launched in the Danube. This boat was the scene of many of his naturalistic observations.

FIG. 69. *Konrad Lorenz (1903–   ), pioneer ethologist*

Lorenz's life of research and contemplation was drastically altered by the Second World War. He served as a doctor in the German army both in Poland and in other parts of eastern Europe until he was captured by the advancing Russian army. Lorenz was held prisoner for three years; he was finally released in 1948. It was difficult for him to pick up the pieces of his work after the war, but he pressed on and worked from the old family home. When an institute for ethological research was established in the 1950s, Lorenz naturally became involved. In 1961 he was appointed director of this institute — the Max Planck Institute for Physiology of Behaviour. He held this post until his retirement in 1973.

Lorenz has been an active researcher all his life and even today he continues to write on ethological subjects. The work for which he is most famous, however, took place in the 1930s. Included in this work is the classic experiment described next.

CLASSIC EXPERIMENT 13:

IMPRINTING

As already noted, Darwin believed that behavioural routines that help organisms to survive are naturally selected and inherited in the same way as anatomical traits. The early ethologists confirmed this belief with their discovery of fixed-action patterns. These patterns appear to be inherited as integrated wholes. The organism need only be exposed to the proper sign stimulus to set one off. Action patterns are so automatic and inflexible that animals can be made to appear stupid simply by altering the environment. Thus robins will threaten a bunch of red feathers and male sticklebacks will attack wooden fish models with painted bellies.

Proving that fixed-action patterns are innate requires that animals be reared in isolation, away from others of their species. In this way they are never exposed to the particular behaviour in question. If such animals, when confronted with a sign stimulus, still perform the fixed-action pattern, they must have inherited the behaviour because they have never been given the opportunity to learn it. Numerous experiments with isolated animals have shown that fixed-action patterns are inherited. A striking example is the behaviour of common North American squirrels. Squirrels raised alone and given a nut for the first time go through the entire act of burying it although they have never seen another squirrel do so. What is more, squirrels perform the burying sequence even if placed on a bare floor. They scratch at the floor as if they are digging in the earth, they push down on the nut with their nose as if trying to force it into the ground and they move their arms about in the air as if covering the

nut with dirt. The entire sequence occurs even though the nut is just as visible afterwards as it was before they began. Nothing could better demonstrate the innate and automatic nature of fixed-action patterns.

Although it seems beyond doubt that fixed-action patterns are inherited, an interesting question is whether the triggering power of sign stimuli is also innate. This question relates back to the broader concern that psychologists have always had about the relative role of maturation and experience in development. Early in this century scientists were divided into two camps on this issue. The first argued that fixed-action sequences and their specific releasing stimuli are inherited together; a genetic package. Holders of the opposing view believed fixed-action sequences and their releasing stimuli to be two different things. Those who held this latter view argued that fixed-action sequences are innate while the sign stimuli triggering them are determined by early experience. The answer to this question comes from Konrad Lorenz's experiments on how young animals recognise other members of their species.

All social behaviour depends on the ability of individuals to recognise others of their own kind. There are often many different species of animals living in close proximity (think of the number of different birds found in any one region) yet the various species appear to have little difficulty determining who belongs with whom. This is beneficial because otherwise animals would not know who to mate with and which young to care for. They might even make approaches to dangerous strangers.

Deciding who is a member of one's species and who is not clearly involves being able to discriminate between similar animals on the basis of their physical and behavioural characteristics. Birds, for example, may be able to tell one another apart by their colours, shape or songs. The best way to determine which characteristics are being used to identify other members of a species is to perform isolation experiments in which offspring are reared apart from other members of their species.

Lorenz's mentor, Oskar Heinroth, performed such experiments with several species of birds. He found that some birds rush away from humans almost immediately after hatching. These birds seem to be born with an innate "image" of what an adult looks like, and it is nothing like a human. The newborns automatically follow after adult birds of their own species, but no-one else.

Although these results seem to indicate that a specific sign stimulus (adult birds, in this case) and fixed-action pattern (following), are inherited together, other experiments have found something quite different. When Heinroth raised greylag geese apart from other members of their species, the newborns were not afraid of humans. In fact they followed after

people in much the same way as geese normally follow behind their mothers and fathers. This finding was just the opposite of his earlier one. The fixed-action pattern (following others) is the same, but the specific sign stimulus that triggers it does not seem to be fixed by heredity. In goslings, at least, following behaviour can be released by humans instead of adult geese provided the newborns are reared by humans. Interestingly, when Heinroth's isolated geese matured they did not mate with other

FIG. 70. *Species often flock in near one another. Social behaviour and survival require that they be able to tell one another apart*

FIG. 71. *Virtually all birds have a fixed-action behavioural pattern that ensures they follow their mothers*

152

geese. Instead they made sexual advances to humans. It seemed that whatever determines who a baby goose will follow also determines appropriate targets for sexual advances.

Lorenz's experiments extended Heinroth's observations in two important ways. First, it showed that timing is crucial in establishing a sign stimulus for following. Second, it showed that movement is important.

Lorenz raised several species of baby birds shielding them from seeing other birds or humans for varying periods. In this way he was able to demonstrate the existence of certain "critical periods" in a young bird's life. If the bird is not exposed to any model during this critical period (the first two days after hatching in goslings), it will not learn to follow anyone. If, on the other hand, the young bird is exposed to a suitable model during the critical period, it will follow that model. Only a brief exposure — 10 minutes is enough — and a sign stimulus will be established; once established it will last for life. Because it occurs so quickly the process of creating a sign stimulus for following is known as *imprinting*. The imprinted animal will always "recognise" the model (and similar creatures) as members of the same species; imprinting can neither be changed nor forgotten.

In addition to timing Lorenz also showed that movement is important. Lorenz exposed isolated greylag goslings to various models during their critical period for imprinting. He found that the baby geese would only follow a model that was bigger than they were and moving. In the natural environment the first large moving object baby geese see is their mother. Normally they imprint on her and follow her around until they are old enough to go off on their own. Thus in their normal habitat goslings follow and recognise members of their own species. In Lorenz's artificial situation the first moving object the goslings saw was controlled by the experimenter; it could be anything from a human being to a motorised wooden decoy. The actual model does not matter. So long as it is the first large moving object the gosling sees, imprinting will occur and last throughout life. Geese imprinted on humans and returned to their natural broods refuse to stay with their parents and run back to the imprinted human or

FIG. 72. *"Mother" Lorenz became the stimulus for following behaviour*

any other human that happens to pass by. When they mature, they will not mate with other geese.

Lorenz followed up his original imprinting experiments with a classic experiment on the jackdaws living in the attic of the family home outside Vienna. One jackdaw was reared in isolation from the others. It knew only its human caretakers. Then, in a series of exposures, the jackdaw was introduced to crows and finally, other jackdaws. The idea behind this experiment was to find out whether different sign stimuli could be established for different fixed-action patterns by selectively exposing the bird to others during the critical periods for imprinting.

One of a jackdaw's distinctive fixed-action patterns is flying in a flock. By exposing the jackdaw to crows during the critical period for imprinting flocking behaviour, Lorenz succeeded in imprinting the jackdaw's flocking on crows. The same jackdaw was introduced to members of its own species during the critical period for imprinting sexual routines. Lorenz later returned the jackdaw to the colony and observed its behaviour. Each day it flew off to flock with a group of crows. When it came to flocking this jackdaw considered itself a crow. However, when it came time to mate the jackdaw preferred its own kind. Actually this bird must have had three critical periods for imprinting because it fed with neither crows nor other jackdaws. Instead it liked to eat with Lorenz.

When this specially reared jackdaw was first exposed to a baby jackdaw, it began to care for it in precisely the same manner as any other jackdaw would. This occurred even though the bird had never before been exposed to a baby of its species. Since the bird had never seen a baby jackdaw it could not have been imprinted on it, and since it had never seen any jackdaws care for their young it could not have learned child-care. So the releaser for fixed-action child-care routines must be innate. In this experiment Lorenz showed that, in the same organism, some releasers were inherited while others were fixed by imprinting.

Lorenz realised that imprinting ran entirely against the views of most experimental psychologists of the time who believed that all learning is gradually built up from repeated stimulus–response connections. Lorenz did not try to reconcile his findings with the prevailing psychological theory. On the contrary, he emphasised the differences. He listed four characteristics that distinguish imprinting from other forms of learning:

1. Imprinting occurs only during a brief critical period.

2. Imprinting is irreversible.

3. Imprinting can establish a sign stimulus well before the fixed-action pattern is performed. (For example, early imprinting establishes a sexual target well before sexual behaviour takes place.)

4. Imprinting occurs not on an individual but to a group of similar individuals. (The geese were not imprinted solely on Lorenz but on humans in general.)

Lorenz's description of imprinting has been modified somewhat by later research. For example, we know today that imprinting is sometimes reversible. We also know that imprinting is not always an all-or-nothing affair. Some animals may be more strongly imprinted than others. Despite these modifications, however, the main point of Lorenz's research remains as important today as it was 50 years ago when it was first performed. Not all significant behaviour is learned through experience. Animals are genetically constructed to behave in certain ways. Lorenz's contribution was to show how such genetic dispositions interact with critical experiences to produce species-specific behaviour patterns.

AFTERMATH

Researchers were quick to follow up Lorenz's experiments. Critical periods for imprinting were studied in a variety of animals. It soon became clear that imprinting occurs mainly in species where the young are mobile. This makes good evolutionary sense because such species have an obvious need for some method of preventing the young wandering away from their parents. Although human babies are not mobile, many writers suggested that perhaps something like imprinting does occur in people. Instead of following, these writers focus on the mother–infant bond as evidence for imprinting. They argue that there is a critical period for forming human attachments — the first year of life. If no attachments are formed during this period, children will have lifelong problems relating to others. Fortunately isolation experiments cannot be done with humans so we do not have any direct test of the imprinting hypotheses. But there is suggestive evidence from natural experiments supporting the notion that human attachments are formed during a critical period early in life.

Most of this evidence comes from observations of children reared in impersonal foundling homes and orphanages. René Spitz, for example, compared children raised by their own mothers in a nursery with those raised in a poorly staffed orphanage. The children in the orphanage had little contact with adults and were left on their own for long periods of time. Although food and medical care were adequate the children in the foundling home had little opportunity to form attachments. During the first four months of life the children in the foundling home appeared to thrive. In fact, they scored higher than children in the nursery on a variety of developmental measures. By the end of their first year, however, this relationship was reversed. Children in the foundling home had fallen well behind (mentally and physically) children being reared by their own mothers. The foundling-home children displayed a syndrome Spitz called hospitalism. They were listless, depressed and very susceptible to infection. As the children grew older those in the foundling home fell even further behind. Developmental milestones like walking or talking were delayed and many failed to grow. Since their medical care and diet were adequate, Spitz blamed the poor condition of foundling-home children on their lack of attachments. He argued that social contact in infancy is crucial for normal development.

Spitz's observations are supported by the occasional discovery of children who, for one reason or another, are raised alone in attics or locked in rooms or allowed to grow up wild in the woods. Such children almost always have severe deficiencies in social relations. The problem is that these children may also be physically abused or mentally retarded and it is hard to determine how much of their problem is due to these factors rather than a lack of parenting early in life. Spitz's observations have also been challenged by others who stated that the medical and dietary conditions in the foundling home were not as good as he stated them to be, and might indeed have contributed to the foundlings' poor development.

Although planned isolation experiments with humans are impossible, such experiments have been done using our close relatives, apes and monkeys. One famous investigation was conducted in Wisconsin by psychologist Harry Harlow. In this experiment infant monkeys were separated from their mothers a few hours after birth. The monkeys were raised in a clean and nourishing environment, but this did not prevent them developing severe behavioural defects. The most severely affected were animals raised entirely alone. These monkeys were fed by a mechanical remote-control device and observed through one-way mirrors. For their first two years they never came into contact with any other

monkeys or humans. When placed back among their own kind, these monkeys found it nearly impossible to adjust. They did not play with others, did not defend themselves from attack and did not mate. This extreme social deviance was found only when monkeys were isolated for prolonged periods. By varying the amount of isolation, Harlow found it took six months alone during the first year of life to produce irreversible social damage. He concluded that in monkeys, at least, the first year contains a critical period for developing attachments.

Harlow's experiment demonstrated that monkeys raised alone do not develop normally. To further investigate the importance of early influences on social behaviour, Harlow constructed two artificial "surrogate mothers". Both were cylindrical with armless and legless bodies. Their heads were wooden balls with faces painted on them. Both mothers had nursing bottles attached to their upper regions and both

FIG. 73. *In Harlow's experiment, even monkeys fed by the wire mother sought comfort from the cloth mother whenever a threatening stimulus was encountered*

were kept warm with heating lamps. The main difference between them was that one was constructed from wire mesh while the other was made of sponge rubber covered in terry towelling. Although both surrogate mothers were equally unresponsive, monkeys given the choice preferred the cloth-covered mother. They spent a great deal of time clinging to her and when frightened they ran to the cloth-covered surrogate for comfort. This was true even when the monkeys received their milk from the wire mother. It seemed as if the terry cloth served as a releaser for affection and security. Even after monkeys raised with the cloth surrogate were returned to their real mothers, they still derived comfort from clinging to the cloth surrogate.

Although the cloth mother provided some comfort, monkeys raised away from their parents and peers were far from normal. They never mated with other monkeys and seemed unable to participate fully in local social life. Thus while Harlow's experiment revealed part of what constitutes mother love, it still left undiscovered some of the important early experiences that lead monkeys to behave like other monkeys.

Of course there is a great difference between monkeys and humans and it is not yet possible to say with certainty that there is a critical period for the formation of attachments in people. However, it does appear that early childhood experiences, particularly social contact, are crucial for normal development. For example, some psychologists have suggested that early childhood is a critical period for language development. It is true that human beings are biologically constructed to learn languages. Our brains are organised to make language possible and so are our vocal cords, throats and mouths but our ability to control our speech apparatus matures slowly. Not until two or three years of age can we exercise the control necessary to speak clearly. This is also the time when our nervous system matures to the point where speedy neural communication is possible. It is of course during this period that children learn to speak a language most easily. In fact children of this age from bilingual homes can learn two languages with no more time or effort than it takes to learn one. What is more, they can speak both with no noticeable accent. Learning a language later in life is an entirely different task. The effort involved is considerable and no matter how proficient we become our accent will always be noticeable to native speakers.

Although critical periods may exist for humans, it is clear that our behaviour is infinitely more plastic than that of lower animals. In fact, one important trait setting us apart from other species is our adaptability. For this reason no examples of fixed-action sequences have ever been identified in humans. Nevertheless, the work of Lorenz and the other ethologists has made us aware of the evolutionary forces affecting behaviour and these do have implications for human beings. Lorenz himself pointed out some of these implications in his book *On Aggression*. He showed similarities between aggression in human beings and animals. Lorenz believed that aggression is an inherited aspect of human behaviour but that it can be modified by creating safe ways to let out hostility. Other ethologists have also tried to apply observational techniques to human beings. Today, thanks to Lorenz, the field of human ethology is flourishing and few psychologists continue to believe that all behaviour is learned.

Lorenz received many honours for his research including honorary degrees from Yale, Loyola, Basel and Oxford Universities, and he has elected as a foreign member of the Royal Society. In 1973 Konrad Lorenz, father of modern ethology, won the Nobel Prize in physiology and medicine.

Further Reading

Lorenz, K., *On Aggression*, Harcourt Brace Jovanovich, New York, 1966.
Lorenz, K., *The Foundation of Ethology*, Springer-Verlag, New York, 1981.

CHAPTER ELEVEN

AGES AND STAGES

Because it is so fundamental, we take our knowledge of the everyday world for granted. We know that dropped objects fall downward, not up. We know that our feet are parts of our bodies. When we close the kitchen cupboard we know that the cups and saucers inside do not vaporise. We know that steel weighs more than plastic; and that we are not strong enough to lift a house; and that the sun and moon are not really alive even though they move around in the sky. But we were not born knowing these things; we learned them when we were very young.

Any parent can testify that little children are curious creatures. They explore their world by manipulating objects with their hands and (all too often) with their mouths. They peer into every corner and, when they are old enough, ceaselessly ask questions. In a few short years children change from primitive to abstract thinkers without any formal plan of study. This last point is very important. All normal children raised in average homes display enormous intellectual growth during their childhood years without any *specific* instruction. This does not mean that a child's environment is unimportant. Children raised in severely deprived environments (poorly staffed orphanages, for example) may be mentally retarded. It just seems that the *unplanned* environment provided by most parents is sufficient to ensure normal intellectual development in most children.

Although parents do not formally set out to "educate" their children, for most of this century psychologists believed that intellectual growth was ultimately controlled by environmental factors. They believed that through conditioning children learn a series of stimulus–response connections which are gradually "built up" into complex forms of thinking. Although there seems little doubt that conditioning occurs in children, it is unlikely to be the whole story behind intellectual development. The speed with which children develop, and the orderly sequence in which intellectual development takes place, suggest that a maturational component may also be involved. In other words, like most human behaviour, intelligence results from the interaction of maturation and experience. Although this conclusion appears self-evident today, it was considered to be controversial when put forward by Jean Piaget 50 years ago. The reason why Piaget's viewpoint ultimately prevailed is the main focus of this chapter.

STUDYING CHILDREN

Developmental psychology as we know it today is an amalgam of information and scientific approaches taken from education and medicine as well as psychology.

In order to understand Piaget's work it is first necessary to have some idea of what preceded it. In this section two important precursors of his work are described — educational philosophy and personality development.

Educational Philosophy

Prior to the seventeenth century there was no real concept equivalent to our modern idea of "childhood". Instead of members of a special age group, children were considered to be simply little adults. There were no children's toys, no children's literature and no special consideration given to children's emotional needs. Child-rearing was mainly custodial and children were sent off to work at a young age. Family portraits painted in those days depict children in adult dress with adult physical features. Often the only way to tell that these figures are supposed to be children is that they are shown as shorter and weaker than their parents.

There have been many attempts to explain why our ancestors had what appears to us to be a very curious attitude toward children. One popular explanation views their behaviour as defensive — parents avoided becoming too emotionally involved with their children because infant mortality was so high. Even as late as 1750 the odds against a European child living past the age of five were three to one. In order to avoid heartbreak and loss parents never treated their children as special in the first place. Of course poverty also played a role. Few parents could afford to indulge their children, or indeed themselves. Economic necessity meant that everyone physically able, including children, worked.

Attitudes toward children began to change during the eighteenth century, and by the nineteenth century all western societies began to view childhood as a special stage of development, different from adulthood. This change in attitude was largely the result of better health care and a consequent decline in infant mortality. Children lived longer and their parents were not so afraid of losing them. With the industrial revolution economic conditions improved and a middle class began to develop. Middle-class parents had the time and money required to take an interest in children. They designed and bought their children toys, special clothes and children's books. In nineteenth-century Britain the Society for the Prevention of Cruelty to Children was founded as an offshoot of the *older* Royal Society for the Prevention of Cruelty to Animals. Its efforts reduced the exploitation of children as a cheap labour resource but did not eliminate child labour altogether. Well into the twentieth century most families even in the West depended on the income earned by their children. In third world countries child labour is still common today. As recently as 1959 the United Nations felt it necessary to pass a resolution affirming that children deserve the same human rights as adults.

Although changing health and economic conditions made it possible to "invent" childhood, political changes were important as well. Democratic revolutions in America and France produced a whole new political and philosophical outlook. Philosophers like Jean-Jacques Rousseau challenged the traditional view that a person's lot in life was determined entirely by heredity and class. In democratic societies, he believed, anyone could move up if given the opportunity. Rousseau compared children with primitive people, "noble savages", who were not shackled by the stultifying class structures that had dominated Europe for centuries. For Rousseau, children were not simply miniature adults, they had their own peculiar ways of seeing, thinking and feeling. Rousseau published his extensive observations of a child in his book *Émile*. He concluded from these observations that if children are given the opportunity to develop in a "natural" manner, they will forge a new, lasting democracy. Rousseau's optimistic view of the essential nature of humankind was in stark contrast to the previously held view that people are naturally uncivilised.

Rousseau's arguments exerted a strong effect on nineteenth-century edu-cators and psychologists, many of whom set out to put his ideas into action. The most famous such attempt began in 1880 when a boy was found in the woods near Aveyron in France. The boy appeared to have had no contact with other human beings for many years. Because of his appearance and manner, the boy was called a "savage" or "wild boy". Professor Itard, a French psychologist, saw the boy as epitomising Rousseau's noble savage and undertook to show how such a child could make a contribution toward society. First, of course, Itard had to teach the boy to communicate with others and take care of himself. Itard's efforts to teach the boy to talk met with only limited success. It seems likely that the child was mentally retarded and unable to learn. Although Itard's goals of educating the noble savage were unfulfilled, his efforts did have one positive effect. They led to an interest in helping "idiots", as the mentally retarded were known at the time. One of Itard's students, Séguin, began treating the retarded in a Paris hospital and wrote a book on his methods. For many years this treatise was recognised as the definitive textbook in the field of mental retardation.

Although of only limited value in educating the retarded, Rousseau's ideas were successfully applied to teaching normal children. The seminal worker in modern early childhood education was Johann Pestalozzi. Prior to Pestalozzi, most educational practices were derived from the belief that children are not born with the faculties necessary to learn and make moral judgements. These qualities must be inculcated by teachers, often using force. In contrast, following Rousseau, Pestalozzi saw the goal of education as helping children to develop their innate powers of observation and perception. To this end Pestalozzi felt that the school curriculum should go beyond lectures to include field trips and other non-traditional experiences. Instead of coercion Pestalozzi encouraged children to become active partners in the educational process — to take a role in deciding how learning should take place. Pestalozzi's ideas were carried further by Fre-derick Froebel, who founded the first kindergarten in Germany. Froebel also believed that children learn best by "discovering" rather than by being lectured to and he arranged his kindergartens to facilitate the discovery process.

Following Froebel's lead kindergartens were soon established throughout Europe and North America. The rapidity of this development was astonishing considering how radically different Pestalozzi's and Froebel's ideas were from the prevailing educational philosophy. By the beginning of the twentieth century kindergartens were established everywhere. An important byproduct of this development was that, for the first time in history, large populations of children were available for investigation. In the beginning these studies were practical. For example, educators observed how children learn in order to refine their curricula, physicians examined them in order to provide parents with child-rearing advice and psychologists studied them in order to develop new intelli-gence measures. Eventually scientists became interested in child development it its own right. An entire field — developmental psychology — was founded solely to study the changes that occur with age. Detailed maturational studies were published and new psychological measures were developed. Around the turn of the present century the idea that children pass through various stages of development, each with its characteristic problems and accomplishments, was introduced. Over the next 50 years the idea of discrete stages was encountered repeatedly in the child-development literature, particularly in the writings of Sigmund Freud.

Personality Development

Sigmund Freud, whose ideas have been encountered several times in this book, was born in what is now part of Czechoslovakia; his family moved to Vienna when he was only four. Although he completed the medical course at the University of Vienna, his major interest was in research rather than practice. He took a research post at the Institute of Cerebral Research and performed some important neurological and drug experiments, but low pay and anti-Semitism eventually led him to take up the private practice of psychiatry.

Even in private practice Freud's major commitment was to science. He was less interested in curing emotionally ill patients than in developing a theory of personality. Freud was a prolific and engaging writer who attracted many admirers and students. He was also an insightful clinician. By listening to his patients Freud tried to construct a theory that would explain their symptoms and, potentially, all human behaviour. As the incident on the train described in Chapter Four makes clear, Freud was a committed determinist who believed that no behaviour is accidental — not even slips of the tongue — and that all behaviour can be explained given enough data. Eventually Freud came to believe that adult personalities are formed very early in life. He felt that a child's early interactions with its environment during certain critical periods of development determine how the child will behave as an adult. He called these critical periods the stages of psychosexual development.

As a nineteenth-century scientist Freud could not avoid being influenced by Darwin and by the work of the early animal behaviourists (ethologists) supporting evolutionary theory. And there are many similarities between Freud's work and theirs. Like the ethologists Freud concentrated on innate drives (or instincts) as the motivating force behind behaviour. He believed that sex and aggressive instincts were most important and so did the ethologists. Freud also believed that the energy produced by these instincts (which he called libido) could be diverted from normal instinctual goals. That is, aggressive instincts need not lead to direct combat, they can be diverted, say, to an appreciation for football. Perhaps the most important parallel between Freud's thinking and ethological theory is the concept of *critical periods* — developmental stages at which specific learning must occur. As discussed in Chapter Ten, the ethologists showed that some young animals (geese, for instance) have a critical period lasting about two days after hatching during which they must be exposed to adult geese if they are ever to behave as ordinary members of the flock. On a more complicated level Freud believed that human beings, too, must pass through critical periods; a failure to meet the demands of each period can affect people throughout their lives.

Each of Freud's critical periods involves a conflict between the developing child and society. These conflicts must be resolved by the child learning to behave in accord with the demands of the external world. The oral stage, which comes first, centres around the child's pleasure in sucking, eating and biting. If for some reason a child is frustrated during the oral stage (perhaps by early or abrupt weaning), it may become "fixated". Some libido energy will remain at this stage for life and the individual will have an "oral personality". Such people are always demanding that others provide a lot of love and affection. They may also reveal their oral personalities by engaging in "oral behaviour" — overeating, nail-biting or smoking.

The next stage, the anal stage, represents a severe challenge to the child from civilisation. Defecation, a reflexive, pleasurable reflex, must be inhibited and regulated according to the demands of society. The child must learn to control his natural biological urge; he must become submissive to the demands of others. Fixation at this stage (perhaps due to inconsistent training) can lead to rebelliousness. Overly harsh training can produce a slavish conformity to social demands.

The third stage brings an even more threatening conflict between the child's natural urges and society's strictures. In this, the phallic stage, males are thought to begin developing sexual feelings toward their mothers, females toward their fathers. Because of the anxiety and guilt feelings this may cause, they must learn to divert their feelings to more appropriate objects. Failure to do so can lead to lifelong social maladjustment. Little Hans, whose phobia of horses was analysed in Chapter One, was (according to Freud) suffering from an unconscious conflict of the phallic stage, which Freud called the Oedipal complex.

According to Freud the final psychosocial stage, the genital stage, sees the development of interpersonal skills, friendships and other social attachments. A fully realised personality requires the successful resolution of the conflicts arising in all four stages.

Freud's psychosexual stage theory exerted a powerful effect on psychiatric and psychological thinking. Naturally the specifics have been challenged and modified over the years. This happens to every theory. But for our present purpose the details of Freud's theory are less important than his general approach which reflects two basic themes. First, underlying all Freud's work is the idea that the early childhood years are a crucial period for later personality development. Second, and even more important, Freud believed that personality development is the result of biological drives (and maturation) interacting with environmental experiences. Both of these ideas also motivated Piaget's work which is described next.

JEAN PIAGET AND GENETIC EPISTEMOLOGY

After Freud, Jean Piaget is the most frequently cited researcher in the psychological literature. Both men made enormous contributions to modern psychology in general and to our understanding of children in particular. Their approach to psychology was similar. Although trained as scientists neither Piaget nor Freud was wholly committed to the experimental method. Instead they preferred to rely on "clinical" evidence and controlled observations supplemented where possible by small demonstration experiments. In addition both men were influenced by evolutionary theory and the efforts of the early ethologists. The result was that both Freud and Piaget produced stage theories in which development was seen to result from the interaction of maturation and environment. It is fair to say that Piaget did for cognitive development what Freud did for personality.

Piaget was born in Neuchâtel, Switzerland, in 1896. His father was a medievalist and, according to his son, something of a perfectionist. Piaget recalled his mother as having a "rather neurotic temperament" and often being in "poor mental health". In fact he credited his mother's emotional problems with sparking his interest in psychology.

Piaget's mother made "family life somewhat troublesome". As an escape the young Piaget followed his father and tried to lose himself in serious work. Fascinated by birds, shells and insects, Piaget spent a great deal of time collecting local specimens. One day he spotted an unusual, partly albino sparrow in a park near his home. He wrote a brief description of his observations which was published in a natural-history journal. This was Piaget's first scientific paper; he was 10 years old at the time. The director of Neuchâtel's natural-history museum was taken by Piaget's enthusiasm and permitted the youngster to work in the museum after school. The director was particularly interested in molluscs (snails and related creatures) and Piaget became interested in them as well. In fact he was more than interested. He collected sufficient information to write and publish a series of papers on the molluscs of Switzerland and France. Foreign "colleagues" wrote to Piaget inviting him to visit them and lecture on his work. He was even offered the job of curator of the mollusc collection at the natural-

FIG. 74. *Jean Piaget (1896–1980), genetic epistemologist*

history museum in Geneva. Piaget had to decline these invitations, however, as he still had not finished high school.

Obviously something of a prodigy, Piaget received a doctoral degree from the University of Neuchâtel when he was only 21. His doctoral research dealt with the structural changes that occur in molluscs moved to new environments. Biological flexibility in response to environmental pressure fascinated Piaget and he soon began to wonder whether similar flexibility can be demonstrated in humans. Thus in 1918 he went to study psychology and psychiatry in Zurich. A year later he moved to Paris where he was put to work by Theodore Simon, one of the pioneers of intelligence testing. Piaget's job was to help standardise verbal reasoning tests on Paris schoolchildren. The main purpose of his work was to determine how many questions average children at various ages can answer. But Piaget was more interested in the reason why children at different ages failed some but not other questions. He would talk to the children about their answers and try to determine their "thought processes". It was at this time that Piaget began to develop the "clinical" research method he was to refine for the rest of his career.

In 1921 Piaget returned to Switzerland where he took up a post at the Institute Jean-Jacques Rousseau in Geneva. The institute was mainly concerned with teacher training. Although originally independent over the years the institute became increasingly integrated with the University of Geneva. In the next four years Piaget produced five books dealing with language development in children. These books made him famous in Europe. Although still in his twenties he was lecturing to experts throughout the world. Piaget's subsequent academic career involved posts at the universities of Neuchâtel, Geneva and Lausanne in Switzerland as well as the Sorbonne in France. Despite all of these moves Piaget always managed to maintain a relationship with the Institute Jean-Jacques Rousseau and this is where he was to spend most of his career.

The institute was an ideal place for Piaget because it had such good contacts with local schools. He trained students at the institute in his research methods and then sent them out to collect data from schoolchildren. These data formed the basis for many of his scientific papers. He was also a keen observer of his own two daughters. Visitors to his home were never surprised to find this tall portly man on the floor playing marbles or some other game with his young children. Piaget published three volumes on cognitive development based almost entirely on data gathered by observing his daughters.

By the end of his career Piaget had published more than 60 books and hundreds of articles on all aspects of intellectual and moral development. All of this work, according to him, was directed at answering a single question — how do children learn? He named his scientific specialty genetic epistemology. The term "genetic" refers to the process of development and the term "epistemology" is philosophical jargon for the nature of knowing or knowledge. Philosophers had of course been interested in epistemology for centuries. Piaget's contribution was to give epistemology a scientific foundation.

Piaget liked to compare his work to embryology, the study of the first stage of biological development. Immediately after conception the fertilised egg begins to divide. Absorbing nutrients from its environment, the egg transforms itself from an amorphous mass to an organised structure with specialised areas each corresponding to the various organ systems. As development progresses the foetus continues to transform itself, passing through periods when it resembles lower animals more than it does humans. Each stage grows out of the preceding one but the result is a different organism. Piaget believed that cognitive development could be viewed in similar terms. Through the interplay of biology and environment intellectual functioning becomes more complex and more effective.

According to Piaget children begin with little intellectual specialisation, just potential. But as children grow, environmental experiences (which are analogous to the embryo's nutrients) provide them with the information necessary to learn about their world. For Piaget the intellect, like the embryo, passes through a regular sequence of stages. At each stage children reconstruct their model of reality. Thus children at a more advanced stage not only know more facts than those at an earlier stage, they actually think differently. It is as if children periodically replace their internal mental "computers" with new, more capable models.

Piaget was ingenious at choosing material to illustrate how thinking changes with age, but it is impossible in one chapter to do justice to the sweeping range of his research. Instead a representative Piagetian investigation is described. This research has to do with what Piaget called conservation.

CLASSIC EXPERIMENT 14:

CONSERVATION

The classic conservation experiment begins with a five-year-old girl seated at a table across from the experimenter. Set before the girl are two short glass tumblers containing orange juice. One glass is filled to the top, the other is empty. The experimenter tells the girl that he wishes to have the same amount of juice in each glass and he wants her to tell him how to accomplish this goal. The girl will give the instructions and the experimenter will follow them.

The little girl tells the experimenter to pour some juice into the empty glass and then she compares the heights of the two liquids. The liquid level in the first glass is still higher, so she asks for a little more. Again a comparison is made (the child carefully aligns the glasses side by side to be sure) and a little more juice is requested. Now the second glass has a bit more juice than the first and the child asks that some be poured back. The process of adding and deleting juice continues until the child is sure the two glasses are equally full.

Now the experimenter makes the task slightly more difficult. He brings out a third glass which is twice as tall as the first two but only half as wide. He empties one of the half-filled short juice glasses into the new tall glass, making certain the child sees that every last drop has been transferred. The experimenter holds the tall glass next to the remaining half-filled short glass and asks the child whether the two glasses contain the same amount of juice. Now since the first two glasses contained equal amounts of juice (the child herself saw to this), and since one was emptied completely into the tall glass, the correct answer to the experimenter's question is: "Yes, they contain equal amounts of juice." But this is not the child's answer. After carefully examining the two glasses she says that they do not contain the same amount of juice; the tall glass contains more.

The experimenter asks the girl for the reasoning behind her answer and receives the following explanation: there is more juice in the tall glass because the juice is higher in that one. The child even points to the difference in the height of the liquids in the two glasses.

It appears that this little girl is basing her judgement solely on the height of the liquid in the two glasses; she seems not to comprehend the idea that the quantity of liquid does

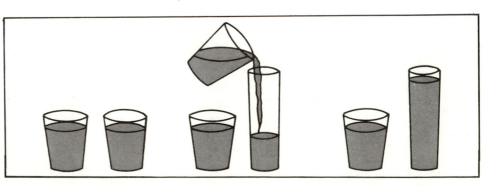

FIG. 75. *In the conservation experiment, a child is shown two glasses equally full of juice. The contents of one glass are poured into a different-shaped glass and the child is asked whether the amount of liquid contained in the two glasses is still the same*

not change with the shape of its container. But there is always the possibility that she does not understand the experimenter's question. Perhaps she is confused by the word *amount*, thinking it applies to the height of the liquid column rather than the quantity of liquid. In order to see whether this is the case the experimenter asks the child to indicate what will happen when the juice is poured from the tall glass back into the now empty short one. Specifically, the child is asked to point to the level the juice will reach. She points to a level higher than it reached previously and higher than the level of juice in the other identical short glass. Thus it really does seem that the girl believes the quantity of juice changes when it is poured into a different-shaped container. In Piaget's terms the child does not realise that the quantity of juice is *conserved* across the pouring operations.

Confusion about the conservation concept is common among five-year-olds. But they do not all answer in the same way as the girl described here. Some actually say there is less juice in the tall glass, explaining that it is narrower than the short one. Whereas the first little girl focuses on the height difference between the glasses, those who answer "less" are focusing on the width difference. What is important, however, is that no five-year-old produces the correct answer; none reports that the amount of juice in both glasses is the same. According to Piaget a correct answer to the experimenter's question requires the ability to consider two dimensions (height and width) simultaneously. These young children pay attention to only one dimension and therefore get the answer wrong. Whether they believe the amount of juice increases or decreases depends solely on chance, that is, on the dimension that captures their attention.

Piaget's explanation for young children's errors sounds plausible, but he could not help worrying that some aspect of the task may have

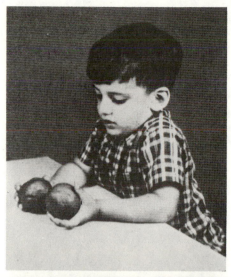

FIG. 76. *The young child acknowledges that the two balls contain equal amounts of plasticine but believes that when one ball is rolled into a sausage shape it gains additional plasticine*

166

confused the children. He knew that other psychologists would have more faith in his findings if he could demonstrate that five-year-olds make similar errors on other tasks. For this reason Piaget went on to investigate the generality of his findings. Instead of liquids he presents a child with two equal-sized balls of plasticine modelling clay. After the child agrees that the balls are indeed equal, the experimenter rolls one in his hands until it takes on a sausage shape. The child is then asked if the quantity of plasticine has changed. All say yes. Most believe there is more in the sausage; they are focusing on its long length. Some say there is less; these children are focusing on the sausage's narrow circumference. These findings are identical to those obtained with liquids — five-year-olds fail to conserve quantity.

Even more powerful support for Piaget's explanation comes from investigations of concepts other than quantity. For example, in one experiment children are faced with two parallel rows of coins. The two rows each have the same number of coins, equally spaced apart. The children agree that the rows have equal numbers of coins. Then the experimenter increases the space between the coins in one row while leaving the other unchanged. The children are asked whether the number of coins is still the same in both rows. "No," they reply, "there are more coins in the longer row." They have failed to realise that number does not change when the length of the row changes. In Piaget's terms they have failed to conserve number. Interestingly, this failure to conserve number can happen even to children who can count accurately the coins in the two rows. It seems that the ability to count and the concept of number are not necessarily related. This shows that the failure to conserve is not specific to a particular task, or even a specific dimension like quantity.

Although Piaget was not always

FIG. 77. *Young children fail to conserve quantity. The same number of coins appear greater when spaced out in a row than when bunched up in a pile.*

concerned with experimental controls, a control group for his observations on conservation does exist — older children. Eight-year-olds, for example, have little trouble answering Piaget's questions; they rarely fail to conserve. Unlike five-year-olds, the older children do not even bother to examine the experimental materials before giving their answer; in fact, they hardly even look at the height of the water in the glass or the length of the plasticine sausage. They do not have to. They *know* that pouring a liquid from one glass to another does not affect its quantity and that rolling plasticine into another shape does not alter its quantity. For them the experimenter's question is not a perceptual problem but merely a matter of common knowledge.

Piaget's conclusion from this line of research is that young children have not yet developed the mental operations necessary to consider two dimensions simultaneously and for this reason they fail to conserve. He believed that learning to conserve means maturing to a higher level of cognitive functioning — a level at which the child looks at the world in a different way. His classic research dramatically demonstrated differences in the way children think at different ages.

AFTERMATH

Piaget was a tireless worker. He arose each morning at 4 a.m. and wrote before breakfast. He spent the rest of the morning teaching, afternoons walking and thinking and evenings were spent reading. The result of his efforts was a prodigious outpouring of research on intellectual development. Using the clinical–experimental technique epitomised in his classic experiments, Piaget would start with a skill adults take for granted and try to find out how and when the skill develops in children. After years of investigations Piaget finally concluded that there are four stages of cognitive development.

Noting the relationship between motor activity and perception in infants, Piaget labelled the first stage of cognitive development the *sensorimotor stage*. During this period, which begins at birth and lasts to about age two, infants are busy learning the relationship between their actions and the consequences of their actions. They learn how to control their hands, how to reach out and grasp objects, how to propel themselves from place to place, and what happens when drink glasses are tipped over. By far the most important discovery the child makes during this period is that objects do not disappear when taken from view.

FIG. 78. *When an object is hidden behind a screen, the infant (who lacks object permanence) acts as if it has disappeared*

According to Piaget young infants (six months old or so) lack the concept of *object permanence*. He demonstrates this by placing an attractive object directly in an infant's view and waiting for the infant to begin reaching for it. If before the object is grasped the experimenter blocks it from view with a screen, the infant does not try to reach around the screen or otherwise go after the object. Instead young babies act as if the object no longer exists. They fail to realise that objects are permanent, that they exist even when they cannot be seen. By one year or so children put in the same situation behave quite differently. Children of this age continue to search for the object, moving the screen if necessary. Through experience children come to realise that objects exist in their own right; they even develop mental images of objects which they can use to guide their behaviour. These mental images free children from reacting only to stimuli in their immediate environment and allow them to construct a mental model of the world.

Once children grasp the concept of object permanence they pass into the next stage of cognitive development which Piaget called the *pre-operational* stage. During this period the child learns to use mental images in a concrete way. It is also during this stage (which lasts from two to seven years)

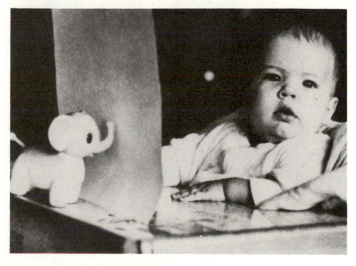

168

that the child gives names to these images and thereby becomes able to talk about them. Although children in the pre-operational stage are much more sophisticated thinkers than children in the sensorimotor stage, they still lack many concepts ("operations" in Piaget's terminology). These are the children who fail to conserve quantity in the juice glass experiments. They also have only a vague concept of time. A "fortnight" or a "week" are meaningless concepts to them; they understand only "before", "now", and "after". Children in the pre-operational stage are also egocentric — they perceive the world only from their own perspective. Piaget illustrated this by having children look at a table on which three paper "mountains" were placed. A doll is seated at the opposite end of the table. The child is then given a set of drawings and asked

FIG. 79. *In the three-mountain problem, young children find it impossible to put themselves in the doll's place*

to choose the one depicting what the *doll* sees. Children younger than seven or so choose the drawing that shows what *they* themselves see, failing to take into consideration the doll's different perspective. Egocentric thinking is also apparent in the pre-operational child's language. Such a child has great difficulty understanding that his father is his grandmother's child. To the child his father is simply *father*, he cannot see him from any other point of view.

After age seven children enter the stage of *concrete operations*. This stage, which lasts to about age 11, is when children learn to use in an effective manner the mental concepts developed in the previous stages. They learn to manipulate their visual images as if they were symbols of real things. In this stage they also learn to conserve quantity and to take the other's point of view, but their thinking is still concrete. Abstract concepts like liberty, love, and even to some extent time, still present problems for them. These final difficulties are overcome when the children reach the *formal operations* stage. During this, the highest stage of cognitive development, adult thought processes develop. Children learn to think abstractly, test hypotheses and apply the rules of logic. Not all people reach this stage; some never progress beyond concrete operations. But for most of us the potential to reach this final stage is given to us at birth — it is programmed into our genes.

Piaget's work made him justifiably famous when he was still in his late twenties and early thirties. But in America, at least, his fame was short-lived. His work fell out of favour in the 1940s and 1950s because it failed to fit in with the behaviourist school that dominated American psychology during those years. Piaget's work was "rediscovered" by the Americans in the 1960s when many of his books were translated into English. Since that time cognitive development has become one of the largest research areas in psychology. (There have been over 500 published investigations of conservation alone.)

Not all of this research has supported Piaget's stage theory. Some experiments have shown that the stages may arrive much earlier than Piaget believed and others have shown that it is possible for a child to be in two stages, exhibiting some of the characteristics of each simultaneously. Many researchers are beginning to believe that the stages are too general and that the development of discrete cognitive skills (memory, for example) should be studied separately.

Some of these new developments will surely alter the model of cognitive development put forward by Piaget, but many will not. For example, American psychologists, perhaps for cultural reasons, have devoted considerable energy to trying to speed up a child's progress through the various stages. Sometimes these efforts appear successful. For example, by intensive training, it is possible to get young children to answer Piaget's "conservation" questions correctly even though they have not yet reached the stage of concrete operations. However, there is some evidence that such children really do not understand the concept behind conservation. In a version of the experiment using two plasticine balls one researcher surreptitiously removed some plasticine, so that when the new sausage-shaped plasticine was put on a scale it weighed less than the original ball. Young children "trained" to conserve did not find this result surprising and immediately reverted to their original answers. Older children who learned conservation without training behaved differently. They continued to believe in conservation of quantity and insisted that either some plasticine was missing or the scale was defective. It seemed that the trained group had only learned to make a response in a specific experimental situation, they had not really grasped the concept.

FIG. 80. *Kittens raised in a restricted environment where all they see is vertical stripes develop a visual system attuned to stripes. Their brains are actually affected by their early environment*

Piaget's basic idea, that the intellect develops through a combination of biological maturation and the child's direct interaction with the environment, also receives support from experiments concerned with brain plasticity. Infant cats raised in restricted visual environments (a world where all they saw were vertical stripes) develop visual systems that are particularly sensitive to vertical stripes but insensitive to horizontal ones. Physiological investigations showed that the organisation of the visual areas of their brains was actually altered by their early environmental experience. This finding provides dramatic support for Piaget's assertion that cognitive development results from the interaction of biological and environmental factors.

Piaget received dozens of honorary degrees and awards for his revolutionary research and continued to be active right up to his death in 1980 at the age of 84. His work put to rest forever the belief that intellectual development is merely a matter of teaching a child a series of stimulus–response connections. Today, no matter what their position on the specifics of his theory, all developmental psychologists believe that intellectual development is the result of an interaction between maturation and the environment, with children themselves being active agents in the process.

Further Reading

Piaget, J., *The Origins of Intelligence in Children*, International Universities Press, New York, 1974.

Piaget, J. and Inhelder, B., *The Psychology of the Child*, Basic Books, New York, 1969.

CHAPTER TWELVE

1528 GENIUSES

Developmental psychologists use several special research techniques to compare subjects of different ages. The most common of these is the *cross-sectional* method which involves selecting representative subjects from different age groups and comparing them on the behaviour of interest. Any differences among the groups are assumed to be the result of their different ages. Although this approach to developmental research is relatively simple and inexpensive, it has certain distinct disadvantages. The most important of these is the impossibility of matching the different age groups on all relevant factors. Since the world is constantly changing no two age groups are ever exposed to exactly the same environments. Most of the time differences between age groups do not affect the experiment, but trouble can arise when environmental differences affect variables the experimenter wishes to study.

Consider, for example, a developmental study of reading habits conducted several decades ago. The experimenter believed that adolescents and young adults in the 1960s read more novels and other types of fiction than the previous generation because they were more interested in "personal relationships". In order to test this hypothesis the researcher randomly selected groups of adolescents and middle-aged adults and surveyed their reading habits. He found little evidence for his hypothesis. In fact older subjects actually read more novels than younger ones. Does this mean that the researcher's hypothesis was wrong? Was the previous generation more interested in personal relationships than the present one? It is hard to say because there is an uncontrolled factor in the lives of these subjects. The older ones grew up before the introduction of television whereas the younger subjects were exposed to television throughout their lives. Since the older and younger subjects actually grew up in different environments (with and without television), it could have been this difference rather than their interest in personal relationships that was responsible for their different reading habits.

The only way to be certain that all subjects in a developmental study are comparable is to use the *longitudinal* research method which involves repeated observations of the same subjects over time. Of course the environment can still change: television can be invented, personal computers can become popular and so on; but these changes will affect all subjects, not just those in a certain age group.

Although most psychologists agree that the longitudinal method is far superior to the cross-sectional strategy, longitudinal experiments are rare. One reason for this is that they are very expensive. Research teams must work (and be paid) for years while data are collected. This requires a long-term commitment of scarce research funds, a rarity in today's uncertain economy. Another impediment to longitudinal research is maintaining subject contact over the long time periods required. Subjects tend to move from one area to another and are often hard to trace. Add to this the possibility that experimenters may change jobs, lose interest or retire and the practical problems involved in longitudinal research are apparent.

Some investigators have tried to get around these difficulties by performing *retrospective* studies in which individuals who display certain behaviours (phobias, for example) are identified and their pasts explored in an attempt to uncover common experiences. Retrospective investigations are easier to implement than longitudinal ones but they are far less reliable. Recollections are often vague and past events are not always accurately recorded. For accurate developmental data there really is no substitute for longitudinal research. It produces data available in no other way. The present chapter describes one of the most famous longitudinal research projects ever undertaken — Lewis M. Terman's study of genius.

MEASURING INTELLIGENCE

Genealogical Approaches

Throughout history it has been recognised that some people have superior abilities — in sport, music, painting and even in thinking. And there is remarkably little disagreement about who these superior people are. Einstein, Newton, Darwin, Beethoven, Michelangelo are well-known names today because it is generally accepted that each has made an important contribution to culture or knowledge. Although we all agree that these people are special there is little consensus about how they got that way. Were they born with special gifts or did they acquire them through training? Can anyone be taught to be gifted? Can we recognise those who will excel later in life while they are still young children?

Philosophers have always been interested in these questions. Plato, for example, noted that able parents produce able children; he interpreted this as indicating that ability is at least partly determined by heredity. But Plato also believed that natural inherited ability was not enough. To ensure greatness Plato believed that intellectual gifts needed to be fostered by training. For this reason he advocated giving young children "intelligence tests" in order to determine which children were most gifted. This select group of children would then be provided with extra education and training so that they could develop to the best of their ability.

The only thing that kept Plato's scheme from being put into action was the lack of an adequate intelligence test; intelligence tests were not developed until the present century. Philosophers, from Plato to the present, who were interested in studying individuals of high achievement had to content themselves with less quantitative data. Their typical approach was to study the lives and families of eminent people,

FIG. 81. *Albert Einstein. We have little trouble agreeing on who geniuses are but there is no agreement on how they got that way*

FIG. 82. *Francis Galton (1822–1911), founder of the Eugenics Society and student of genius*

looking for clues to their greatness. Such biographical studies of "geniuses" were particularly popular in the eighteenth century when many treatises on intellectual ability appeared.

Ideas began to change, however, with the introduction of the theory of evolution. The idea that the fittest survive, which was originally applied to animals and plants, was soon seen to be applicable to people as well. The Social Darwinists of the nineteenth century were particularly vocal, claiming that mental abilities, like intelligence, are subject to the same evolutionary forces that shape physical characteristics. According to the Social Darwinists some people inherit a great deal of intelligence, others very little. Since those with high intelligence are more likely to thrive (find the best sources of food, attract the best mates), those with little intelligence will eventually die out. In this manner the human race continually improves. It is probably no surprise to learn that the Social Darwinists opposed most welfare programmes. From their point of view misguided humanitarianism only interferes with natural selection.

The dog-eat-dog world of the Social Darwinists was captured early in the century by William Wordsworth in his poem "Rob Roy's Grave":

> The good old rule
> The simple plan
> That they should take who have the power
> And they should keep who can.

The Social Darwinists favoured careful control of population growth and hoped to encourage only the most "fit" to reproduce. Their social views led to the founding of the Eugenics Society which was dedicated to promoting "ideal" matings (and, on some occasions, sterilisation of those who were not so ideal). A prime mover in the Eugenics Society and in nineteenth-century English science in general was Francis Galton, whose "breakfast-table" memory experiment was described in Chapter Four.

Galton, Darwin's cousin, was totally convinced of the heritability of virtually all human traits including intelligence. In a series of books, *Hereditary Genius, English Men of Science, Natural Inheritance,* Galton developed the thesis that eminent individuals almost always come from eminent families. His approach was to study biographies of famous men (women were largely ignored) looking for evidence that their relatives were also very able. Sometimes of course this was very easy. Kings had a habit of giving birth to kings; bishops to other bishops. But Galton went even further, uncovering evidence that great poets, statesmen, scientists and even wrestlers were related.

The flavour of Galton's work can be appreciated from his treatment of Mozart which appeared in *Hereditary Genius* and is reproduced below:

Mozart, J.V. [sic] Wolfgang; was exceedingly precocious as a child — quite a prodigy in music. He played beautifully at 4, and composed much of real merit between the ages of 4 and 6. He overworked himself and d. at 35.

F. *Leopold Mozart; famous violinist. His method, which he published, was considered for fifty years to be the best work of its kind. He composed a great deal.*

b. *[Sister] Was a hopeful musician as a child, an excellent pianist, but she did not succeed in after-life.*

S. *Charles Mozart; cultivated music as an amateur, and played with distinguished talent, but nothing more was heard of him.*

S. *Wolfgang Amedée; born four months after his father's death; was a distinguished performer, and has composed a good deal, but has not risen to high eminence as a composer.*

Galton believed that since intelligence is inherited "each generation has enormous power over the natural gifts of those that follow". More specifically he believed that we all have a duty to "humanity" to exercise our power in a way that would "be most advantageous to future inhabitants of the earth". As a eugenicist (he actually coined the term) Galton believed that evolution could be hurried along by selective mating and by permitting "inefficient human stock" to be supplanted by better strains. Among those he hoped to supplant were the black races. According to Galton "the number among the negroes of those whom we should call half-witted men is very large". While travelling in Africa Galton noted that: "The mistakes the negroes made in their own matters were so childish, stupid, and simpleton-like, as frequently to make me ashamed of my own species." Moreover, "The Australian type is at least one grade below the African negro".

In retrospect Galton's ideas seem amazingly naive. We appreciate the role of money and connections in maintaining a family's eminence and we know that we cannot estimate the intelligence of members of different cultures (Africans or Australian Aborigines, for instance) by applying the standards of a foreign society. Nevertheless, the importance of evolutionary theory — and the conservative social climate of his times — ensured that Galton's ideas were taken quite seriously.

Although Galton devoted great amounts of energy to studying the biographies of eminent men, he was never entirely satisfied with a purely genealogical approach to the study of intelligence. Like Plato he longed for tests which would allow him to measure intelligence quantitatively. Unlike Plato, however, Galton set out to develop such tests.

Galton's Measure of Intelligence

Since Galton believed that intelligence is largely inherited (although adequate schooling is necessary to help the intellect develop) he searched for biological traits that might produce superior mental ability. He reasoned that since we are born knowing nothing everything we learn must somehow be noticed by our senses. Thus according to Galton those who are most knowledgeable must also possess the most acute senses. Putting this hypothesis to the test, Galton devised a number of simple sensory discrimination and physical strength tests. He set up a booth at the London Exhibition of 1884, where for a fee visitors could have their visual acuity, hearing, head size, breathing capacity and grip strength measured. By the end of the exhibition Galton had examined over 9000 people. Unfortunately the data he collected did not support his theory. Eminent scientists and men of letters could not be distinguished from ordinary citizens on the basis of traits such as sensory acuity and grip strength. Although Galton's intelligence tests proved invalid his research did produce a legacy which continues to serve psychology to this day: in the course of developing his tests Galton invented the correlation coefficient.

Galton may have failed, but his attempt to develop intelligence measures inspired others. For example, James McK. Cattell, a psychologist at the University of Pennsylvania, expanded Galton's tests to include colour vision, memory, coordination and even imagery. He found considerable differences among students on all of his measures but, once again, these differences did not appear to be closely related to intellectual ability. Cattell's main contribution turned out to be the term "mental test" which he first used in 1890 to describe the sort of measures he and Galton were trying to produce.

By the turn of the century psychologists in laboratories throughout England and America were hard at work trying to develop mental tests. But the big breakthrough took place in France — in Alfred Binet's psychology laboratory at the Sorbonne. Binet's early work on human abilities closely resembled Galton's; it was concerned largely with physical measures and simple sensory discriminations. However, Binet soon became disenchanted with this approach. He came to believe that useful mental tests must be aimed not at sensory functions but at psychological processes. The earlier tests had failed, he argued, because they did not approach intellectual functioning at the proper level. Instead of visual acuity, grip strength and the like, Binet believed that intelligence tests should measure psychological processes such as imagination, reasoning, memory, knowledge of facts, verbal comprehension and so on.

Although Binet's views were clearly different from Galton's, it is likely that nothing practical would have come of them had he not been commissioned by the French government to study mental deficiency among Paris schoolchildren. In 1881 the French government made school attendance compulsory for all children. This meant that slow learners who had previously been kept at home were now the schools' responsibility. The education authorities were willing to provide extra assistance and special classes for such children, but first they had to identify them. This is where Binet fitted in. The Minister for Public Instruction asked Binet to develop a test that could be used to identify slow children. It is somewhat ironic that the test Plato wished for was eventually produced not to select geniuses for special training but in order to identify the mentally retarded.

FIG. 83. *Alfred Binet and his daughters*

Binet's Mental Test

Binet's first step was to abandon Galton's research approach. Binet turned from investigating the physical and sensory "elements" of human ability to the development of an overall index of mental functioning. Actually Binet discarded more than just Galton's research approach; he also gave up trying to develop a theory of how intelligence develops. Galton had such a theory: he believed that intelligence grows by taking information in through the senses. Binet never said where intelligence came from; instead he adopted a purely empirical approach. As far as he was concerned, his job was to develop a test that predicted who would do well in school and who would do poorly. Theoretical questions could be left to others.

Binet realised that to produce a useful instrument — one that would identify those children who are likely to have trouble in school — he had to include measures of the skills necessary for school success (language skills, mathematics and so on). On the other hand since the test was supposed to measure ability (aptitude) rather than the results of special tutoring (achievement), test items should not depend on any special training beyond normal everyday experience. Meeting both these requirements simultaneously was not easy and Binet had to experiment with a number of items before producing his first test in 1905. This first test, and a subsequent revision, represented a radical departure from previous efforts. The tests created by Galton, Cattell and others were meant to be applied to adults, whereas Binet's test was designed for children. The most important difference between tests designed for adults and those created for children is that the latter must take into account changes in intellectual performance with age. By quantifying these age-related performance changes on a variety of specific tasks, Binet developed an overall ability index — the first modern intelligence test.

Perhaps an example would help clarify Binet's approach. As a test of memory Binet read a long sentence aloud to more than 500 children (who were all between the ages of nine and 12). He then asked the children to write down as much of the sentence as they could recall. As you might expect, he found that as children grew older they could recall more words. For Binet this finding meant that the sentence-recall task could be used as a measure of mental ability. He reasoned that since older children are more capable than younger ones, and since older children recall more words than younger ones, then word recall can serve as an index of mental ability. This interpretation of the relationship between recall and mental ability was an important corollary — if a child recalls more words than average for his or her age, perhaps as many as a child one year older, then he or she must be more intelligent than average. If on the other hand a child recalls fewer than the average number of words for its age, Binet believed the child was subnormal.

Of course Binet realised that there is more to school performance, and intelligence, than just recalling words. For this reason he compiled an entire library of test items, each of which he tried out on children of different ages. Ultimately Binet organised the most useful items (those that discriminated best between children of different ages) into a test. This test consisted of 30 items reflecting a child's ability to understand and reason about common objects and situations. The test items were clustered into "age levels" (items that could be answered by the average child of a particular age), and increased in difficulty from those that could easily be solved by the very young to those that were difficult even for older children.

It should be obvious that Binet's approach to measuring intelligence was largely empirical. He constructed a scale comprised of items that were related to school performance but which required no particular training. He then tested these items on children in order to determine average performance at different ages. The final step was to apply the test and see how well it worked. Children beginning their school careers were given Binet's test and their test performance was compared with school performance ratings made by the children's teachers. Binet found that those who scored above the mean for their age were rated as bright by their teachers, those who scored below the mean were rated as dull, and those who scored at the mean on his test were considered by their teachers to be average. From these findings Binet concluded that his test measured what it was intended to.

In a later revision of his test Binet introduced the notion of mental age. Mental age is defined as the highest age level at which a child can still answer most questions. A child whose actual age is five but who answers questions designed for 10-year-olds is said to have a mental age of 10; a child of 10 who can only answer questions up to level five has a mental age of five. The introduction of the mental age concept ignited the first of many controversies to surround Binet's test. Critics objected to the concept of mental age on the grounds that a 10-year-old whose performance on the test matches that of the average five-year-old (that is, a mental age of five), is not really intellectually equal to a five-year-old; the 10-year-old is retarded. In fact Binet never actually claimed that the two children are the same. He believed that since the normal five-year-old is healthy whereas the older child who scores at this level is "sick", the two children cannot be considered equivalent. Binet advised psychologists to ensure that children were evaluated medically and educationally (as well as psychologically) before any conclusions were reached about their intellectual ability. He viewed his test as merely one source of data and was well aware that children can differ in many ways not reflected in his test.

Intelligence Quotients

After Binet's age scale the most important development in the field of mental testing was the introduction of the intelligence quotient by the German psychologist William Stern. Stern argued that mental age alone is not a sensitive enough index of intellectual ability. He pointed out, for example, that although they are both the same number of years behind in mental age, a six-year-old whose mental age is four is more retarded than a 12-year-old whose mental age is 10. Because this important fact is not conveyed by their respective mental ages, Stern advocated using a proportion constructed by dividing mental age by chronological (calendar) age (multiplied by 100 to eliminate decimals). Stern called this proportion the intelligence quotient or IQ.

To see how the intelligence quotient works let us consider Stern's example of two children who are each two years behind. The child who is two years behind at age six has a mental age of four and a chronological age of six producing an IQ of 66 ($\frac{4}{6}$ × 100). The child who is two years behind at age 12 has an IQ of 83 ($\frac{10}{12}$ × 100). Although both children are two years behind their peers in mental age, their IQ scores show that they are not equally retarded; the younger child is far worse off than the older. Using Stern's formula the average child at any age has an IQ of 100 (try the arithmetic and you will see why). IQ scores greater than 100 indicate above average performance; those lower than 100 indicate below average performance.

Although the IQ score represents a distinct improvement over the mental age score, Stern's formula is far from perfect. Its most serious drawback is that it breaks down as children approach adulthood. This is because intellectual abilities do not continue to grow throughout life. The number of words recalled from a sentence, the number of digits held in immediate memory and so on are essentially the same at age 40 as they were at age 20. To see the problem imagine what happens as a precocious eight-year-old girl who scores 100 per cent correct on the Binet scale grows up. At age eight this child receives the top mental age possible on the test, 16, which produces an IQ of 200 ($\frac{16}{8}$ × 100). If she still gets all the items correct at age 16 then according to Stern's formula her IQ has shrunk to 100 ($\frac{16}{16}$ × 100). Even worse, the same performance at age 32 produces an IQ of 50. Clearly the formula is only workable for young children. For this reason today's intelligence tests do not use Stern's formula to calculate IQs. Instead IQ scores are calculated by comparing an individual with a larger peer group. Using this modern method a person who scores higher than 99.9 per cent of others who have taken the test is assigned an IQ score of 145 or higher. Those who score at a level reached by 50 per cent of the population are given an IQ of 100 and those who score in the lower one percentile are assigned IQs of 45 or below. Percentile scores and IQ scores are easily convertible, so an IQ score can be assigned to any level of performance.

IQ scores proved very popular among psychologists and they soon replaced Binet's mental age score. Although they make it easy to consider a person's performance relative to his or her age, IQ scores can also be somewhat misleading. Many uninformed people believe that an IQ score refers to some fixed amount of intelligence. However, it should be clear that someone with an IQ of 100 at age 10 is not intellectually equal to someone with the same IQ at age five. One must score higher on the test at age 10 than at age five to achieve

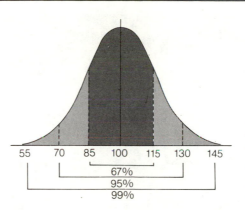

FIG. 84. *Distribution of IQ scores in the population. Most individuals fall around the mean of 100, only a small percentage score higher than 130 or lower than 70*

the same IQ score. In other words, an IQ is a *relative* measure. It indicates where a person stands in relation to a peer group (say, white eight-year-old girls); it does not indicate any fixed amount of knowledge. Think of it this way: if we were to measure height using an IQ-type scale, we would assign a "height quotient" value of 100 to the average height in a population of pygmies or a population of Amazons. The average person in both populations would receive the same height quotient even though in an absolute sense they are not the same size.

Psychologists who understand the relative nature of IQ scores have criticised them for precisely that reason. They argue that since IQ scores are relative they cannot really be measuring an entity called intelligence. Binet agreed with this criticism. He admitted that he was not measuring intelligence, whatever that might be, but merely trying to predict school performance, which is quite a different thing. Binet avoided using the term "intelligence test" and deplored the use of IQ scores because they gave the impression that they represented a psychological trait called intelligence. Unfortunately Binet's distinction between intelligence and what his test measures has not always been maintained by other psychologists.

Perhaps the most controversial aspect of Binet's work was his assumption that children who were below average early in their school careers would remain below average unless they were provided with extra instruction. Of all the criticisms made about Binet's test this was the most telling, because Binet really had no evidence to support his assumption that the *relative* mental ability of an individual (with respect to others in a population) is constant over time. It was not until many years after Binet's tests were introduced that evidence supporting this assumption became available. Part of this evidence was provided by a classic longitudinal study conducted by American psychologist Lewis Terman.

LEWIS M. TERMAN AND THE STANFORD-BINET

Despite sometimes heated controversies, Binet's test of intelligence had tremendous impact. His method of discriminating those children who could benefit from normal school experiences from those who were likely to have trouble was rapidly emulated by psychology clinics, the armed forces and industry. The tests were soon exported to America, Britain, Belgium, Italy and Germany where they were continually improved. Interestingly, minimal change was required (other than translating the items) to transfer the tests between these countries. This fact alone testifies to the generality of Binet's tests, at least among European cultures. Each new user improved the tests, tossing out poor items and replacing them with those better able to discriminate among different age groups. Eventually the tests reached the maximum predictive power obtainable, given the usual

FIG. 85. *Lewis Terman (1877–1956) directed the genetic study of genius*

restrictions on testing time and expense. The person who did most to improve and popularise Binet's test was Lewis M. Terman.

Terman was born in rural Indiana in 1877. He was the twelfth of 14 children and was raised on a fairly prosperous farm by loving parents. Perhaps because of the size of his family Terman was not given a great deal of special attention when young. Although interested in others he tended to be shy and introverted, traits that stayed with him for the rest of his life.

Terman's early education was in a one-room rural schoolhouse so Spartan that it contained not a single library book. For seven years he attended this school for a few months each year. The rest of the year was devoted to farm chores which generally involved getting up at 5 a.m. and working to 7 or 8 p.m.

Terman's first contact with psychology occurred during his early childhood when a travelling book-pedlar stopped at the farmhouse. Not only did the salesman have a book on phrenology, he also gave the family phrenology readings — foretelling their future by examining the bumps on their heads (see Chapter Two for more on phrenology). He saw a great future ahead for young Lewis who was so impressed he studied phrenology for the next four years (the family bought the book).

There were no high schools in Terman's part of Indiana, so at age 15 his family sent him to Central Normal College in Danville, Indiana. Normal colleges were teacher-training institutions in those days and a teacher is what Terman eventually became. He taught in country schools in Indiana for several years and even married a fellow teacher, Anna Minton. In 1901 the young couple and their newborn child moved to Bloomington where Terman attended the University of Indiana. After two years there he received both bachelor's and master's degrees and also developed a strong interest in the new science of psychology. Terman's interest was not in laboratory experiments (he was mechanically inept and hated working with laboratory apparatus) but in mental testing. Terman's distaste of working with his hands stayed with him throughout his life. Later, when he developed a negative attitude toward behaviourism (he believed it was a fad), at least part of the reason was his aversion to their intricate experiments and their complex apparatus.

Terman's two years at Indiana were financed by a $1200 loan which he worried about ever being able to repay. Nevertheless, when offered a fellowship to attend Clark University, Terman borrowed another $1200 and moved his family (which had grown to two children) to Massachusetts. In 1903 Clark University was the place to study psychology in America. Its president, G. Stanley Hall, was one of America's most famous psychologists and he filled his staff with other luminaries. Its library and laboratory facilities for psychology were also second to none. Clark was also an unusual place for someone used to the formalities of American education. It patterned itself on the European approach to higher education. Professors gave lectures on subjects that interested them and students attended when they pleased. There were no class lists, attendance records, final exams or marks. When they were ready students took a four-hour oral exam; if they passed they received their doctoral degree. This was the only exam given at Clark.

Terman's research at Clark dealt with Binet's mental tests which he had adapted and revised for use with American subjects. About the same time he received his doctorate Terman was diagnosed as having tuberculosis and advised to seek out a warm climate. For this reason in 1904 he moved his family to southern California, where he became principal of a high school. But he did not stay in this position long. Within two years he took on a post with the nearby Los Angeles State Normal School as Professor of Child Study. In 1910 he moved to Stanford University in northern California where he joined the department of education. Except for a break during the First World War, when he worked for the army developing mental tests for recruits, Terman spent the rest of his career at Stanford, first in the department of education and later in the department of psychology. Even after retiring from the university in 1942 Terman remained actively involved in psychological research.

Terman performed research and wrote on many psychological topics during his long career, but he is best remembered for his research on intelligence tests. This work began when he adapted and revised Binet's test for American children and it culminated in his classic longitudinal study of high-scoring children. It is this study more than any other that supports Binet's assumption that relative mental ability stays constant throughout life.

CLASSIC EXPERIMENT 15:

THE GENETIC STUDY OF GENIUS

When Terman launched his research project in 1921 his aim was not to fulfil Plato's dream of a test that could identify gifted children early in life; his purpose was considerably more modest. He wanted to dispose of some common misconceptions about gifted children. At that time intellectually precocious children were viewed as freaks. They were seen as physically weak bookworms who were socially inept and certainly eccentric, if not mad. It was widely held that many gifted children "peak" too soon and were destined to fail later on in life ("early ripe, early rot"). Terman believed none of this. He felt that a careful study of gifted children would dispel such myths once and for all. Armed with a grant from the Commonwealth Fund of New York he set out to identify and study a sample of gifted children. Because he lived in California his subjects were all selected from among Californian schoolchildren.

Terman and his co-workers sifted through 250,000 schoolchildren who were preselected by their teachers as being potentially gifted. These children were tested with intelligence tests in order to identify those with the highest IQs. Terman selected 1528 children this way. The mean IQ score of the children selected for the study was 150 with 80 having scores of 170 or higher. The lowest score in the group was 135. Since only one in 200 children has an IQ score of 150 or above, you can see that Terman's subjects were very special. The group consisted mainly of children between the ages of eight and 12, but a few

were younger and several were teenagers; 857 were boys, 671 were girls.

Within a few years it became quite obvious that these children (who became known as the Terman Gifted Group) were neither socially nor physically inferior to their less gifted classmates. In fact the children in Terman's gifted group were taller, had broader shoulders, stronger hand grips and greater breathing capacity than average children. They also tended to reach sexual maturity at a younger age. In essence they were found to be just the opposite of the stereotypic scrawny short-sighted bookworm.

While Terman's observations dispelled some common myths about bright children, they did not reveal what would happen to these children as they grew older. Would they "burn out" early as many thought or would they continue to excel? Were they psychologically healthy or would they succumb to madness? The only way to answer these questions was to keep in contact with the children as they grew up. And this is what Terman set out to do. The result is the most elaborate longitudinal research project ever conducted. Terman's gifted group has been continuously followed since it was first constituted over 60 years ago. The study will probably continue until everyone in the original sample has died.

Terman was in his forties when the study began. Over the next 40 years he published a series of volumes detailing the progress of his subjects. These volumes formed a series called *Genetic Studies of Genius*. The title conveys Terman's main purpose — to study the growth of children with great intellectual ability. When Terman died in 1956 the children in his gifted group were themselves in their mid-forties. Since Terman's death several additional follow-up reports on his gifted group have been prepared by other researchers. This huge compilation of data (as many facts about the subjects were recorded at each follow-up as possible) cannot be fully discussed in the space of a single chapter. Instead what follows is a summary of some of the main trends in the findings. Before getting to these, however, a caveat is in order.

Terman's gifted group was clearly not a representative sample of the California school population of the 1920s. For instance, as already noted, there were many more boys than girls in the gifted group although their numbers in the schools were about equal. There were also very few Mexican, black or oriental subjects; much fewer in fact than one might expect considering their numbers in the school population. Jewish children, on the other hand, were over-represented in the gifted group. While only five per cent of Californian schoolchildren were Jewish, 10 per cent of the sample was. Also most of the children in the gifted group had fathers who were professionals — lawyers, doctors and so on. Less than one per cent were the children of labourers and virtually all were from urban rather than rural communities. It is hard to know what to make of these facts. It is possible that white, urban, male children with professional fathers are smarter than black, rural children whose fathers are labourers, but other possibilities also exist. For instance, teachers may have been biased when they pre-selected promising children for IQ testing, choosing only those who met their stereotype of a gifted child. If this were the case many children with

potentially high IQs may never have been tested. Another possibility is that the IQ tests themselves were biased in favour of certain groups. Since it is not possible to choose between these possibilities on the basis of the data available, it is impossible to say why the gifted group was not representative. Nevertheless, it is worthwhile keeping this fact in mind as the study's findings are described.

In addition to their physical stature children in Terman's gifted group were healthier than average children. They had fewer childhood illnesses and accidents than the population as a whole. They also had a lower incidence of alcoholism and criminality. The gifted group maintained its health advantage over the general population throughout life. Even in their sixties they had lower death rates and much lower accident rates than the rest of the population.

As might be expected, children in the gifted group did well in school. They excelled in academic subjects, particularly reading, mathematics and science. Interestingly, they were no better than their less gifted classmates in non-academic subjects such as physical education or woodworking. Contrary to popular mythology the gifted children's academic abilities did not diminish as they grew older. They did not "burn out". In fact 70 per cent of the group received university degrees compared with only eight per cent of the population as a whole. Out of the entire gifted sample only 11 subjects failed to finish high school and eight of these attended some sort of technical school. Of those who finished a university degree 35 per cent did so with high honours. Periodic retestings confirmed Binet's assumption — the gifted group continued to achieve scores that placed them in the top one or two per cent of the population.

Even compared with other university graduates the gifted group excelled. Thirty-five per cent received at least some postgraduate university training and gifted group members were five times more likely to hold a Ph.D. than average university graduates. Their professions also served to distinguish them from the rest of the population. Among the males of the group the most common occupation was lawyer, followed by university lecturer, engineer, physician, school administrator, teacher, chemist, physicist, author, architect, geologist and clergyman. Overall 40 per cent were lawyers, physicians or held doctorates. Only three per cent held semiskilled or labouring jobs. Fewer female than male group members pursued careers. However, among those who did 66 per cent were also professionals. Interestingly, almost all of these career women married and raised families.

Since the gifted group did well academically and chose prestigious careers it should come as no surprise to learn that they also fared well economically. At mid-life about 30 per cent of the group had family incomes greater than $15,000, placing them in the upper one per cent of American earners in 1954. In that year, when the average yearly wage for professionals was $6000, the professionals in the gifted group averaged $10,500. Even those in semiskilled jobs were making 25 per cent

RANK ORDER OF OCCUPATIONS
ACCORDING TO 1954 EARNED INCOME (MEN)
(Includes only fields in which 5 or more men were engaged)

OCCUPATION	N	MEDIAN
1. Physicians (practising)	36	$23,500
2. Executives in major business or industry	73	17,680
3. Radio, TV, or motion picture arts: producer, director, engineer, writer, etc	19	17,500
4. Lawyers	65	15,970
5. Architects	8	15,000
6. Economists	5	13,750
7. Executives in banking, real estate, finance, insurance	41	12,500
8. Owners and executives in building and construction trades	9	11,500
9. Chemists and physicists	26	10,835
10. Musicians and actors (i.e., performers)	5	10,830
11. Geologists and related	7	9750
12. Personnel, labour relations, vocational placement officials	9	9500
13. Advertising, publicity, public relations	17	9250
14. Engineers	45	9100
15. Sales Managers, technical or engineering salesmen	22	9000
16. Army or Navy officers	14	9000
17. College or university faculty	52	8167
18. Authors or journalists	14	8000
19. Accountants, statisticians, and kindred occupations	26	7600
20. Office managers, purchasing agents, traffic managers, etc	10	7500
21. School teachers or administrators	29	6792
22. Draftsmen, surveyors, specification writers, etc	7	6250
23. Owners and managers, retail business	11	6125
24. Protective service occupations*	11	5900
25. Agricultural occupations	9	5850
26. Skilled trades, craftsmen, and foremen	25	5700
27. Clerical and retail sales occupations	25	5125
28. Clergymen	5	4500

FIG. 86. *Occupations of the gifted group at mid-life*

*Members of police and fire departments with rank of sergeant and above and noncommissioned officers in military services.

more than others in similar positions. Overall the gifted group's income was twice the average income for middle-class white families. Although we expect to find a correlation between academic achievement and income, this relationship did not hold throughout the income range. Of the six men making over $100,000 per year only one graduated from a university; the highest income ($400,000 yearly in the 1950s) went to someone with no education beyond high school. Thus high income in this sample was not solely the result of good schooling and professional occupations.

Periodically through the years members of the gifted group completed questionnaires and gave interviews about their contentment with life. Even as they approach old age 90 per cent report feeling content and satisfied with their lives, thereby bringing into doubt the view that highly intelligent people are more likely to develop psychological problems. High contentment ratings were characteristic of women as well as men, even women who had not pursued careers. One woman who had an IQ of 192 and who had raised eight children, including three sets of twins, had little contact with the world outside her family and yet reported high contentment.

As might be expected Terman's gifted group has been highly productive. By their mid-forties they had produced thousands of scientific articles, 60 non-fiction books, 33 novels, 375 short stories, 230 patents, radio and television shows, art works and music compositions. Although the identities of gifted group members have been kept confidential, the reports describe one as a leading science-fiction writer who has produced dozens of stories and many volumes of fiction. Another has been described as a famous motion picture director and winner of several Academy Awards (Oscars). Many are (or were) listed in *Who's Who* and *American Men of Science.*

Obviously Terman's gifted group has accomplished much compared with the general population. But what about differences within the group itself? Although all were gifted as measured by an IQ test, not all group members used their gifts in the same way. In 1960 one of Terman's colleagues, Melita Oden, set out to determine what differentiates those gifted children who achieved a lot in life from those who did not. Oden separated out 200 men from the original gifted group (women were not studied because too few had pursued careers). Half of these men were designated the A group and the other 100 made up the C group. The A group consisted of successful men who had pursued high status careers; the C group contained those men whose careers were much less spectacular. In 1959 the members of the A group had a median income of $24,000 while the members of the C group made only $7178, almost a threefold difference. (Just to keep this in perspective, however, it is worth noting that the median income for the nation that year was only $5000, so even the gifted group's low earners were still almost 50 per cent ahead of everybody else.) The A group was made up mainly of lawyers, doctors, scientists and executives. Most of the C group were non-professionals, clerks and salesmen.

So what was responsible for the difference between the groups? One factor was health. Although their health records were more or less identical in the early years, by 1960 nearly twice as many C group members than A group members had died. Among those who lived the A group seemed more full of life. They took part in more cultural, political and social activities, belonged to more societies and were also more physically active. (The Cs, unlike the As, preferred watching to participating in sports.) The backgrounds of the two groups were different as well. The As tended to come from professional families with lower levels of sickness and marital discord than the Cs. There had been more books in the A group's homes and stronger encouragement to excel in school. This encouragement appears to have fostered an ambition and need for achievement that stayed with the As throughout life. Even at age 40 they described themselves as more persistent and goal-directed than the Cs.

The members of the C group expressed less contentment and happiness at age 50 than those in the A group. Not surprisingly, they were also more concerned with money. C group members also had a higher incidence of those problems that are associated with discontentment — alcoholism and divorce. Thus although members of both groups had exceptionally high IQs, other factors in the background of the As produced a drive to succeed that made them more likely to get ahead.

As might be expected, a study of this magnitude carried out over more than 60 years could not fail to attract criticism. Some of this criticism has been directed toward the unrepresentative nature of the sample, which has already been mentioned. Other critics have focused on problems inherent in the longitudinal methodology itself. The gifted group grew up during very special times — the Great Depression and the Second

World War. We have no way of knowing the extent to which these events coloured their lives. It is entirely possible, for example, that gifted children raised in the postwar era and the affluent 1960s would have an entirely different attitude toward work and success. Without doing another longitudinal study on a different group of gifted children, there is no way of knowing.

Another criticism of the study is that simply having been chosen for an experiment may have changed the way the children behaved. Pointing to the results of the famous Hawthorne experiments (see Chapter Nine), some critics have argued that just knowing they had been chosen to participate in a study of geniuses may have spurred group members to do their best. There is also no way of assessing this criticism as it, too, points to a problem inherent in psychological research.

A final criticism, one that also cannot be answered, is that the study was not really an experiment at all as it had no control group. Although this is not entirely accurate (Oden's subsamples — the A and C groups — were controlled), it is certainly mostly true. An adequate control group would presumably consist of a sample of people with low or average IQ matched on all other relevant variables. You can imagine how difficult it would have been to construct such a group. Nevertheless, its absence makes Terman's project more of a demonstration than a true experiment.

Despite these criticisms the results of Terman's longitudinal study tell us a lot. In addition to the specific data gathered about the gifted and the various stereotypes it failed to confirm, the study shows very clearly that a paper and pencil test given to children at age eight can predict their school performance, health, income and achievements at age 40 and beyond. The study demonstrated that, just as Binet claimed, bright children remain bright throughout life.

FIG. 87. *Relative importance of six sources of life satisfaction as reported by members of the gifted group in a 1972 follow-up*

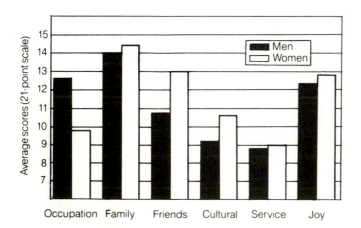

AFTERMATH

The years during which Terman inaugurated and supervised his longitudinal study were growth years for mental tests, especially in America. Terman's work in developing the US army mental testing programme during the First World War meant that for the first time IQs were measured on great numbers of people. By the end of the war nearly two million recruits had been examined. Terman and other psychologists also developed other mental tests aimed at special populations. By the 1930s mental testing had become the major occupation of psychologists, not only in America but in Britain as well.

The success of the mental testing movement did not bring with it any great breakthroughs in the scientific understanding of intelligence. Most psychologists chose to follow Binet's lead and adopted a largely atheoretical approach to their subject matter. For them it was enough to know that mental tests predict academic performance. Many psychologists justified their work on democratic grounds. They pointed out that, in the past, intellectual assessments had been made subjectively and some capable students had been barred from furthering their education because of class distinctions and prejudice. Mental tests, they maintained, would end such unfair discriminations. All students would now compete on equal terms because assessments would be made scientifically using mental tests. In other words tests were viewed as instruments of egalitarianism. This view was eventually changed but not until people became much more sensitive to racial prejudice than anyone was in Terman's day.

Although psychologists in the mental testing movement were never entirely clear about what intelligence is, they were certain that, whatever it is, it is inherited. It is only a small step from this belief to the view that differences in intelligence test scores must be due to poor heredity. In Terman's own words, "... the major differences in the intelligence scores of certain races ... will never be fully accounted for on the environmental hypothesis".

The notion that some races are genetically inferior received a boost from Terman's army testing programme. His results showed that whites score higher than blacks and northern Europeans perform better than southern and eastern European immigrants. Although it does not appear that these findings were given much credence by the army's top brass, they did have a lasting effect on the public and on contemporary psychology. In the 1930s group differences in IQ were put forth as a scientific rationale for curtailing immigration, particularly from eastern Europe. The finding that immigrants' IQ scores improved with the number of years they spent in the USA (they did better as they learned the culture) was largely ignored.

By the 1950s American, Canadian, Australian and British students were getting accustomed to receiving intelligence tests. And the school systems in all four countries routinely made educational assignments on the basis of IQ test scores. The tests were considered to be objective; thus placements made on the basis of tests were supposedly more democratic than placements made subjectively. Few of the psychologists using these tests concerned themselves with whether scores were determined by inheritance or by environment until they were forced to do so by the events of the 1960s and 1970s. During those years the American civil rights movement began to challenge the notion of racial inferiority. It was only a matter of time before this challenge confronted intelligence tests. Blacks on average were scoring 15 points below whites on most intelligence tests. While Galton and Terman were fairly sure that most of this difference was the result of racial inferiority, the civil rights activists were not so certain. They maintained that since blacks grow up in different subcultures, differences in IQ test scores may be the result of cultural rather than genetic differences between the races. Whites do better because the tests are biased in favour of white middle-class students.

The last 20 years have seen this issue debated in many forums. Data from studies of twins raised apart have been analysed for evidence of heritability, and cross-racial adoption studies have also been examined. Some of this research has been challenged as faulty and some is liable to more than one interpretation. The overall result is that no answer to the question of the heritability of intelligence is yet available. Moreover, even if intelligence is found to be largely inherited within a group, this does not mean that racial differences are the result of environmental effects. As Plato knew, what is inherited is simply a genetic potential; it takes suitable learning experiences to permit this potential to develop. If some people lack these experiences their intellectual performance will be affected.

Intelligence testing has become so entangled with politics it may be many years before we know where the field is heading. At present some jurisdictions have banned intelligence testing while others still permit it. At the same time many research psychologists have given up Binet's atheoretical approach and have gone back to trying to understand intelligence from a theoretical point of view. Following Piaget (see Chapter Eleven) these psychologists are less interested in predicting school performance than in finding out how children think. The goal of their research is not to place children in categories but to improve instructional practices by tying teaching techniques to children's learning strategies.

Despite the controversy, Terman's study remains a classic. Although not a true experiment (it lacked adequate controls) it did show that intellectual performance can be predicted and that high intellect is not related to illness, madness or other peculiarities. Terman died in 1956 at the age of 79 but his work is being continued by colleagues and students. Before he died he received honorary doctorates from the University of California, University of Southern California and the University of Pennsylvania. When he died he was Professor Emeritus of Stanford University.

Further Reading

Terman, L. (ed.), *Genetic Studies of Genius* (Vols 1–5), Stanford University Press, Stanford, California (Oxford University Press, London) 1921–1959.

EPILOGUE

The 15 experiments discussed in the preceding chapters cover a broad range of topics, everything from child development to neurophysiology to conformity. Yet there are many psychological topics that have not even been mentioned in this book. Psycholinguistics, moral development, geriatric psychology, psycho-pharmacology, parapsychology; the list can go on and on. As these fields mature they too will produce experiments worthy of being called "classics".

One area of psychology that has grown very quickly since the 1960s takes its major ideas from computer science. Psychologists working in this area view the computer as a kind of metaphor for human thinking. Since both computers and people process information, these psychologists have tried to *simulate* cognitive processes on computers and to think of their computer programmes as complex theories about how people think. Information-processing theories have come to be recognised as an important breakthrough in knowledge about behaviour. One leading proponent of this research, Herbert Simon, has won the Nobel Prize for his work.

Another trend in modern psychology is an emphasis on practical research and applied problems. We saw a little of this in Chapter Four where research on eyewitness testimony was discussed. In recent years psychologists have also become involved in aviation research, in designing machinery to be "user-friendly" (ergonomics) and in planning environments to suit people's needs.

Psychology, as you can see, is continuing to develop and change. There is great excitement in the field as new theories replace old ones and new generations of researchers come forward to carry on where the previous ones have left off. To a great extent the healthy state of modern psychology is owed to the researchers discussed in this book. Three (Pavlov, Sperry and Lorenz) received the Nobel Prize; the others have also received many scientific honours. Although they have all performed research relevant to psychology (and an exceptionally large proportion lived to their eighties), the classic experimenters do not constitute a homogeneous social group. They come from many different countries (America, Australia, Austria, Britain, Germany, Poland, Russia, Switzerland) and they lived during very different times. There is, however, one important trait they all share — a curiosity about behaviour and the determination and drive necessary to produce high-quality research. So long as psychology continues to produce researchers like these, the science cannot help but thrive.

BIBLIOGRAPHY

In addition to the references given at the end of each chapter the following sources were consulted in writing this book.

American Psychological Association, "Distinguished Scientific Contribution Award Citation" (S. Asch), *American Psychologist*, 22, pp. 1128–30, 1967.

American Psychological Association, "Distinguished Scientific Contribution Award Citation" (J. Piaget and S. Schachter), *American Psychologist*, 25, pp. 65–81, 1970.

Aronson, E., *The Social Animal*, W. H. Freeman, San Francisco, 1972.

Atkinson, R. L., Atkinson, R. C. and Hilgard, E. R., *Introduction to Psychology* (eighth edition), Harcourt-Brace-Jovanovich, New York, 1983.

Baddeley, A., *Your Memory: A User's Guide*, Macmillan, New York, 1982.

Bartlett, F. C., "Autobiography", in C. Murchison (ed.), *A History of Psychology in Autobiography* (Vol. III), Russell & Russell, New York, 1961.

Blakemore, C. and Cooper, G. F., "Development of the Brain Depends on the Visual Environment", *Nature*, 228, pp. 477–8, 1970.

Boring, E. G., "Mind and Mechanism", *The American Journal of Psychology*, 59, pp. 173–92, 1946.

Boring, E. G., *A History of Experimental Psychology* (second edition), Appleton-Century-Crofts, New York, 1950.

Bramel, D. and Friend, R., "Hawthorne, the Myth of the Docile Worker, and Class Bias in Psychology", *American Psychologist*, 36, pp. 856–66, 1981.

Bronowski, J., *The Ascent of Man*, Little, Brown, Boston, 1973.

Brown, R., *Social Psychology*, Collier-Macmillan, London, 1965.

Cofer, C. N., "Properties of Verbal Materials and Verbal Learning", in J. W. Kling and L. A. Riggs (eds), *Woodworth and Schlosberg's Experimental Psychology* (third edition), Holt, Rinehart & Winston, New York, 1972.

Cotman, C. W. and McGaugh, J. L., *Behavioral Neuroscience: An Introduction*, Academic Press, New York, 1980.

Cuny, H., *Ivan Pavlov: The Man and His Theories* (P. Evans, trans.), Souvenir Press, London, 1964.

Davies, J. D., *Phrenology: Fad and Science*, Yale University Press, New Haven, Connecticut, 1955.

Dworetzky, J. P., *Psychology*, West Publishing Co., St Paul, Minnesota, 1982.

Ekman, P., *Darwin and Facial Expression: A Century of Research in Review*, Academic Press, New York, 1973.

Engen, T., "Psychophysics I: Discrimination and Detection", in J. W. Kling and L. A. Riggs (eds), *Woodworth and Schlosberg's Experimental Psychology* (third edition), Holt, Rinehart & Winston, New York, 1972.

Eysenck, H. J. and Eysenck, M. W., *Mindwatching*, Michael Joseph, London, 1981.

Frisby, J. P., *Seeing: Illusion, Brain and Mind*, Oxford University Press, Oxford, 1979.

Fodor, J. A., "The Mind–Body Problem", *Scientific American*, *244*, pp. 124–33, 1981.

Forrest, D. W., *Francis Galton: The Life and Work of a Victorian Genius*, Paul Elek, London, 1974.

Freud, S., "Analysis of a Phobia in a Five-year-old Boy", in *Sigmund Freud: Collected Papers* (Vol. 3) (Alix and James Strachey, trans.), Hogarth Press, London (original published in 1909), 1959.

Galton, F., *Hereditary Genius: An Inquiry into its Laws and Consequences*, Watts & Co., London, 1869.

Gazzaniga, M. S., *The Bisected Brain*, Appleton-Century-Crofts, New York, 1970.

Gazzaniga, M. S., "1981 Nobel Prize for Physiology or Medicine", *Science*, *214*, pp. 517–18, 1981.

Geschwind, N., "Specializations of the Human Brain", *Scientific American*, *241*, pp. 158–71, 1979.

Gibson, J. J., "Autobiography", in E. G. Boring and G. Lindzey (eds), *A History of Psychology in Autobiography* (Vol. 5), Appleton-Century-Crofts, New York, 1967.

Goleman, D., "1528 Little Geniuses and How They Grew", *Psychology Today*, Feb., pp. 30–43, 1980.

Gregory, R. L., *The Intelligent Eye*, McGraw-Hill, New York, 1970.

Haber, R. N. (ed.), *Contemporary Theory and Research in Visual Perception*, Holt, Rinehart & Winston, New York, 1968.

Haber, R. N. and Hershenson, M., *The Psychology of Visual Perception*, Holt, Rinehart & Winston, New York, 1973.

Harlow, H. F., "The Nature of Love", *American Psychologist*, *13*, pp. 673–85, 1958.

Harré, R., *Great Scientific Experiments*, Phaidon, Oxford, 1981.

Harris, B., "Whatever Happened to Little Albert?", *American Psychologist*, *34*, pp. 151–60, 1979.

Hernnstein, R., "IQ", the *Atlantic*, Sept., pp. 43–64, 1971.

Hochberg, J., "Perception II: Space and Movement", in J. W. Kling and L. A. Riggs (eds), *Woodworth and Schlosberg's Experimental Psychology* (third edition), Holt, Rinehart & Winston, New York, 1972.

Hofling, C. K., Brotzman, E., Dalrymple, S., Graves, N. and Pierce, C. M., "An Experimental Study in Nurse-physician Relationships", *Journal of Nervous and Mental Disease*, *143*, pp. 171–80, 1966.

Hohmann, G. W., "Some Effects of Spinal Cord Lesions on Experienced Emotional Feelings", *Psychophysiology*, *3*, pp. 143–56, 1962.

Hollander, B., *The Mental Functions of the Brain*, Grant Richards, London, 1901.

Houston, J. P., Bee, H., Hatfield, E. and Rimm, D. C., *Invitation to Psychology*, Academic Press, New York, 1979.

Hovland, C., "The Generalization of Conditioned Responses", *Journal of General Psychology*, *17*, pp. 125–48, 1937.

Hunt, M., *The Universe Within: A New Science Explores the Human Mind*, Simon & Schuster, New York, 1982.

Lorenz, K., *King Solomon's Ring*, Methuen, London, 1961.

Marshall, J. C., "On the Biology of Language Acquisition", in D. Caplan (ed.), *Biological Studies of Mental Processes*, MIT Press, Cambridge, Massachusetts, 1980.

McHenry, L. C., *Garrison's History of Neurology*, C. C. Thomas, Springfield, Illinois, 1969.

McLeish, J., *The Development of Modern Behavioural Psychology*, Detselig Enterprises, Calgary, Alberta, 1981.

Milgram, S., "Behavioural Study of Obedience", *Journal of Abnormal and Social Psychology*, 67, pp. 371–8, 1963.

Morgan, C. T., King, R. A. and Robinson, N. M., *Introduction to Psychology* (sixth edition), McGraw-Hill, New York, 1979.

Neisser, U., *Cognitive Psychology*, Appleton-Century-Crofts, New York, 1967.

Piaget, J., "Autobiography", in E. G. Boring, *et al* (eds), *A History of Psychology in Autobiography* (Vol. 4), Clark University Press, Worcester, Massachusetts, 1952.

Plutchik, R., "A Language for Emotions", *Psychology Today*, Feb., pp. 68–78, 1980.

Russell, P., *The Brain Book*, Routledge & Kegan Paul, London, 1979.

Samelson, F., "J. B. Watson's Little Albert, Cyril Burt's Twins, and the Need for a Critical Science", *American Psychologist*, 35, pp. 619–25, 1980.

Schwartz, S. and Johnson, J. H., *Psychopathology of Childhood*, Pergamon Press, New York, 1985.

Terman, L. M., "Autobiography", in C. Murchison (ed.), *A History of Psychology in Autobiography* (Vol. 2), Russell & Russell, New York, 1961.

Terman, L. M. and Oden, M. H., *The Gifted Group at Mid-life* (*Genetic Studies of Genius*, Vol. 5), Oxford University Press, London, 1959.

Thornton, W. P., *Heads and What They Tell Us*, Sampson, Low, Marston, London, 1891.

Watson, J. B., "Autobiography", in C. Murchison (ed.), *A History of Psychology in Autobiography* (Vol. 3), Russell & Russell, New York, 1961.

Woodworth, R. S. and Schlosberg, H., *Experimental Psychology*, Holt, New York, 1938.

INDEX

ACKNOWLEDGEMENTS

Permission to use the following text extracts and illustrations is gratefully acknowledged.

Text extracts

P. 29: J. Watson, *Behaviorism,* W. W. Norton & Co., New York, 1925.

P. 37: R. W. Sperry, "Cerebral Organization and Behavior", *Science,* vol. 133, pp. 1749-57, American Association for the Advancement of Science, Washington, DC, 2 June 1961.

P. 51: G. Fechner, *Elements of Psychophysics,* Holt, Rinehart & Winston, New York, 1966. Reprinted by permission of CBS Publishing.

P. 63: H. Ebbinghaus, *Memory,* Dover Books, New York, 1964.

P. 65: W. James, *Principles of Psychology,* Holt, Rinehart & Winston (Henry Holt, 1890). Reprinted by permission of CBS Publishing.

Pp. 67, 68, 69: F. C. Bartlett, *Remembering: a study in experimental and social psychology,* Cambridge University Press, Cambridge, 1932.

P. 87: C. Darwin, *Expression of Emotion in Man and Animals,* J. Friedmann, London, 1890.

Pp. 116, 117: S. Milgram, *Obedience to Authority,* Tavistock Publications, London (Harper & Row, New York), 1974.

P. 138: E. Mayo, *The Human Problems of an Industrial Civilization,* Harvard University Press, Cambridge, Mass., 1933.

Pp. 172-3: F. Galton, *Hereditary Genius,* J. Friedmann, London, 1869.

P. 185: L. Terman, "Autobiography", *A History of Psychology in Autobiography,* vol. 2, Clark University Press, Worcester, Mass., 1861.

Illustrations

Figs 1, 2, 3, 6, 7: The Granger Collection, New York.

Fig. 8: Courtesy of Professor Benjamin Harris, from Watson's 1919 film, *Experimental Investigation of Babies.*

Figs 9, 13, 14: From L. C. McHenry, *Garrison's History of Neurology,* 1969. Courtesy of Charles C. Thomas, Publisher, Springfield, Illinois.

Fig. 12: John Davies, Princeton, New Jersey.

Fig. 15: From N. Geschwind, "Specializations of the human brain", *Scientific American,* 241(3), 1979. © 1979 by Scientific American, Inc. All rights reserved.

Fig. 16: Wild World Photos.

Figs 17, 18: M. Gazzaniga and J. E. Le Doux, *The Integrated Mind,* Plenum Publishing Co., New York, 1978.

Fig. 19: R. Sperry, "Hemispheric deconnection and unity in conscious awareness", *American Psychologist,* 23, 1968. Copyright 1968 by the American Psychological Association. Reprinted by permission of the publisher and author.

Fig. 20: P. Russell, *The Brain Book,* Routledge & Kegan Paul, London (E. P. Dutton, Inc., New York), 1979.

Fig. 21: Photo courtesy of Stoelting Co., Chicago, Illinois.